Looking for

MR.

10686694

Looking for
MR.SMITH

A Quest for the Truth Behind
The Long Walk,
the Greatest Survival Story
Ever Told

Linda Willis

Skyhorse Publishing

Copyright © 2010 by Linda Willis

All Rights Reserved. No part of this book may be reproduced in any manner without the express written consent of the publisher, except in the case of brief excerpts in critical reviews or articles. All inquiries should be addressed to Skyhorse Publishing, 307 West 36th Street, 11th Floor, New York, NY 10018.

Skyhorse Publishing books may be purchased in bulk at special discounts for sales promotion, corporate gifts, fund-raising, or educational purposes. Special editions can also be created to specifications. For details, contact the Special Sales Department, Skyhorse Publishing, 307 West 36th Street, 11th Floor, New York, NY 10018 or info@skyhorsepublishing.com.

Skyhorse® and Skyhorse Publishing® are registered trademarks of Skyhorse Publishing, Inc.®, a Delaware corporation.

www.skyhorsepublishing.com

10 9 8 7 6 5 4 3 2 1

Paperback ISBN: 978-1-62636-541-4

Library of Congress Cataloging-in-Publication Data

Willis, Linda.
  Looking for Mr. Smith : seeking the truth behind The long walk, the greatest survival story ever told / Linda Willis.
    p. cm.
  Includes index.
  ISBN 978-1-61608-158-4 (hardcover : alk. paper)
  1. Rawicz, Slavomir. Long walk. 2. World War, 1939-1945--Prisoners and prisons, Soviet. 3. World War, 1939-1945--Conscript labor--Soviet Union. 4. Rawicz, Slavomir. 5. Escaped prisoners of war--Russia (Federation)--Siberia--Biography. 6. Prisoner-of-war escapes--Russia (Federation)--Siberia--History--20th century. 7. Prisoners of war--Poland--Biography. 8. Prisoners of war--Europe, Eastern--Biography. 9. Prisoners of war--Russia (Federation)--Siberia--Biography. I. Title.
  D805.S65R395 2010
  940.54'72470957--dc22
                                2010028080

Printed in the United States of America

AUTHOR'S NOTE: Reader, kindly note there are various spellings of the transliterated words throughout the book. The spellings I have chosen are the most commonly used.

CONTENTS

PREFACE

I first read *The Long Walk* when it was reprinted and distributed to book shops in the summer of 1999. "What a story!" I thought, as I finished reading the last sentences in the book. In the next instant I wondered if that was it. Was there not another page? Was there really no more to the story? No, there didn't seem to be any more. The story ended, the book was closed; but the essence of the story didn't fade away. Over time it took on a life of its own, a life that prompted me to look into its origins in search of the truth.

Curiosity was the initial driving force. Concurrently, earlier in 1999, I became seriously involved in family research. I discovered the two interests complemented one other: My skills in genealogy provided a sound base for investigating the story behind the *The Long Walk*. As months and then years went by while I tracked down more and more details, curiosity combined with a desire to discover the truth behind the events related in the book. I joined the ranks of readers around the world who, for decades, had attempted to research the contents of the story. I wondered if my skills would be up to the task and whether I would find the answers I looked for. Ultimately, I believe I did. The quest for the truth behind *The Long Walk* is now laid out in the following pages, beginning with a summary of the story itself.

The story of *The Long Walk* involves a group of men who were imprisoned in a Siberian labor camp at the beginning of World War II. The group consisted of a variety of East European nationalities, imprisoned on the basis of being in the wrong place at the wrong time, and desperate enough to want to escape despite all the odds against accomplishing such a feat. The book is a page-turner, compelling the reader to speed through the narrative, share the misadventures and hardships of the escapees, and breathe a sigh of relief at the end when the survivors of the walk reach freedom in India.

Having lived and traveled all over the world for thirty years, and having been to some of the places named in the book, I felt a profound attachment to the story: My feet had thudded and plodded in some of the same lands on which the feet of the escapees had left their footprints. I reread the book carefully, searching for details, thinking about the sequence of events, and wondering if there was more to the tale. In fact, there was an Afterword in my edition in which the author had tried to answer oft-repeated questions by readers such as myself. The answers fell flat, though, and his explanations left many questions still unresolved. This was unsatisfactory to me as a reader with a profound attachment to the tale! So, having been born with endless curiosity, I set out to find some answers.

By the year 2000, I thought the Internet would be a big help to get me started on my quest for answers. I quickly found, however, that the great search engine of the twenty-first century was still in its infancy and would never grow out of childhood until every piece of printed paper had been scanned into it. I believed I could find anything with just a click of a button but soon found this to be an unrealistic expectation, even in the new millennium. While the Internet has been an incredible research tool, it hasn't taken the place of good old-fashioned sleuthing, of laboriously writing letters, waiting months for replies, searching for translators, making phone calls, and meeting and speaking to people directly, all in the search for answers.

Little by little, answers did come. Little by little, barriers broke down—but not easily. One of the hardest barriers to overcome was getting documentation from the former Soviet Union. I soon learned to give thanks to the magnificent efforts of The International Volunteer Public Organization "Memorial Historical, Educational, Human Rights and Charitable Society" (hereinafter referred to simply as "Memorial"), whose answers did eventually begin to reach me, though months would go by before a letter would arrive in the mail; sometimes there would be a single sheet of paper, sometimes a thick packet of photocopied documents. Translations would have to be made, replies thought out, and the search would proceed with another interval of months before a further letter would come, covered with Russian stamps.

Other groups that slowly but surely brought their collections up to date and made them available through the Internet and accompanying e-mail included Karta Indeks, a sister organization to "Memorial"; the Hoover Institution in California; the archives of Belarus at Pinsk; the Public Records Office (universally known as the PRO but now renamed the National Archives) at Kew outside London; the British Library; the various libraries at Cambridge and Oxford; and the quaint but delightful treasure trove of the Sikorski Museum/Polish Institute in London. One of the best discussion forums on the Internet began to take shape after 2000, when the Kresy-Siberia Web site came into being, dedicated to the millions of Poles and others who, at the start of the War, were deported from Eastern Europe into the Siberian tundra. Some lived to tell the tale, recounting their stories for future generations; millions, unfortunately, perished, their voices silent forever. Meanwhile, readers from the four corners of the globe questioned and commented on the walk. My voice joined theirs.

At the beginning of my research I took it on faith that the walk had taken place. It was the most amazing escape and survival story I ever read. It was only as I learned details of the story that questions arose in my mind. Using the walk as my starting point, I began questioning who had been on that walk and what had actually taken place along the way. As my research gained momentum, I accepted that there were differences between the story and the book, differences that were compelling and intriguing and that spurred my sleuthing efforts to uncover long-buried or forgotten facts.

My original idea was to carry on telling the tale of the walk—to extend the walk, as it were. To relate the rest of the story depended on doing an awful lot of research and, principally, in tracking down the people involved in the walk. Then, over time, I began to realize that I wanted to write about the long, slow process of researching the story as well as learning the fate of its participants. What was originally a story by and about the men of an exceptionally long walk to freedom slowly became my own story, as well as that of hundreds of other people whose lives I touched along the winding road of research. Their stories and memories added new and sometimes invaluable dimensions to the original story.

In taking my first steps along the research road and combining curiosity with investigative skills, I was not held in thrall by preconceived ideas. My research goals shifted over the years, as each new piece of documentation came to light. I first concentrated on learning about the men who had escaped from Siberia and walked to freedom in India: Who were they? What were their backgrounds? This led me on a path toward verifying the details of the story as well as tracking down, if possible, people who might have known the escapees. Throughout the process, new avenues of research sprang up: dates and times of events centering on the escapees; relationships between the escapees as well as with other people and entities; contacts with associations and organizations involved with World War II matters, and so on. My questions multiplied and led to more questions instead of solid answers.

The lack of answers was frustrating at times, and when answers finally came, they were full of information that inevitably led to further queries. These queries broadened my quest to seek out any facts that were left out of the book and to try to understand them. I speculated about the truthfulness of the story from so many conflicting bits of data that were unearthed and wrestled with the dawning realization that there was certainly more to the story than first appeared. I was on a fact-finding expedition to discover more about the men who undertook the long walk, to attempt to reconcile discrepancies that came to light, to expand my network of information to accept and appreciate help from others, and to continue to probe and question every bit of information that surfaced. I searched for answers:

What had happened to the survivors? Were any of them still alive? And, if so, what were their versions of the story?

I found it hard, at first, grappling with the research and understanding where to go to obtain information and what to do with it once I had it. The information discovered, the conversations held, the communications received always brought surprises and alluded to further mysteries in the unraveling of the story. Who could have imagined that partway along the research road I was to learn that the spokesman of the story appeared never to have been on the walk? Why? What had happened? How had he learned the details of the walk? At about the same time, I learned that other men had been on that walk but had kept silent about it for decades. The mysteries abounded and led to more detective work, tracking down missing pieces.

Investigating *The Long Walk* required many, many steps to be taken, beginning with following the footsteps already set out in the story. Walking in another's footsteps is always a precarious exercise. One has to adjust one's own steps to match the original imprints. The exercise becomes even more of a challenge when it's not just a single set of footsteps that one is trying to match but several sets at a time.

Finding the truth would be a huge endeavor, but be that as it may, I set myself the task of getting to the heart of the tale, of unraveling the story, skein by skein, to learn what had really happened. To do so meant casting my research net back to the beginning of World War II while taking a firm stance and keeping my balance and feet on the ground some sixty-five years later.

Part I

A WALK RETOLD

Chapter 1

~~&~~

THE WALK

For those readers not familiar with the book, *The Long Walk* details the story of a group of men who were caught up in the events of World War II. Arrested for being in the wrong place at the wrong time, they ultimately joined forces while in a labor camp in Siberia to escape their collective fate and regain their freedom. "Escape" is the key word. They escaped from the camp, and four of them reached their final goal—freedom—by walking from Siberia to India in 1941–42, bringing to an end their individual ordeals that had begun some years earlier.

Like most escape stories, this one uses a first-person narrative and is written in a fashion that compels readers to keep turning the pages. Over the course of roughly a year, the group of escapees flees south from Russia across China and Tibet to India. They experience harrowing difficulties and hardships, suffer defeats and deaths, and finally, as a much shrunken band of survivors, they triumphantly reach India and freedom.

The men who begin this incredible walk to freedom are all East Europeans: Slavomir Rawicz, a young Polish cavalry officer—and the author of the book; Anton Paluchowicz, an older man, also a Polish cavalry officer; Sigmund Makowski, another member of the Polish military; Zacharius Marchinkovas, a young Lithuanian architect; Eugene Zaro, a clerk from the Balkans; Anastazi Kolemenos, a Latvian landowner; and Mr. Smith, an American engineer, the oldest escapee at fifty. Along the way they encounter another escaped prisoner, a Polish teenager, Kristina Polanska from Ukraine, who joins their ranks. Over the course of the many months it takes to reach India, half of the above-named escapees perish, leaving only four survivors at the end of the walk to recuperate in Calcutta. What happened to the survivors after the walk ended has been the subject of ongoing speculation by readers ever since the book first emerged in 1956.

For more than fifty years, the guesswork surrounding the survivors has been unceasing. Who were these remarkable men and woman? How had they interacted with one another? What were their intimate thoughts and dreams beyond escape? And most importantly, what happened to them at the end of the walk? Before reaching the end of this journey, however, we need to start at the beginning.

❦❦

The Long Walk spans the years 1939–1942 and focuses on the life of young Slavomir Rawicz. As the story opens, Rawicz finds himself under arrest and the subject of brutal interrogations by the Soviets at the infamous Lubyanka prison. His interrogators, the Soviet Secret Police (initially called the NKVD and later the KGB) show the young man no mercy. Rawicz describes his feelings of helplessness, anger, frustration, and fear against a backdrop of being moved from one prison to another between 1939 and 1940. Over that one-year period, he tries to resist the pressure of his tormentors to confess to spying against the Soviet Union. His refusal to cooperate and admit his guilt infuriates the police, and he's punished for his obstinacy by various means of torture. After days and weeks of abuse, Rawicz succumbs, signs a confession stating he is a spy and, therefore, an enemy of the U.S.S.R., and outlines his experience of the mock trial he is given.

While yearning for the past—including his involvement in the Polish army and his bride, Vera—Rawicz still has to cope with the present. With the conclusion of his trial and the receipt of a twenty-five-year sentence with hard labor, his feelings of desperation are replaced by a choking grief over the unfair treatment he's endured, fear of the unknown, and worries about his survival as a twenty-four-year-old prisoner heading for a Siberian labor camp. These thoughts and feelings assail him as he's forced into a cattle car on a train carrying hundreds of convicts east to Irkutsk, near Lake Baikal.

Rawicz, though in despair, movingly reports the horrendous conditions in the cattle car: the lack of toilet facilities, the scarcity of food and water, the overcrowded conditions, and the overpowering uncertainty of what fate has in store for him. All is not doom and gloom, however. Descriptions of fellow convicts and his observations of their plight broaden the narrative. Arguments as well as laughter are noted, conversations recorded, and tales of personal tragedies recounted. Rawicz dwells on his time as a student and as a military cadet and wonders at the state of the war in which he is no longer involved.

The convicts disembark from the train at Irkutsk, and there begins several weeks of trudging through the snow as part of a chain gang to their destination—a forced labor camp with no name. Rawicz only knows it as Camp 303 somewhere near the Lena River and goes on to describe it as a new camp, recently built, with thousands of prisoners representing many European nationalities. The contacts he makes in the camp change the course of his life, the most important being the camp commandant, Colonel Ushakov, and his wife. The meeting between the prisoner and the commandant is a fluke, based on Ushakov's broken radio and Rawicz's technical expertise. For Rawicz, the encounter will eventually save his life, although he has no inkling of the great adventure still to come.

While repairing Ushakov's radio, Rawicz makes the acquaintance of Ushakov's wife, who sympathizes with his plight. At this time, communication is made between Rawicz and a few of the other convicts who, like him, can't see themselves surviving twenty-five years of hard labor and the hardships of life in Camp 303. As Madame Ushakov increasingly hints at the possibility of his escape, Rawicz meets two fellow Poles, Anton Paluchowicz and Sigmund Makowski, both military men; a Lithuanian, Zacharius Marchinkovas, a Latvian, Anastazi Kolemenos, and a Yugoslav, Eugene Zaro. He also meets an older man, Mr. Smith—an American. This group of seven begins plotting its escape and preparing for the journey with as much food and warm clothing as each member can possibly stow away without notice from the guards and other prisoners.

The roll of the dice favors the seven escapees, and they flee one evening during a winter storm, their strength holding up long enough to put distance between themselves and the hell they leave behind. They head south, toward freedom.

Increasingly, the book transforms into an outstanding example of the classic escape story—a real page-turner. Rawicz set the time of their escape as having been in April 1941, with winter still extending its icy grip throughout Siberia. The men made it over and under the many layers of barbed wire fencing surrounding the camp and ran, stumbled, and fell until their legs and lungs gave out. The escapees doggedly kept going, mile after mile, day after day despite their growing exhaustion. The pace of their efforts gradually slowed to alleviate their fatigue, but they kept pressing south in long, steady, hungry marches. Within days of their escape there were problems with shortages of food.

Within a fortnight the escapees encountered their first major obstacle, the Lena River. Fortunately, it was still icebound and easily crossed, and the group continued south toward Lake Baikal. The men were by turns fearful and adventurous, and their personalities soon emerged. The Poles tended to be serious and grouped together; Marchinkovas was reserved; Zaro and Kolemenos were the jokers of the group; Smith kept his own counsel; and Rawicz—the self-purported leader—spun the tale.

Their efforts to survive not only spurred them on but also sharpened their wits. They learned to make fire by rubbing twigs together, to fish through the ice of streams, and to hunt small game while pushing themselves to the limit with marches of 30 miles per day.

By the middle of May, the escapees had reached Lake Baikal. Far in the distance they could see villages, smokestacks, telephone poles. They wanted to avoid civilization and all its dangers, and so chose the eastern route around the lake. No sooner had their course been set than they ran into the final member to comprise their group: Kristina Polanska. She was only a teenager who had had the bad luck of being rounded up and deported from her home in Polish Ukraine during the upheavals of 1939, after her parents were killed. She was sent to a *kolkhoz,* a state-run farm, in Siberia. There, she had been harassed by the foreman, and matters came to a head when he attempted to rape her. She fought back, then fled for her life. She had been wandering around for weeks when fate intervened and her path and that of the escapees crossed. Their humanity and her pleas found common ground, and Kristina became the eighth escapee.

She got on well with the group as all moved rapidly around the eastern shore of the lake, crossing the Barguzin River several days later. The escapees pressed on, finding food when they could and battling exhaustion. They continued onward, crossing the Trans-Siberian Railway and entering Mongolia, where they determined, after an encounter with two Mongolian travelers, to make Lhasa their final destination.

Throughout the narrative, Rawicz describes the surrounding countryside, incidents that happened along the way, and the feelings of and interactions between the escapees in great detail. They all developed a strong attachment to Kristina, treating her as their mascot, and they frequently looked to her for cheerfulness during their bleakest moments. She was considered their good-luck charm.

Once the group realized they were out of the Soviet Union, the intense fear that someone might be tracking them and planning their capture diminished. The escapees had time to draw breath, take stock of their situation, and decide on their future course. There was discussion of aiming west for Afghanistan or south toward India. They talked of heading east into China. Eventually they set their course for Tibet and Lhasa, even though none of them had any accurate idea of its location. All they knew was that there were still many miles to tack on to the thousand they'd already covered the past two months.

Over time, food became their chief concern. They walked on empty bellies and hunger accompanied them in the face of a changing climate and terrain. The landscape might have been free of ice and snow, but they now had to contend with heat by day and freezing temperatures by night as they traversed the deserts of Mongolia and northern China. Along the way, the group had chance encounters with gracious strangers, and even though there was a significant language barrier, these strangers were always willing to provide the band of weary escapees with food, drink, and, at times, shelter for the evening. Rawicz recalled many of these meetings with admiration for the generosity of the people they met. He also referred to surprises, such as being shown a pocket watch made by the famous Russian watchmaker Pavel Bure and being given tobacco wrapped in a Russian newspaper—a treasure in itself.

Hunger and thirst were problems. There was no more snow to melt as they moved southward, so their marches carried them from one water hole to another. They learned to catch fish, dig for eels in the mud, and to ease their aching feet in cool water whenever possible. They were no longer pushing themselves to cover 30 miles per day and were lucky if they made 20 miles before collapsing at the end of each day.

Without a map or compass, none of the escapees had any idea where they were. They did know the sun came up in the east and set in the west, and were thus able to keep going in a more or less southerly direction—as long as they traveled by day. The heat, lack of water, fatigue, and poor diet began to take their toll. The terrain became more desertlike, with sand and dunes; the rough going further drained their reserves of energy. In spite of their growing weakness, they continued walking, managing as best they could to encourage and help one another along. From time to time they stumbled upon a small oasis or a bit of water oozing from the ground. It was just enough to slake their thirst and boost their morale so they could continue on their way the next day.

Food and water were foremost in their thoughts as they crossed the Gobi Desert. They tried to maintain a collective will to survive, but their individual fates began to assert themselves. Everyone in the group had experienced sore feet during the long marches, but Kristina's feet became infected. They didn't heal, and the infection spread up her legs. Rather than abandon her, the men took turns carrying Kristina for several days until, during a rest stop, they put her down, and she closed her eyes and died.

Kristina's death frightened the men, and they grieved at her loss as they pushed themselves onward. They didn't have more than a couple of days to dwell on Kristina when Makowski fell by the wayside. Although he was able to stagger on for several days on swollen feet and legs, he succumbed to the same fate as Kristina.

Days of searing heat and exhaustion followed, and the escapees knew they faced death unless they could find water. Rawicz estimated they went thirteen days without it before they came across a dry watercourse in which a trickle of water was discerned. The trickle saved their lives, as did the snakes they found nearby, which, when caught and cooked, gave strength to the starving men.

Starved, sick, and crawling with lice, the group kept walking. Their feet were blistered and sore, they suffered from diarrhea, their teeth were falling out, their eyes became inflamed from sand and glare, yet they pressed on—there was no point in stopping. Gradually they came out of the desert and onto higher elevations with views of far-off mountains. Streams became more prevalent, taking care of their thirst, while snake meat and chance encounters with local people kept them nourished. Rawicz expressed the group's gratitude and humility toward the local people who so unstintingly shared what little they had with the escapees. He marveled at the welcome he and the others received at the hands of nomads and villagers.

They kept walking, and Rawicz guessed they entered Tibet sometime during October. The far-distant mountains were coming closer; villages were passed; they saw their first yaks. Hunger and thirst were no longer constant companions. Their next contact with people proved fruitful. As they came into a small village a well set-up headman greeted them—in Russian. Alarm on the part of the escapees quickly gave way to gratitude as the Circassian man welcomed them into his home. He fed them, answered their questions, and set them on the road to Lhasa, a road that began to ascend into the mountains.

Weeks passed, hunger and weariness again reared their heads, and the group reviewed which direction they should take. Marchinkovas and Paluchowicz thought it best to set their sights on Lhasa itself and rest up before pushing on to India. Rawicz, Kolemenos, Zaro, and Mr. Smith thought otherwise. At last the group agreed to bypass Lhasa and continued on its way, staying away from large settlements.

They had an opportunity to discover where they were when they chanced across a European missionary. Because of suspicion on both sides, however, the opportunity was lost. Days later, the group came across a great lake that stretched as far as the eye could see. They skirted the lake in slow, leisurely marches, enjoying its cool water and flat terrain. They felt refreshed after a few days and once again took the trail south. The climbing became arduous, the weather turned cold and rainy, and one morning Marchinkovas didn't wake up. He had died in his sleep.

After the shock of this unexpected death wore off, with a grave dug and a prayer said, the men continued their walk. Several weeks passed before the group found itself in a good-sized village. Rawicz guessed their arrival took place in late December. They were greeted by an educated man, either Tibetan or Chinese, who spoke to them in French. He introduced himself only as a teacher and treated them kindly, helping them on their way when the time came.

Another month passed, and the reader finds the five survivors being punished by severe weather conditions as they struggled over the Himalayas, crossed the icebound Brahmaputra River, and wondered when they were going to reach India. They were treated one more time to warm Tibetan hospitality when, during February 1942, they found themselves in another village. Being housed and fed for a couple of days was a welcome respite. Before they left, the headman made sure they took supplies of food with them. Thereafter, day followed day, week after week. Crossing the Himalayas tested the worn-out men to the limits of their endurance. The cold was piercing, and hunger reappeared.

They continued climbing over the Himalayas, sensing, hoping, that they were nearing India. It was all they could do to keep going. Altitude sickness affected them with nosebleeds and dizziness; their breathing became labored and painful. They scarcely noticed when they stopped climbing and began descending, the realization finally dawning that they were approaching their goal: India.

Though out of the mountains, there were series of foothills still to cross. During a break from climbing, the men became aware of animals in the distance. They drew closer and observed the creatures from a vantage point. They weren't bears or dogs. They were huge and walked upright. Rawicz estimated their height at around eight feet. The men speculated among themselves about what it was they were seeing, but no conclusions were drawn. It would be years later before Rawicz heard about yetis—abominable snowmen—and realized that's what he and the others had seen.

Leaving the creatures behind, the group continued on its way. As they detoured around the yetis, tragedy struck again: Paluchowicz fell off a cliff to his death. As with the previous deaths, they paused only long enough to say a prayer before picking up their feet and proceeding south. Within a week they were looking into the faces of their rescuers: a native patrol led by a British officer. They had reached India at last.

❦❦

The last pages of the book describe the men's journey to Calcutta, their recuperation in the hospital, the kindness of the medical staff, the separation from and return of Mr. Smith and, lastly, Rawicz's farewell to his companions. Zaro, Kolemenos, and Mr. Smith remained in Calcutta; Rawicz, after having been interrogated by British officials, was allowed to board a troopship and join the Free Poles in the Middle East. Tears were shed, good-byes were spoken, and a page of history was turned. Thus *The Long Walk* ends, impressing thousands of readers around the world with its story of courage and perseverance, yet leaving in its wake questions that remain unanswered to this day—questions that began in 1939.

Chapter 2

RAWICZ

Nineteen thirty-nine, a year to remember. Globally, it's significant as the start of World War II. For our purposes, 1939 marks the beginning of a series of events that led to *The Long Walk*.

The late summer of 1939 heralded the tramp and thud of millions of feet stepping out and connecting with the ground. It heralded the movements of millions of people whose lives were about to be disrupted forever. The slap of all those feet hitting the earth has echoed in my mind for years while researching *The Long Walk*.

The last few months of 1939 and the first few months of 1940 were significant for the number of arrests that took place throughout Europe, both by the Nazis and by the Soviets. Those involved in *The Long Walk* were caught up in this chain of events. Who were these men named in the book: Slavomir Rawicz, Anton Paluchowicz, Sigmund Makowski, Zacharius Marchinkovas, Eugene Zaro, Anastazi Kolemenos, and Mr. Smith? Where did they come from? What had they done? What were their thoughts and feelings? Although particular names were mentioned in the book, those names, I later found out, were not necessarily the same as in the actual events. The name of one of the two men who collaborated on writing the book was actually a composite name; and the name of the man who physically wrote the book has almost been lost to history. And what about the names of the men who escaped to freedom? As the story unfolded to me, I found that each of the men was hesitant to give his true name. I then began to wonder about the validity of the names in the book. How far could the researcher assume the names given were "real," especially in the case of the supposed American, Mr. Smith, who, of all the characters in the book, was the only one professing outright anonymity through the use of a nickname? Were all the other names assumed as well? As I subsequently found out, the name of the principal character and co-author of the book, Slavomir Rawicz, certainly was.

Slavomir Rawicz is a shortened version of Rocieslav Slavomir Rusiecki-Rawicz—quite a mouthful. It was also quite a unique name with a variety of spellings. There were few like it, whether one searched in Russia, Ukraine, Belarus, Poland, or in any other place in Eastern Europe. Considering the bad memories of the War and the imposition of communist rule in Belarus and Poland after 1945, it was little wonder that Mr. Rusiecki-Rawicz preferred another name—a composite name as it were—to protect not only himself but also his family from recriminations and threats. (There were references—in interviews during 1956—that he wished to protect the privacy of his English family, since his Polish family had all been killed in the War.) But was Slavomir of Polish descent? On making linguistic inquiries, it was discovered that, yes, part of the name was Polish while the other part of it was certainly Russian. What did that mean? Could the hyphenated name indicate one of those old aristocratic families that had intermarried with others of their class, had landholdings across half of Europe, and were now scattered to the four winds? Was this double-barreled name even real? One had to assume so as it appeared on birth certificates as well as in obituaries. But I wasn't to know about any of this until well into my research.

❧❧

With excitement and anticipation, I launched myself straight into a variety of Web sites, posing question after question in conjunction with the book. The replies were initially deafening by their silence.

My queries were eventually acknowledged, albeit by more queries. While answers were scarce, the number of replies and further questions took me by surprise. I quickly deduced that there were many readers of the book, and believers in the story, who were desperate for answers. Many of these readers, I later learned, kept up correspondence with Rawicz from the first publication of the book to his death some fifty years later. At that time, there were file cabinets, boxes, bags, and so on at his home overflowing with letters and general correspondence from all over the world. The story captivated the imaginations of thousands of people. It was a story that appealed to anyone rooting for the underdog, cheering on a precarious escape from injustice, and admiring the courage and dedication necessary to attain the goal of freedom. There was also the grand mystery at the end of the story that was still open to investigation: what happened to those four who survived the walk? Many of the readers of *The Long Walk* gradually went beyond pen and paper and were, like myself, exploring cyberspace in an effort to solve the mystery.

My own efforts began with posting queries on genealogical Web sites in hopes that someone with one of the last names of those who had escaped from Siberia might know what became of his or her ancestor. These efforts were fruitless. However, my generic query to Web sites in which I could include the words "Moscow Metro" (where Mr. Smith claimed to have worked in the 1930s) somewhere within the text proved more successful. Thus, the Moscow Metro became my first step toward finding out the truth behind the book.

Simultaneously with the Moscow Metro link was the link I unearthed through looking at old book reviews from 1956. Instead of finding any comment or mention of the Moscow Metro, however, the one word or phrase that appeared in all of the reviews was either "yeti" or "abominable snowman." Now, one can question the veracity of yeti sightings and still speculate on the creature's existence. Basing a true story around a central theme of escape and flight, and throwing in comments about yetis, does cause the reader—never mind the critics—to pause and question the truthfulness of the storyteller.

World-famous traveler and mountaineer Eric Shipton knew all about skepticism when his photographs of a yeti's "footprint" were first published in 1951, during his unsuccessful attempt to scale Mount Everest. Whether Shipton voiced real skepticism or there was professional jealousy involved (bearing in mind that Shipton never saw a yeti, only a footprint), he made light of Rawicz's claim to have actually seen the creatures. Although there followed discussion of travel in Asia under difficult circumstances, no conclusions as to routes taken or yetis sighted were reached.

Other critics of the book, such as Peter Fleming—another renowned traveler and brother to Ian, of James Bond fame—challenged Rawicz on his story from start to finish, concluding the book was "moonshine" and most of the journey invented. Fleming, like Shipton, continued to doubt the story but came round to the possibility that some of it might ring true. Still other critics, such as Freddie Spencer Chapman, a guerrilla fighter in Malaya during the War, would have nothing whatsoever to do with the book, according to his widow, Faith.

Three years before the publication of the book, in 1953, Sir Edmund Hillary and Tenzing Norgay had struggled to the top of Mount Everest—an astounding achievement. The general public focused on that remarkable feat, and remained focused on the Himalayan Mountains for the next couple of years. During 1954, the Daily Mail in England decided to sponsor a trip to the Himalayas—the Yeti Everest Expedition—in search of the abominable snowman. Sir Ralph Izzard, who had covered the Everest Expedition in 1953 for the Daily Mail, was put in charge of the yeti search. (I watched the documentary as a young schoolgirl on my family's very small television screen, and I remember being thrilled by the adventure of it all.)

One of the people instrumental in getting that expedition off the ground was a journalist working for the Daily Mail named Ronald Downing. Downing had been a journalist before the War and after 1939 had entered the military as a Royal Navy (R.N.V.R.) officer who served on a variety of ships in and around home waters while continuing to pursue journalistic duties for the war effort and the British government. Those duties included an opportunity to go along on one of the Normandy landings and report on what he saw.

After the War, Downing returned to journalism full time at the *Daily Mail*. It was during 1954, with the increasing interest in Mount Everest, that word trickled down through contacts, either in the field of journalism or through returned servicemen, that there was someone living in the English Midlands who had been through an incredible adventure, including sightings of abominable snowmen. The subsequent collaboration between Ronald Downing, an experienced journalist, and Slavomir Rawicz, an escaped convict and survivor, resulted in one of the most gripping true adventure stories of the last century. *The Long Walk* was printed in early 1956 and has never been out of print since.

Chapter 3

~~❧~~

DOWNING

Ronald Charles Thomas Downing was the next name on my search engine list. I had considerable trouble finding out anything about him. While Slavomir Rawicz's name appeared on the cover of *The Long Walk,* Downing's name, as ghostwriter, was found on one page only in the Foreword to my 1997 edition. The 1956 edition of the book prominently displayed Downing's name; other editions all but dropped it. Aside from the Foreword in which Downing detailed his introduction to and collaboration with Rawicz to write the book, there was very little about Downing the man.

I put out all kinds of queries on genealogical sites looking for Downing and got nowhere. I tried contacting the *Daily Mail,* writing a letter to them asking that it be forwarded to Mr. Downing. I never received a response to my letter. I decided to phone the *Daily Mail* and speak to someone who might know Ronald Downing. I was passed from one person to another before some kind soul looked up his name on an index card—pre-computer staff member that he was—and suggested I contact the Newspaper Press Fund. It was then that I learned Downing had been a sub-editor at the Press Association and had died in 1961. With that information in hand, I came across an obituary in *The Times* detailing his death. It was a short step after that to contact the General Register Office (GRO) in London and ask for a copy each of his birth and death certificates.

Once I had those certificates, I was able to focus on genealogical sites for Downing's family in Llanelli, Wales. This time round I received replies from a number of people. E-mail messages passed back and forth, a couple of phone calls were made, and soon I spoke to someone who said she had been contacted by a distant Downing relative on a genealogical quest a few years prior. She gave me the name and phone number of a man in the Shrewsbury area who proved to be a close cousin of Downing's. He, in turn, gave me the name and phone number of one of Downing's nephews in London.

At last my research had borne fruit, and it was a satisfying feeling to know that I had tracked down this particular family. I counted myself lucky in that this first successful breakthrough in the research arena put me into contact with such a welcoming and interested audience as the Downing family. When I made contact and explained my quest, I learned that Downing and his wife, Edna, had been childless; Edna died sometime in the 1980s; and there were four nephews, all living—the children of Downing's brother. It became clear from the beginning that the brothers thought very highly of their uncle and that he had been the object of their hero worship. Aside from these observations on my part, I asked if they remembered any comments Downing made while writing *The Long Walk* or before, when he traveled back and forth to the Midlands to interview Rawicz once a month for more than a year. Did they participate in any discussions about the book, about his research . . . anything?

Regrettably, it transpired that the four nephews were all too young during the early 1950s to have participated in adult conversations such as these. That was not to say they didn't hear things when their uncle and their father got together before the two men went off to the pub. Their memories included hearing their uncle comment on how frustrating it was not to be able to verify the information Rawicz passed along to him. Downing apparently tried and tried to contact British authorities who had been in India during the time Rawicz and his group stumbled into the country and subsequently recovered in the hospital. (In later letters to the American publisher of *The Long Walk*—Cass Canfield of Harper & Brothers—Downing put that frustration into print and stated he had contacted Brigadier Nigel Dugdale, Director of Publicity at the War Office, to inquire about wartime hospital administration records and which officers were responsible for the same in the Calcutta area. The outcome of the inquiry was that Dugdale had no evidence at hand to dispute or accept Rawicz's claim that he had been hospitalized in Calcutta. Bearing that in mind, Downing informed Canfield that he could neither "knock down" Rawicz's story nor corroborate it.)

Through my interviews with Downing's nephews, I gleaned that their uncle had been excited to write a book about such an adventure. Apparently, Downing felt that the story was true, and he pursued many avenues to obtain more detailed material about the other survivors of the walk—and, ultimately, hit dead ends for many of his inquiries. Not only had Downing contacted Brigadier Dugdale but in one of his many letters to Canfield, he mentioned asking his friend at the *Daily Mail*, Noel Clark, to approach the State Department in Washington to ask them to contact U.S. Consul General Howard Donovan in Zurich. The reasoning for this contact was that Donovan had been the primary U.S. consul in Bombay during the War and, if Mr. Smith were really an American, then Donovan might remember him. Again, Downing came up empty-handed as Donovan could find no trace of any of the survivors of the walk in his records.

The letters between Downing and Canfield were dated 1956. When I came across them it was 2001, Brigadier Dugdale had passed away many years before, and I had no luck in contacting his family or, indeed, anyone who might have known him. With Noel Clark, I had more luck. I was able to contact Clark and ask him about his approach to the State Department in Washington in 1956. I quoted part of Downing's letter that pertained to him contacting Donovan. To my surprise, Clark got back to me affirming that he had worked in the United States from 1954 to 1957 but he had no idea what I was talking about. He stated the content of Downing's letter was news to him and that, to the best of his memory, Downing had never approached him for his help vis-à-vis contacting the State Department, Donovan, or anyone else. Clark went on to say he had never read the book, although he was aware of Downing having written it, and he had no idea about the authenticity of the account ever being in question.

At the time I was in touch with Clark, I was also in touch with other colleagues of Downing from his days at the *Daily Mail*. Joan Gabbeday Kirby worked in the same office as Downing, and she and her husband socialized with Downing and his wife from time to time. Paul Rossiter worked at the reference library of the newspaper for many years and knew Downing, as well as one of his nephews. Both of these people kindly aided my efforts by making suggestion after suggestion regarding other people to contact: Ralph Izzard's family, Jan Morris, Brian Freemantle, Don Anderson, Jack Starr's widow, Anthony Cave Brown, Christopher Lucas, John Gold, Jeffrey Blyth, and more. Similarly, one of Downing's nephews also began to add names of colleagues to the list: Mike Browne, Riley Moger, Bill Hardcastle, and Noel Barber. He brought me up to date on the family's efforts to obtain more recognition for their uncle's role as the co-author of the book.

With the popular success of *The Long Walk* in 1956, both Downing and Rawicz promptly sold the film rights to Laurence Harvey, a well-known British actor at the time. Fifty years on, no film was ever made, although many attempts to write a film script and produce a movie took place over the years, and the film rights were sold and resold every few years.

During those early days of their collaboration, from 1954–1956, Downing visited Rawicz on a monthly basis. According to Marjorie Rawicz's letter to me in 2002, Downing initially came to interview Rawicz regarding the yeti sighting. Actually, another reporter was supposed to have gone to the Midlands to interview Rawicz but, at the last minute, he became ill, and Downing went in his place. He and Rawicz developed a warm relationship, one of empathy and patience. Rawicz would talk, Downing would make copious notes, then the two would part ways at the end of the weekend. Downing returned to his job at the *Daily Mail*, where he used the office typewriter to type out his notes and send them to Rawicz and his wife for editing. Marjorie Rawicz corroborated this claim by writing that Downing sent the manuscript to her and her husband so that they could make corrections and return the edited version to him. Both Marjorie and

Rawicz restated the fact that they had the last word regarding Downing's edits to the manuscript.

The insistence that the Rawicz family had editorial control over the content and facts of the story dampened subsequent attempts by some readers to blame Downing for any inconsistencies. (One such point of controversy centered on the statement that the escapees had gone nearly two weeks without water while crossing the desert. Rawicz later claimed that Downing had inaccurately described this event—while stating at the same time that Rawicz and his wife had editorial control.) Those inconsistencies and the speculation they fueled only heightened the appeal of the book—so much so that while controversy dogged *The Long Walk*, it was propelled from one reprinting to the next. From the moment of publication, questions were asked as to whether the story was true, whether people could survive walking through a desert for days on end with no water, whether they could have crossed the main east/west road that bisects China without having noticed it, and so on. These questions, and many more, remain unanswered in the public sphere, though answers have been forthcoming privately, in letter form and in interviews with Rawicz. Although Downing died young, at age fifty in 1961, there were still five years from the time of publication until his death in which he had the opportunity to make corrections, do more investigating, and put out feelers for more information. For whatever reason, his interest in pursuing any of those avenues to further elucidate the facts of the story waned. Alternatively, Rawicz lived until 2004, saw the demise of the Soviet Union and the liberation of Poland and Belarus, and could have asked for additional information about his past. He had decades in which to make corrections to the many reprints of the book, but he never bothered. Perhaps it was inevitable that both men decided to allow the controversies to continue as an enticement to future readers, though their true intentions cannot be known.

The popularity of *The Long Walk* notwithstanding, long-term monetary success from its publication seemed to elude both Downing and Rawicz. In Downing's case, he initially bought an automobile and a typewriter, and enjoyed an outgoing lifestyle with his wife and friends for the few years left to him. Sadly, "living beyond one's means" caught up with him in the end. At the time of his unexpected death, he was cleaning and tinkering with his car in order to sell it and pay off debts. Rawicz and his wife fared somewhat better, using the proceeds from the book to buy a larger house and continue renting rooms as an additional source of income. However, according to Marjorie Rawicz's letters, there were sad episodes of frustration with HM Treasury over rights and proceeds from the book. At the end of the day, the book brought notoriety and fame to both families but not very much in the way of monetary benefits. Neither family was ever able to live exclusively from the book royalties.

After Downing's sudden death, his widow, Edna, had to fend for herself as best she could. She had been an actress during the 1920s and 1930s, treading the boards in places like pre-war Berlin, and had known the likes of Beatrice Lillie and J. B. Priestley. She was a good deal older than her husband. From the census of 1901, her name appeared as Ethel Birtwell, daughter of William Gibson Birtwell, surveyor, born in Rochdale; there were two older sisters, Nellie and Edith, listed on that census. At some point Ethel changed her first name to Edna and also adopted the stage name of Laurence, so that her name on the marriage certificate to Downing, dated 1938, was recorded as Edna Laurence Birtwell. Her date of birth on the marriage certificate was shown as 1903; however, in the census records, she was born in 1900.

Despite a rather glamorous life before the War and fun times with Downing during her marriage to him, once he died Edna was left emotionally and financially bereft. Very little money came in from book royalties, and she was too old to go back to the stage. Edna became a barmaid, working at a popular watering hole near the *Daily Mail,* where she kept in touch with her late husband's colleagues. Gradually, she dropped out of sight and seemed to vanish into thin air, according to the Downings. For unfathomable family reasons, Edna wanted nothing to do with her Downing in-laws, although they attempted to contact her on more than one occasion to offer some financial help. To their frustration during one such attempt at contact in the 1970s, they found the building on Cathcart Road completely empty. Edna and all the other occupants were gone; the premises were being gutted, renovated, and put up for sale. (The

Newspaper Press Fund indicated in a letter to me that they had been in touch with Downing's widow until 1980. They helped her out financially from time to time, as best they could.)

It eventually transpired that Edna met a neighbor, a man by the name of Harold Ward, with whom she developed a relationship after Downing's death. Once the premises in which she had lived for years were sold out from under her, she moved in with Ward and remained with him until her death in 1982. By the time my research got under way and I was interested in learning about Edna, it was clear from the Downing family that they knew little about her antecedents. My interest revolved around any manuscript or raw notes left to Edna after Downing died; then, when I discovered she had died some twenty years later, I attempted to track down any of her family members in hopes they would have inherited something from their aunt.

I quickly discovered there was little in the way of an inheritance. Downing had died suddenly in middle age without a will. As with most intestate deaths, Downing's estate went directly to his widow, Edna. Although "estate" is the word commonly used on these occasions, there was precious little of it at the end of the day. The car had to be sold, there was a large piano that went, the typewriter disappeared, and there weren't many other items that would fetch any money. My concern, however, was not with money but with paper—manuscript notes, journals, diaries, and so forth. When I asked the Downing family if they knew whether their uncle's notes from writing *The Long Walk* were still in existence, they said they had no idea; they went on to add that they knew their uncle had been working on another manuscript at the time of his death. I had no luck tracking down Edna's nieces and nephews to see if they had inherited any of these items from her, and because of the family estrangement between Edna and her in-laws, the nephews never knew what happened to any of the items in question either. In other words, Edna never mentioned what became of her husband's belongings on the rare occasions she and the Downings communicated after Ronald's death.

(After their uncle's sudden demise, the Downing family felt awkward about the rebuff they suffered at the hands of his widow. One or two of

Downing's nephews, teenagers at the time, remembered accompanying their father to Cathcart Road, where Edna lived, trying to make contact with their aunt and offer help, financially and emotionally. Edna consistently declined those offers.)

Before I could ask the Downing family about Edna's "estate," I was told she had also died intestate, though, unlike Downing, her death was not unexpected by the time it occurred. She died in a hospital well into her eighties. What happened to Edna's estate? Because of the peculiarities of the intestacy laws in Britain, her estate came under the umbrella of HM Treasury and remains there to this day.

At one point, Harold Ward's son talked to me at length about his father and Edna. Though no light was shone on what became of Downing's manuscripts or notes, it was heartening to learn that Edna had been looked after and cared for by Ward in her twilight years.

Probing into other people's lives made me aware of the need to be cautious. My queries into past lives sometimes aroused old memories that were less than happy, sentiments that were not benign, feelings that were still sore after several decades, and wounds that should have remained closed. Instead of seeing a wide-open field of research ahead of me whenever I made contact with a subject, I began to see a minefield of emotions. It was an important lesson to learn as I continued to question the veracity of *The Long Walk*.

Chapter 4

〜

KOLEMENOS, ZARO, AND
MR. SMITH

A ll along the research route I tried to follow the old adage about leaving no stone unturned. I kept going back to revisit genealogical Web sites pertaining to Rawicz and two of the other men who made it to India with him: Kolemenos and Zaro. Over time I received replies from researchers who stated that Kolemenos, as spelled in the book, was most definitely a Greek name. Later on, however, I was contacted by genealogists who thought the spelling was wrong and that it might, indeed, be more like Kolymenous, Kalminis, Kalamanas, Kalmann, or something similar, which I was informed was a Lithuanian name, and possibly Jewish. Zaro, it turned out, had many adherents from the Mediterranean, primarily Yugoslavia and Italy. Then there was the name of Ushakov, the commandant of the camp from which the men escaped. I had a few replies from researchers who mentioned that Ushakov was the name of an old military family in Russia, but no one had ever heard of the particular Ushakov and his wife mentioned in the book. Little did I realize at the beginning that the number of names I received to follow up would grow exponentially.

While delving into names and various spellings, I began to branch out and contact groups such as the British Red Cross and its American counterpart. These organizations in both the U.K. and the United States do admirable work, but only if one can prove that the research is on behalf of a relative, not just a personal interest in someone. The organizations hide behind something called the Data Protection Act, a relic of the Cold War that has no place any longer in modern research. (By 2007, even the war records of the Nazis in Germany were at last thrown open to relatives and researchers alike.) Considering that most national archives around the world adhere to either a seventy- or one-hundred-year ban on personal data, and all the birth information on the people whom I wanted to research was outside that ban, mentioning protection rights was a little out of place. The International Red Cross in Switzerland was more accommodating, but they came up with nothing in the way of documentation about the men who had made the long walk to India. They did, however, suggest that I try to contact the Indian Red Cross to see if their records would shed any light on the subject. Although daunted by the thought, I went ahead and wrote to that organization, only to learn later that records from the time of Indian independence were not centrally located and the information I was seeking could be anywhere.

On that encouraging note, I then tried to contact the Royal British Nurses' Association as Rawicz mentioned nursing staff in the book. This time I received notes to contact the Royal College of Nursing and ask about retired nurses. I followed up that e-mail with a phone call, but got no results. I had the same sorry repetition of events with the Royal Medical Association.

At the same time I was pinpointing mainly British medical associations in 2000 and 2001, I also began to focus on the American angle. As stated in the book, Mr. Smith had been separated from the others once they were in Calcutta. Could he have been taken to an American medical facility? Were there any such things in Calcutta in 1942? I found a Web site that led me to the Office of the Surgeon General, U.S. Army. The person who replied to my query was full of facts, very detailed, but the dates were for American medical facilities much later than 1942. (I had to keep in mind that the book's mention of March 1942 was only the approximate time for when the small group of escapees finally stumbled into India.)

What next? I reasoned that if Mr. Smith were an American and the book mentioned that he was separated from the others and later returned with new clothes and a new look, then someone must have paid for those clothes and that look. I set about trying to find a *Diplomatic List* for pre-war India. Gradually I tracked one down, listing diplomats at their posts right up to the beginning of 1942—just after the bombing of Pearl Harbor in December 1941. I flipped through the pages to India, then Calcutta, and there were names—lots of names—of diplomats stationed at the U.S. consulate in Calcutta for 1941–42.

Any name that was fairly common, such as Smith, Jones, Williams, Davis, I immediately put aside as being too time consuming to track down. Two names, however, were quite unusual and, perhaps, more easily traceable: Colquitt and Hillenbrand. As it turned out, in all of the United States there was only one Adrian Colquitt listed on the Internet. I found myself engaged in more than one long conversation with Colquitt, who was full of charming reminiscences and memories of Calcutta before and during the War, up until the time of his death in 2002 when he was well into his nineties. He was unable, however, to shed any light on Mr. Smith. He encouraged me to contact the next name on my list, that of Martin Hillenbrand, the former U.S. ambassador to West Germany.

Both Hillenbrand and his wife were delightful to talk to. They were full of stories of the past. They had met in Burma in the 1930s—he "a young whippersnapper" of a diplomat; she the daughter of missionaries. As the Japanese were pouring into northern Burma in early 1942, they both managed to jump on one of the last transport flights out of the country and ended up in Calcutta. Hillenbrand was assigned to be a vice consul in charge of, among other things, helping Americans in distress; his wife later became a secretary at the Hastings Mills headquarters of the U.S. Army Air Force in Calcutta, and eventually worked with such larger-than-life figures as General Wedemeyer.

They both told marvelous stories of dancing at consular parties while dodging Japanese bombs falling on Calcutta, and many other adventures. Hillenbrand, himself, was busy trying to aid drunken American merchant seamen in returning to their ships before those ships left them to the mercy of the oncoming Japanese. He frequented many of the low dives and bars in the Calcutta area trying to keep track of any American who may have been stranded. We had long discussions as to who Mr. Smith could possibly have been, because it became immediately apparent that, as in the case of Colquitt, Hillenbrand had no knowledge of any American who had escaped from a prison camp in Siberia and turned up in India a year later. Hillenbrand also stated that he was in charge of emergency funds and repatriation, and any paperwork regarding travel documents or passports would have gone through his office. Despite all the activity with Japanese bombs falling, the appearance of an American citizen who had walked from Siberia to India, never mind sighting yetis along the way, would have been a nine-day wonder, and Hillenbrand felt sure he would have heard about it.

Before finishing with the diplomatic angle, Hillenbrand suggested I look into the possibility that Mr. Smith went to either New Delhi or Bombay, for whatever reason. In 1942, the seat of American interests in India was centered in Bombay. I put out feelers via the National Archives and Records Administration (NARA) in Washington, D.C., at the same time as I kept looking at the names on the *1941–1942 Diplomatic List.* Hillenbrand also thought that an approach to the American Foreign Service Association (AFSA) might be beneficial. He thought I might be able to ask them to include a query in their monthly newsletter concerning my research. I followed that suggestion, had a positive reply from AFSA, but never heard a peep from anyone about Mr. Smith.

In the meantime, NARA came back empty-handed, but I did manage to track down more names via the *Diplomatic List.* One of the people I subsequently contacted was Frances Brotzen, secretary to U.S. Consul General Howard Donovan, who was mentioned in Ronald Downing's letter to his American publisher. Donovan was the doyen of the American consular staff in India at the time, and Brotzen worked for him for quite some years. Brotzen had a wonderful memory for people and stories but had no knowledge of anyone resembling Mr. Smith, either in Bombay or New Delhi, seeking help from the American authorities. She did, however, mention another couple of names of people she knew who were in U.S.

intelligence at that time, stationed at the U.S. consulate in Bombay. One of those people was Coulter Huyler.

Searching through records concerning this man proved to be a long and fruitless venture. The episode of Coulter Huyler became my first, but not last, example of a true "dead end." I contacted the family and friends of Huyler's—who passed away in the 1990s—at the same time as one of the archivists at NARA found documents, stamped Top Secret, about Huyler and his intelligence activities in India during the War. During this flurry of activity, Huyler's name came up in the writings of Richard J. Aldrich, *Intelligence and the War Against Japan,* and of Professor Windmiller at San Francisco State University. Both men kindly helped me to discover something about Huyler's career as an intelligence officer and, later, as a CIA operative.

Huyler, it turned out, was the scion of a chocolate manufacturing family in New England. He went to India as a member of the U.S. Army Counter Intelligence Corps and was attached, like many others in those early days of 1942, to a unit of British intelligence in Bombay. He shared a bungalow with U.S. vice consul Charles Adair, who later married Huyler's cousin. Huyler reported to a British officer at this time whose name no one could remember except for his nickname: Coffee Cup. While all this information swirled around me in a fascinating but meaningless cloud, Frances Brotzen got back to me with yet another name, that of Phillips Talbot, who was later the U.S. ambassador to Greece. I spoke to Talbot on two occasions about his wartime activities, and he stated he was the first U.S. naval liaison to the British, sent out to Bombay right after Pearl Harbor. He remained on duty in Bombay for several months and was unaware there had been any other U.S. intelligence people in India at that time. Although he knew Brotzen and Donovan at the U.S. consulate, Huyler's name, not to mention that of Mr. Smith, did not sound familiar. So, at the end of the day, the Coulter Huyler tangent turned into a waste of time.

❧❧

I began veering toward the military edge of my inquiry. With contacts established between myself, NARA, and AFSA, I started to place queries on military intelligence/World War II Web sites, especially those dealing with the China-Burma-India (CBI) theater of operations. I received all kinds of replies to those queries, many of them pointing me in the direction of Wild Bill Donovan (no relation to Howard Donovan in Bombay), who organized the Office of Strategic Services (OSS), the forerunner of the current CIA; however, none of them were able to address my questions concerning *The Long Walk*.

So, after floundering through the shallows of a variety of wartime Web sites, and the shifting sands of diplomatic tittle-tattle, I took the plunge and began to look at the overall military picture, both American and British. Coincidentally with receiving replies and reports from NARA, I contacted the Imperial War Museum in London. They sent me information about their collections and what they might have pertaining to World War II operations in the CBI theater. As the book mentioned the escapees had been picked up by a British patrol (British officer leading native soldiers) in the foothills of the Himalayas, I thought it made sense to begin delving into military matters, especially those pertaining to the British Empire. I received lots of information, but little of it was relevant to my search.

I also poked around on Web sites concerning the "other side" of the British Empire forces, the Indian Armed Forces, and soon found myself receiving an invitation to submit a query to *Sainik Samachar (Military News)*. I followed up on that in early 2002 and did receive replies but, again, they were more on the order of the replies I had received to my genealogical queries—namely, what had I found out so far in my research.

(Whether my queries pertained to military matters, family names, nursing, historical narratives, and so on, the replies I received from people around the world impressed me. Most of the people who replied had read or heard about *The Long Walk* and wanted to find out what new information had come to light. They looked on my efforts as a research mystery. Their questions in reply to my online queries made me realize there was a large, worldwide audience with a real interest in *The Long Walk*.)

Chapter 5

FROM MOSCOW TO SIBERIA

At the same time e-mail messages were whizzing across the globe to
the U.K. and the Indian subcontinent, other messages were being
received from my postings on those first genealogical Web sites. One day,
I received a message from a small group of people who asked if I would
like to join them and collaborate on investigating the story. They realized
my efforts were serious and that I was receiving responses from around the
world. They, in turn, began to share with me what information they had.
Ultimately, one of them contacted Yahoo!, and *The Long Walk* (TLW) forum
was established, to which anyone could contribute.

While I had managed to track down and discover the Downing family,
they had been busy contacting Rawicz directly. Some of the members of
the TLW group had already corresponded with Rawicz years before. They
were early readers of the book, which had sparked their imaginations,
and now, through the Internet, they were hoping to do a little research
on their own into the story. Aside from the group's interest in the book,
there was an added impetus. Some of the group members knew and were
friends with a Hollywood scriptwriter. This particular scriptwriter was
enraptured by the story and wanted to shape it into a film script. To that
end, he requested help from this small group and also hired a professional
researcher to begin digging at NARA and elsewhere. The researcher came

up empty-handed, though. There didn't appear to be any formal docu-mentation at NARA pertaining to Mr. Smith or to the other participants of *The Long Walk.*

❧ ❧

This would be a good place to review the unanswered questions raised by the members of the group over the years. At the end of considerable discus-sion, it was decided that each member of the group would draw up a list of questions we would like answered. The questions were mostly clones of one another, confirming that we were all definitely on the same wave-length. Many of the TLW group had already asked their questions in letter form to Rawicz at earlier dates but took the opportunity to ask for more details. The questions were grouped into three categories. The first cate-gory consisted of questions about Rawicz's early life, his arrest and impris-onment, the fate of his first wife and family, and led up to his arrival at a labor camp in Siberia. The second category had more pointed and specific inquiries: Where was Camp 303 actually located? What was the camp like? What kind of person did the camp commandant, Ushakov, appear to be? More importantly, just how much did Ushakov's wife encourage and/or outright help the prisoners to escape?

While the first two categories dealt with Rawicz exclusively, the third category—questions about the escape and subsequent walk—encom-passed the entire group of men. This part of the story prompted all kinds of questions dealing with the practicalities of escape and survival: How well planned was the escape? How well did the men know and get along with one another? Why hadn't they taken more food with them, and uten-sils? How was it possible to walk for almost two weeks without water, never mind food, in the desert?

The last set of questions surfaced once the survivors finally staggered into India and were taken to Calcutta: Why hadn't the survivors kept in touch? What happened to them? And, of course, the ultimate question: Who was Mr. Smith? Every reader of the book had asked that question since 1956—and there was still no answer.

Mr. Smith was certainly the sticking point. Just how many American engineers had there been in Russia in the 1930s and 1940s? In addition to typing queries into Internet sites concerning the American engineers who had worked on the Moscow Metro, I was also trawling through book reviews and library catalogs for any information about those men. *The New York Times* ran several articles throughout 1931, stating that six thousand Americans were to join an estimated thousand U.S. workers already in Russia to work on a variety of projects: some would go with their families, others on their own; many, if not most, were Europeans of German or Russian descent who had become U.S. citizens but were going back to Europe to help build a new country; and nearly all of them went as skilled laborers—miners, carpenters, railroad workers—to destinations scattered all over Russia. The *Economic Review of the Soviet Union* also ran endless articles on the need for and recruitment of foreign engineers to work in the U.S.S.R. throughout the late 1920s and early 1930s. These articles focused on the concept of "job opportunities" offered by the nascent communist country and compared those opportunities to the alternative available in 1931 in the capitalist West—becoming a permanent fixture on a bread line. The writing targeted American laborers with news and praise about the "good life" awaiting them in the Soviet Union as contract workers.

One such worker was John Scott Neering, writing as John Scott. His book, *Behind the Urals,* was published in the 1940s and described his life as a mining engineer. Along with fifty-nine other foreigner workers, Scott also contributed an essay to *60 Letters: Foreign Workers Write of Their Life and Work in the U.S.S.R.,* published in 1936. All of these essays contained a sense of gratitude to the Soviet government for job opportunities as well as a sense of being needed and respected as the specialists many of them were. That's not to say there weren't complaints, mainly about living conditions as well as work standards. Scott, for instance, had returned to the United States with his wife and family. I wondered if he might still be alive, or if anyone in his family would remember life in the early days of the Soviet Union? Would they have heard of the American engineers in Moscow? How was I to track down this family?

Quickly, the real dilemma became how to track down any of the engineers who worked in pre-war Moscow! Searching for those engineers led me to Michael Gelb. I came across a reference by Gelb to a work he edited concerning Zara Witkin and Amtorg, the American Trade Organization. Amtorg, in lieu of the U.S. government, officially did business with the U.S.S.R. in those long-ago days before diplomatic relations. Their board of directors contained only Russian names, men who acted as go-betweens and managed overall trade relations with respect to both countries. The saga of Witkin, Amtorg, Alfred Zaidner, and a host of others requires writing a book of its own. Suffice it to say that it made fascinating reading; there were lots of names, but nothing that pointed to a Mr. Smith. Unfortunately, Witkin died in 1940, and his family declined to comment on his past history, having burned all his records after his death; records for Amtorg were either housed at the Hoover Institution at Stanford or scattered to the four winds; and Zaidner, an Amtorg executive, was reportedly taken out and shot at the foot of a wall behind the Lubyanka during one of the Moscow purges in the mid-1930s.

Gelb proved to be a great source of information. With his help, I tracked down one of John Scott Neering's daughters and learned that her Russian-born mother was still alive, though not able to talk for long on the phone. Though the family tried to be helpful, they had not lived in Moscow for any length of time, nor did Neering's widow remember anything about a Mr. Smith.

Another suggestion from Gelb pointed me to Professor Bill Wolf at Ohio State. He had dared to breach the portals of Soviet-era police archives while doing research in Moscow in the early 1990s. He came across a dozen or so names of those legendary American engineers who once worked on the Moscow Metro. Wolf kindly passed on those names, which I added to my genealogical queries, and guessed that, in all, no more than perhaps fifty Americans ever worked on the Moscow Metro in the 1930s. Nearly all of the names he came across sounded either German or Russian, possibly Jewish. Once I cranked up my trusty search engine, I did manage to track down the families of four of those names. Disappointingly, none of the men who had actually worked on the Moscow Metro were still alive, though their family members remembered hearing about the famous underground system.

One family in particular, Weiner, got back to me to say that their grandfather's papers were still intact. In other words, the family still had their grandfather's Soviet-issued I.D. card that had allowed him to come and go while working on the Metro. I also learned from another family that the American engineers, a number of whom were in Moscow with their wives and children, were all housed together and were thus segregated from their Soviet counterparts in housing for foreign specialists. Some of their wives had taught English to Soviet officials. Assessing the wide variety of sources and comments, the general consensus from these families was that their relatives were idealistic (not all were card-carrying communists); they went to the Soviet Union to follow a dream; and they came home disillusioned. Returning to the United States, the descendants of these men heard nothing but complaints about the Soviet system and their treatment at its hands. The engineers came back disenchanted and frightened in the aftermath of the many purges they had witnessed and were lucky enough to escape.

It was suggested I make further inquiries of professors who had ferreted around the archives of the KGB while pursuing academic careers in Russian and Soviet studies. J. Arch Getty, Adam Hochschild, and Antony Sutton were names of academics that I contacted and who passed on valuable thoughts and pointers. Hochschild and Sutton both warned me about the frustrations of trying to do actual research in Moscow at the KGB archives, which, in the many years since the two academics had delved into it, had moved and changed its name. I was also warned that it would be another frustrating experience to try to do research long-distance through a fellow researcher in Moscow—a hard fact I later found to be true.

Along with my own individual efforts at research, the TLW group that had contacted me about The Long Walk kept me posted regarding their collective efforts. So far, those efforts had not been as far reaching as hoped. Several members of the group were going through the same frustrating steps as I was, sending e-mail messages and letters around the world with scarcely a reply to show for all the effort. The pace and scope of our collective efforts picked up and broadened, however, when the Hollywood scriptwriter contacted us to say he had arranged to visit Rawicz and his wife in England with the objective of conducting a lengthy interview (backed up by the TLW group's input) before settling down to write the film script. During the time in which the logistics of the plan were being hatched, news came about a woman who reviewed the book in 1956 while working as a book reviewer in Calcutta for *The Statesman*. Her name was Shirleyanne Cumberledge.

❧❧

My first conversation with Shirleyanne and her husband, the first of many conversations and e-mails, was very informative. She was down to earth, had great stories to tell, and made many worthwhile suggestions. The gist of her comments, though, had to do with her review of *The Long Walk*. She was already aware that people such as Peter Fleming were dubious about the book's content. So she put out an appeal for information concerning the story. A man came forward who stated that he was the British intelligence officer mentioned only as "the British officer" in the book. It was he who had questioned the escapees while they convalesced in Calcutta. That man turned out to be Rupert Mayne, who died in October 2001.

Thanks to Cumberledge and David Gore, the author of a monograph on Mayne with the title of "Death on the Pale Horse," I managed to locate a copy of Mayne's obituary and, thus, track down his children. With the encouragement of Cumberledge and Gore, I also took the opportunity of contacting the Special Forces Club in London, the Special Operations Executive (SOE) Archives, the Burma Star Association, and a host of other organizations. More names were soon to appear, as if by magic, from a seemingly endless reservoir. However, the name at the top of my list was that of Rupert Mayne.

Chapter 6

MAYNE

Rupert Eric Mosley Mayne—another long and singular name to remember. Mayne came from a family whose history stretched back some two hundred years in India. A photo of him as a child astride a camel, attended by an Indian servant, adorned the cover of Charles Allen's *Plain Tales of the Raj*. His was a name associated with Mayne's Horse, later the Central India Horse, and the Deccan Horse, cavalry units of the British Raj. His name was also connected to that of General Sir Ashton Mosley Mayne, an uncle. Where exactly did Mayne fit in with British intelligence? From the monograph "Death on The Pale Horse" I gathered that he was a captain during the War; however, from his obituary, I learned he was in Force 136, a clandestine intelligence outfit in the China-Burma-India (CBI) theater, with a subsequent rank of lieutenant colonel. It was stated that Mayne liaised directly with General Sir William Slim of the 14th Army. His name was also listed in the (British) Army List for 1950 under the heading "Emergency Officers (ex-Indian Army)" with the rank of 2nd Lt. I also came across references to him as Major Mayne. The confusion as to rank, and the duties attached thereto, deepened each time I tried to get clarification—from his family, his friends, colleagues, history buffs, and the like.

Mayne's children were helpful, but knew nothing specific about their father's part in questioning the men who had made such a long walk to

India. His son read the book as a teenager when it first came out and was thrilled to learn his father was "the British officer" mentioned therein. His memory of Mayne's comments complemented that of Cumberledge, the book reviewer, namely, that the escapees were in a dreadful state, and there had been some doubt about their story, but by and large their adventure seemed plausible. While Mayne did not go into detail with Cumberledge, stating he was bound to silence under the Official Secrets Act, he might have done so with his son; however, what teenager could possibly remember, fifty years later, something his father said to him? The details, if any, were lost.

That is not to say there was no more to be heard from the Mayne family. There were further links to explore in the effort to contact anyone who might have known or even spoken to Mayne over the years. One of the most important people in this search was the head of the Indian Army Association, Patric Emerson. Through him, as well as Mayne's children, contact after contact was made. Emerson put out an annual newsletter to members of the Association and kindly included a query regarding Mayne and *The Long Walk*. Emerson also had access to the Indian Army lists as well as to contacts at the National Army Museum in London. He went out of his way over the years to dig, make suggestions, dig some more, and prod me along when necessary. He was a wealth of information about army life in India and helped me immensely to understand ranks, emergency commissions, units, regiments, and all the specific expressions that pertain to the military.

One suggestion, though, came from a member of the Special Forces Club who recollected that someone named Boris Hembry had been a great friend of Mayne's. Unfortunately, Hembry had died many years before. However, I located his son, who filled me in on his father's careers as a rubber planter in Malaya and as an intelligence officer with V-Force and ISLD (Inter-Service's Liaison Department) in the CBI theater. Hembry kindly passed on a copy of his father's unpublished memoirs, which were a delight to read—full of information and insight; but the memoirs raised more questions than they answered, and Mayne's name did not appear in them.

While I was in contact with the Hembry family, I also had the good fortune to be in touch with Terence O'Brien, author of *The Moonlight War* and other accounts of World War II. He interviewed both Mayne and Hembry in the 1980s prior to writing one of his books on the CBI theater. O'Brien came across as quite a raconteur, both over the phone and in his long e-mail messages. O'Brien went on to supply yet more names of people I should contact about Mayne's role in *The Long Walk*. He, like so many other people, heard about Mayne's appearance in the book as the British intelligence officer. Mayne, himself, made no secret of his part in the story, apparently mentioning it every time the book was reprinted. The odd thing was that no one could recall any details Mayne may have let slip at that time. But it was O'Brien who let valuable information "slip" in one of his very long e-mail messages, full of names and details. In one such e-mail, there was one little phrase that eventually unlocked the mystery of Mayne's role during the War.

Mayne first came across in my research as something of a mystery man, albeit a man who occasionally appeared larger than life. Some of his old friends, such as Bob Wright, who still lived in Calcutta at the Tolly-gunge Club when I contacted him, remembered him fondly as "Roaring" Rupert because of his loud parade-ground voice. His friends remembered a man who could tell a good story and who was a mainstay of the Special Forces Club. Other people were not so kind to Mayne's memory. Over the ninety-one years that Mayne was alive, suspicion crept in about his bona fides, primarily because there were inquiries from time to time by friends and acquaintances about what he actually did during the War. No one seemed to know—I was told numerous theories, such as he had been in ISLD, or that he was in Force 136, or that he had been in the Secret Service. I got hints of Mayne having become the "club bore" in more than one e-mail and letter. Whether he bored people or titillated them made no difference to me; what I was after had to do with verification of his role in *The Long Walk*. To discover that, I had to backtrack and dig into his military background—and this proved to be long and rather exhausting.

As references to Force 136, SOE, and General Slim were sprinkled here and there in monographs, obituaries, e-mails, letters, and the memories of his friends, I decided to start the search for Mayne's wartime military career with Patric Emerson of the Indian Army Association. It was he who pointed out that the magnificent photograph of Mayne, as shown in his obituary, had one flaw. While Mayne proudly stared out at the camera, dressed in an immaculate military uniform with his hair slicked back and his moustache trimmed—the very picture of a pukka World War II officer—there was something missing. I scoured the photo but couldn't figure out what was amiss. Mayne seemed to be "all there." Emerson, who had only glanced at the photo, immediately put his finger on the problem: there was no insignia on the collar tabs. What did that mean? "His insignia's been airbrushed out of the photo," Emerson replied.

Speculation ran rife between us and later between me and several people who, like Emerson, were attuned to the hierarchical nuances of the military. In other words, most World War II military men have only to glance at someone's collar to glean volumes of information about rank and regiment. I spoke to Mayne's son about this, and he was surprised. He was unaware of the omission. Members of the Special Forces Club, however, saw the same as Emerson and commented on the lack of insignia. Perhaps it really did point to his inclusion in an intelligence outfit. It was certainly puzzling.

During this particular time I began to receive feedback from the Burma Star Association, both from Paul Loseby, who managed the Web site, and from the Association's secretary, Capt. Paddy Vincent. Letters went back and forth, and soon I received a note from Vincent, who had elicited a response from the current Viscount Slim, General William Slim's son. The gist of the response was that, indeed, Mayne had been on General Slim's staff during the 1942 retreat, as a G.2 intelligence officer. He went on to add that the Burma Star Association would be happy to incorporate a query into their magazine *Dekho* concerning Mayne and his wartime activities. The edition with my query was printed and, once again, I received responses from people asking what I had learned so far. Much to my dismay, no new information came of that effort.

Other efforts, though, proved a bit more fruitful. Through the offices of O'Brien, Wright, Emerson, Cumberledge, and Mayne's children, I also made contact with people such as the Gemmell family, tea planters in India before and during the War; Lady Jardine Patterson, who was in Calcutta during the War and knew the Mayne family from that time onward; Dr. Maurice Shellim, a doctor in Calcutta right after the War; Theon Wilkinson of the British Association of Cemeteries in South Asia (BACSA); Ranjit Gupta, a commissioner of police in Calcutta during and after the War; Ian Gardiner, Lionel Severy, Alan Hoe, and Don Palmer, all of the Special Forces Club—the names flowed endlessly, one after the other. Bits and pieces of information accumulated but the actual question as to what Mayne did in the War was still not answered.

The Imperial War Museum, the Oriental & India Office Collection (part of the British Library), the PRO (Public Records Office, which later became the National Archives), and the SOE Archives (which soon closed its doors and transferred its holdings to the PRO) all returned my queries and essentially said that they had nothing on Mayne; in fact, they had never heard of the man. The National Army Museum in London threw in its lot with the rest, stating that his name did not appear anywhere in its records.

With so much discouraging news, I was momentarily at a loss as to where I should turn. I began to grasp at straws, sending queries to the publishers of *Plain Tales of the Raj* in hopes of contacting Charles Allen; the flurry of e-mails and phone calls between myself and members of the Special Forces Club reached monumental proportions. I clutched at any prospect, no matter how remote. Faith Spencer Chapman, widow of the renowned Freddie, kept in touch with me, providing yet more names to research. In the end, my impetus ground to a halt. Had Mayne actually ever existed? There was the evidence of photos and of his children, but trying to get a grip on Mayne was like trying to catch hold of a slippery eel.

That is not to say the inflow of facts and fantasy dried up. While the Burma Star Association and the Indian Army Association were both running queries on my behalf, not to forget the appeal in *Sainik Samachar,* I took Shirleyanne Cumberledge's advice and wrote to *The Statesman* in Calcutta with a query similar to the one she had placed in 1956. (Not long after this, a member of the TLW group discovered a useful Web site:

www.allreaders.com. Someone by the name of Ramesh Nayajee wrote in stating that a member of his family had either been on the patrol that came across the escapees when they entered into India or was on the medical team that cared for them. Ramesh contacted allreaders.com with this information, then promptly vanished into cyberspace without replying to any of the subsequent queries his comments had elicited.)

More information arrived in the guise of suggestions to contact diverse nursing organizations located in the Calcutta area during the War. Perhaps someone working as a nurse remembered Mayne or the men who made the long trek from Siberia. Letters and e-mails were written once again. I was in touch with the Lady Minto Nursing Service as well as the Queen Alexandra's Imperial Military Nursing Service, the QAIMNS. Mention of these organizations was made through the Burma Star Web site. It was on that particular Web site that I also found quite a bit of material about nursing in field hospitals in Assam during the War. There was a lengthy memoir about a nurse by the name of Ivy Prichard. She was at the field hospital in Panitola, Assam, at that time.

Delving into the nursing facet of the research brought me into touch with Elizabeth Kaegi, Prichard's daughter, and this led to contacts with Len Thornton, who recently had his memoir, *Another Brummie in Burma,* published. Both of these people were extremely helpful to me in my floundering efforts. Kaegi suggested I contact the Koi-Hai Web site that encompasses the families and histories of tea planters in Assam. Through that organization I came into contact with Sandy Cleland, who had been in the Assam Rifles. Thornton suggested the Friends' Ambulance Unit, wartime pacifists (British Quakers) who were brave enough to ship out to the CBI and drive ambulances while ducking Japanese bombs. Name after name proceeded: Bill Brough, Laurie Baker, George Parsons, Henrietta Thompson, and Pete Lutken, among many others. Hand in hand with these outfits were the FANYs and the Chinthe Women, aka WAS(B)s (First Aid Nursing Yeomanry and Women's Auxiliary Service Burma, respectively). I was beginning to sink under the weight of names and accompanying acronyms.

Part II

ESCAPE FROM SIBERIA

Retelling the Tale

The new year of 2002 began with the anticipation that solid information regarding *The Long Walk* would soon be at hand. The Hollywood scriptwriter was preparing for his visit to England to interview Rawicz. I and the rest of the TLW group received a long e-mail from him. We were all in a state of excitement, pinning our hopes on concrete facts and answers coming forth from this meeting.

Prior to the visit, we each contributed lists of questions, often duplicated. The lists sprouted with "whens, whys, and wheres." We also swapped information we'd gathered from other sources. Books such as Victor Hermann's *Coming Out of the Ice* and Josef Bauer's *As Far As My Feet Will Carry Me* were mentioned. Web sites dealing with a variety of subjects including the POW/MIA Gulag Study site looked after by Michael Allen were noted. Articles were passed around about missing Americans in Russia, their histories, and their fates.

Comparing stories with other firsthand experiences helped to define questions we all had about the book. Our questions dealt with the group's escape from the Siberian labor camp, the walk across China and Tibet, and the arrival of the survivors in India. Had the escapees definitely gone thirteen days without food and water? Had the commandant's wife really helped them escape? Who exactly were the other escapees with Rawicz?

Were their names, as spelled out in the book, true, or were they false? Once in India, did the four survivors really not talk to each other about their pasts or futures? *Who* was Mr. Smith? What happened to the two other survivors of the walk? The questions went on and on but, in general, they were mere echoes of the same questions that had been asked since 1956.

One difference, however, became startlingly clear. While the book brought on an avalanche of speculation at the time of its publication about the existence of yetis, thanks to the alleged sighting of them, not one of us raised that particular question. We all had enough on our plates, grappling with the logistics of those thudding footsteps throughout the story; there was simply no interest in this day and age to speculate on yetis.

So, with questions galore, the scriptwriter from Hollywood headed for England in early 2002. Within a short time he was back, with many pages of interview notes. Those of us in the TLW devoured every word.

ℰ✺℥ ℰ✺℥

It seemed that Rawicz, his wife, and their family lived outside Nottingham, England, since the end of the War. In 2002, Rawicz was in his late eighties and still vigorous, despite some health problems. Although he wrote to many in our group, only one member had actually met him. He was described as being tall and lean, with thick gray hair, a neat beard, and eyeglasses. He still spoke with a heavy Polish accent after more than fifty years in England. He took pride in his surroundings and in his family. Rawicz pointed out the filing cabinets in his home that were overflowing with fifty years' worth of correspondence. He spoke about the charity work he did to benefit Polish orphanages and to fight against global hunger. He referred to the many newspaper articles and reviews of his book. He was voluble and easy to listen to.

The interviewer showed Rawicz a photo of Rupert Mayne and asked if he remembered the man as being the British officer who interviewed him in Calcutta. Apparently, tears came to Rawicz's eyes as he recalled that period in his life but, all the same, he shook his head and said he didn't recognize the man in the photo. He went on to explain that while recovering in or near Calcutta he hovered between life and death. He had no idea where he was nor what was going on around him. He repeated phrases from the book that indicated he hoarded food under his mattress and then forgot about it until the nurses found it.

During the interview with the scriptwriter, Rawicz's eyes welled up with tears on more than one occasion. Passages from his life still deeply affected him in the retelling. However, as the scriptwriter talked about his own hopes of writing a screenplay and of seeing *The Long Walk* become a movie, smiles and laughter came to the fore. Rawicz said he had heard it all before. There had been nearly twenty attempts over the years to make the book into a movie since he had sold his film rights to Laurence Harvey. He would believe it when he saw it.

⌘⌘

Movies aside, Rawicz began to relate his story to the scriptwriter. It was one of horrendous bad luck, the bad luck of anyone living in Eastern Europe, and Poland in particular, in 1939. Millions of people like him were caught between two huge armies led by megalomaniacs who tossed people aside like straws in the wind. Human life was cheap and had little or no meaning, and Rawicz soon found himself under arrest. He repeated the main facts of his young life as stated in the book: he studied architecture and surveying at Wawelberea and Rotwanda Technical School in Warsaw before the War; he attended cadet school and became a lieutenant in the Polish cavalry when the War started; he was recently married and soon after was arrested. He also spoke at some length about his boyhood and his family. His father had been a painter and an artist, as well as a landowner; his mother was Russian, and it was from her that he learned to speak that language. He also mentioned a nanny who sang Russian folk songs from the Lake Baikal region, which held him in good stead when he later found himself in a camp in that area. All in all, he spoke of a near idyllic boyhood outside Pinsk, in what is today southern Belarus.

Rawicz continued the recitation of his story, following the narrative in the book. Basically, he was arrested, tortured, and transferred from one prison to another, until he found himself on a train headed for Siberia.

He and hundreds of other prisoners disembarked at Irkutsk and began walking. That initial walk took weeks and covered hundreds of kilometers until they reached their destination near the Lena River: Camp 303, a labor camp in which the main occupation of the inmates was to cut timber.

It was the escape from the camp and the subsequent series of events that was of most interest to me and to the members of the little group who encouraged the scriptwriter. The question-and-answer sessions were based on our lists of queries. They began with a review of Rawicz's days in the camp and the time spent getting acquainted with the other potential escapees. They also included questions about the commandant, Ushakov, and his wife.

Rawicz repeated the depiction in the book regarding his work making skis at the camp, then his introduction to commandant Ushakov because he knew something about fixing radios. His relationship with them developed after each successful meeting. Finally, Madame Ushakov spoke of escape. Rawicz described her as having been in her forties and very attached to and protective of her husband. Ushakov had slipped up elsewhere, allegedly because of his drinking, and had been sent to Siberia to take command of a labor camp as punishment. Thanks to family connections, his wife was able to join him in his "exile," though she was not happy to be there. Rawicz related an unguarded comment made by Madame Ushakov in which she stated she dreamt of herself as having wings with which to fly away from the camp and from Siberia itself. However, while encouraging him to escape, she wanted any such attempt to take place when her husband was away so no blame would fall on him.

Rawicz proceeded to talk about his fellow escapees. As in the book, he mentioned the people he approached, and those who approached him, about escaping: Sigmund Makowski, Anton Paluchowicz, Zacharius Marchinkovas, Eugene Zaro, Anastazi Kolemenos, and, of course, Mr. Smith. When asked if any of the others, especially Makowski who was a captain and in his late thirties, resented Rawicz being their nominal leader, the latter replied there had been no actual leader. He said they all contributed thoughts and suggestions on how to escape and what to do afterward.

However, it's apparent to any reader of *The Long Walk* that Rawicz was, in effect, the true leader of this band of escapees.

The common thread Rawicz wove throughout this part of the interview dealt with the necessity for secrecy, which was based on his fear of capture and of being returned to the labor camp. The risk of escaping was only slightly less than the risk of capture and the certain torture that would accompany it. Rawicz recalled that he learned a little bit about each of the above men and never asked for more information, nor did he contribute any about himself. During their collective time in camp, their thoughts were solely focused on preparations for their escape: food and clothing.

Of course, the major question for any American interviewer would have to do with the identity of Mr. Smith. As set out in the book, Rawicz stated that initially he and the others thought the name Smith was actually Schmidt, a good German name! They were astounded to learn he was an American; and there was a rumor of at least one other American in the camp at the time of their escape. Then came the information that was *not* included in the book, namely that Mr. Smith told them his name was Herbert Smith and they could call him Herb. (At this point there was some discussion about the names Herbert and Herb, and somewhere in the mix Fitzherbert made an appearance—later to be disavowed by Rawicz.) At any rate, Rawicz went on to say he and the others did not like the name "Herb," thinking that it signified "grass," even though none of them could speak English and would have known what the name implied. In the event, they continued to call him Mr. Smith.

This man appeared to speak English, although none of the other escapees had enough knowledge of the language to be sure, while at the same time he spoke colloquial Russian as a native speaker would. He was possibly in his late forties or early fifties and did not talk much about his past except to refer to having been an engineer on the Moscow Metro, having had a Russian girlfriend, having been arrested in 1936 during a purge, and having eventually ended up in Camp 303 after already spending years in other camps. He did, however, tell Rawicz that he loved the United States and that he had made a trip to Mexico, during which visit he bought a saddle with silver trimming. From that one comment, Rawicz speculated that Mr. Smith might have come from Texas. He also replied to a question about Mr. Smith's faith by suggesting that he was a Christian rather than a Jew. The question arose because so many of the men who worked on the Moscow Metro were from Jewish families; many of them had been born in Russia and emigrated as children to the United States, only to go back as adults to help build socialism in the young U.S.S.R. Lastly, after some thought, Rawicz became specific about Mr. Smith's age, stating he had been fifty-one. When asked why that particular number stuck in his mind, Rawicz couldn't say.

Speculation about Mr. Smith and his actual identity was laid aside as the interview picked up speed. The escape itself was gone over in detail; the days of racing into the unknown, wondering if the group would make it, afraid of capture, led to the mention of coming across a trapped elk. The meat from this animal and its hide to make moccasins proved to be lifesaving.

Rawicz also detailed how they tried to trap small animals and gradually learned to catch fish by using Kolemenos, a big man, to block shallow sections of streams and, in effect, dam the fish into a confined space so they were easy to grab. Later on their flight, Rawicz mentioned finding the eggs of ground-nesting waterbirds that were edible.

Following the recitation of some of the obstacles they encountered as they fled south, Rawicz flatly denied they had gone thirteen days or more without water as alleged in the book. He declared that during the crossing of the desert there had been thunderstorms, which the book failed to mention, and the escapees dug holes in the sand and used their jackets to catch the water. They also used those jackets to catch condensation that formed during the night, or simply licked any condensation from rocks in the early hours of the morning. At the same time as they were trying to trap enough water to drink, they had to think about food. Not only had they caught and eaten snakes, as outlined in the book, but they also caught and ate earthworms. The worms, when cleaned, had been a good source of protein and not too gritty.

The comments about unexpected water from rainstorms and food from earthworms prompted the scriptwriter to question why these details were never inserted into the book. Surely, with so much criticism leveled at it in 1956 by men who traveled in the Gobi, in China, and in Tibet, and knew the rigors of such travel, it would have made sense to include these details. Rawicz supposed Downing left them out either through oversight or because of squeamishness. The interviewer made a counterargument pointing out that Downing died in 1961 and the book continued to be reprinted for another fifty years. In all that time it would have been possible for Rawicz, on his own or through the services of another ghostwriter, to correct the record and lay many of the criticisms to rest. Rawicz agreed that corrections should be made to the narrative in the future, but he made no effort to take on that task.

Leaving details of survival to one side for a moment, the interview then centered around the appearance of Kristina in the story. Kristina Polanska. Her story still brought tears to Rawicz's eyes after more than five decades. He again described how her escape route crossed their own, how fate threw them all together as they continued on their flight south. At this point, however, Rawicz digressed. Not only did he talk about Kristina but he also mentioned that, initially, he had not told Downing very much about her. At the time, he could not bring himself to go into any detail about her with Downing. It was later, after most of the book was written, that Rawicz broke down and told his wife, Marjorie, Kristina's full story. He dictated to Marjorie the entire chapter in the book pertaining to Kristina: the men's encounter with the runaway teenage girl, their travels together, and the subsequent death of Kristina from, in all probability, malnutrition, which led to gangrene from infected blisters. He spoke of her tearfully throughout the interview, obviously wishing that something could have been done to save her life. As to hard facts about her identity, though, he knew little more than what was written in the book.

With the death of Kristina began the diminution of the group. Due to the hardships of the escape and travel through hundreds of miles of snowbound terrain and waterless desert, the group began to weaken. Any previous health problems came to the fore. The result was that after Kristina's death there were three more: Makowski seemingly died from the same cause as Kristina; Marchinkovas died in his sleep; and Paluchowicz fell to his death at the time of the yeti sighting.

While speaking of the escape and the hardships endured, the interviewer asked Rawicz whether he or any of the others knew where they
were during all their wandering. He insisted, as he had since 1956, that
they had no idea where they were, only that they were heading south, away
from Siberia. Rawicz again went over some of the high points in the book,
namely, meeting caravans of local people into which the leaders welcomed
them and fed them; of being welcomed by a Circassian man, and later
by shepherds and townspeople; of an enigmatic meeting with a German-
speaking missionary; and of ultimately stumbling into India where they
were met by a British officer leading a native patrol. (One interesting note
came to light at this juncture. Although, as stated above, Rawicz had no
idea where he and his companions were and they blundered blindly along
until their encounter with the patrol, during the interview he expanded
on his mention of seeing birds in trees and spoke of walking through
tropical vegetation and seeing beautiful butterflies. He then remarked that
Mr. Smith later told him they were in the vicinity of Bhutan or Sikkim.)

The scriptwriter asked about any stresses or conflicts that occurred
between the escapees on such an arduous trip. Rawicz replied that, of
course, there were disagreements from time to time. Some of their discussions became heated when debating pre-war politics: Why hadn't Poland
been more prepared for the blitzkrieg? Why had the world not seen what
was coming? Why was everyone turning a blind eye to Stalin? Yet, under
the circumstances, they agreed that escape was their primary concern, and
escape they did. Any disagreements that arose were mainly over the direction of their escape. Early on there had been talk among themselves about
veering east and heading into China, but they had all heard rumors of
civil war in that country. They were afraid of encountering the Chinese
military on their travels and of being handed over to the Russians, so they
continued due south or southwest. Then, at one point, Mr. Smith had the
idea to strike out much farther west and make for Afghanistan, though
none of them had any idea where Afghanistan actually was. After some
debate, they decided to stick to their southerly route in hopes of reaching
India, a fairly big target.

Near the end of the interview, the focus shifted to the last part of the trip: their rest and recovery in India. Rawicz revisited the story of bumping into the British patrol in the foothills of the Himalayas and of initially being taken to some kind of field hospital where he and his comrades were checked over and released for further travel. They then went to a larger medical facility somewhere in or near Calcutta.

For decades, people speculated that this larger medical facility was the Presidency General Hospital in Calcutta; however, Rawicz said he was sure he was never in any such grand hospital (the scriptwriter had a photo of the gates and main entrance of the hospital taken from an album of World War II photos, which Rawicz did not recognize). He remembered being in a ramshackle medical facility with wooden or bamboo gates rather than an imposing set of metal gates, as suggested in the book. Having been delirious from hunger and ill health, his memories were vague about places and people who attended to him and his companions.

Rawicz pointed out that while in the hospital he weighed in at less than 100 pounds. As stated earlier, he and his comrades hoarded food. He had little memory of the people who came to interview him, although he did remember that the Polish interpreter who came with the British intelligence officer to question him wore a British uniform. He then said it was possible the man was a Polish Jew, although he could not explain why he thought so. In retrospect, he also stated that the native patrol led by the British officer were most likely Gurkhas. It was while he and his comrades were recovering that they learned about the Japanese invasion of Burma and that the Japanese were bombing Calcutta. Rawicz repeated his wish to the scriptwriter that he had wanted to join the Free Poles, although the others, Zaro and Kolemenos especially, only wanted to find a safe haven where they could recover and wait out the War.

When asked about Mr. Smith, Rawicz remarked that he was separated from the others once they were in the hospital recovering, although in the book this separation took place earlier, right after they were found by the British patrol and taken to a field hospital. He stated that while the three comrades remained in or near Calcutta, Mr. Smith went off or was sent to Bombay to meet with American authorities. (This piece of information was left out of the book.) When asked how he knew this—whether Mr. Smith had mentioned this side trip all the way across India and back—he couldn't say. He did state that Mr. Smith was in Calcutta at the time he, Rawicz, left and that apparently Mr. Smith was given new clothes; he was wearing a gray suit and a panama hat while Rawicz had an Australian uniform to wear, complete with a hat with an upturned brim.

At their final parting, the members of this incredible long walk to freedom embraced, with tears running down their faces and with promises to keep in touch. Mr. Smith rode with Rawicz on a bus to a nearby transit camp, where the latter was to await transport on a troopship to the Middle East. (Although not in the book, Rawicz declared that he was put—"carried" was his word—onto a troopship, but he did not know the name of the ship nor did anyone on board speak Polish. After a pause, he then said he thought the name of the ship was "Empress of something.") Rawicz reported that he gave Mr. Smith his Warsaw address and extracted a promise to visit after the War. In return, Mr. Smith gave Rawicz a silver cigarette case. When the scriptwriter asked to see the cigarette case, Rawicz explained that it had been "pinched" along with some of his other gear when he landed in England, after his sojourn in the Middle East.

Rawicz was again asked why, at the very end, none of the men made any serious attempt to learn more about each other or to exchange addresses, for instance. Rawicz had no answer except to state that "not knowing" had become a part of their being. Even though they were safe in India, they were out of the habit of questioning one another. He also stated they really had no addresses to exchange. Although he wanted to go back to Europe and fight with the Free Poles, Zaro and Kolemenos wanted to stay where they were or perhaps go to Australia after the War. Rawicz assumed Mr. Smith would return to America. He also assumed his real name was Herbert Smith and, therefore, did not press the matter.

⁓

Thus the interview ended, with little new material to add to the story of *The Long Walk*. Yet, there were tidbits that raised many new questions regarding the events in the book and why certain passages were never corrected. For instance, Rawicz dismissed the account in the book of traveling nearly two weeks without water and declared Downing must have "got it wrong." At the same time, he stated over and over again that he and Downing had a very warm relationship, and he and his wife admired Downing's prose immensely. From the very first interviews with Downing for articles in the *Daily Mail*—regarding the sighting of yetis—he and Downing hit it off. He felt Downing was a very responsible journalist who was meticulous in sending him and his wife monthly drafts of what he had written for their review and editing. What's the explanation, then, of why corrections were never made? It is easy enough to point out that Downing died young in 1961; however, the book had already been reprinted more than once by that time, so surely it would have been possible to submit an Afterword as, in fact, later occurred. Rawicz concurred with this assessment when questioned by the scriptwriter and agreed that future corrections should be made to the story.

So what happened? No corrections were made; no updates were added to the current Afterword. Rawicz's wife, Marjorie, passed away in early 2004, and Rawicz soon followed in April of that year. The questions about the story and what happened to the other three escapees continue to linger.

Chapter 8

〜♾

SPECULATION AND CRITICISM

After all the firsthand information was digested from the interview with Rawicz, it was time to move on to other avenues of research. I sorted through the information I had gathered up to this point, looking again at my written communications with the Downings, with the Maynes, with the TLW group and the scriptwriter, and with a host of other people. There were lengthy and detailed messages to and from the POW/MIA people concerning possible sites for Camp 303 in Siberia. Contact was made with someone in U.S. intelligence who wished to look into the identity of Mr. Smith. (It turned out this man had actually met Rawicz and his wife some years earlier and became interested in the story. He wanted to probe into what little was known about the American escapee in hopes of reaching a better understanding of Mr. Smith's character and personality.) At this juncture, I took a fresh look at anything that had been uncovered researching *The Long Walk* since 1999.

I noted that in the correspondence referred to previously between Downing and his American publisher, Cass Canfield, mention was made of Downing's approach to U.S. Vice-Consul Neil Ruge in London in 1956. As a sequel to that, I contacted Ruge's widow but she couldn't recall her husband ever having mentioned the names of Downing or Rawicz. She graciously made further suggestions as to whom I might contact including colleagues of her husband at the embassy, but nothing came of those suggestions. No one I contacted remembered Ruge ever referring to *The Long Walk*. However, it turned out that Rawicz mentioned to the scriptwriter during their recent interview that in early 1956 two intelligence men from the U.S. Embassy arrived at his house to ask him about Mr. Smith. They listened to Rawicz's reminiscences, asked questions, and finally left with a request that Rawicz get in touch with them should he remember anything else or should he ever hear from Mr. Smith. In the end, Rawicz neither heard anything from Mr. Smith nor from the U.S. Embassy again.

There continues to be serious speculation that Mr. Smith may have been a U.S. intelligence operative. This speculation has fueled the general air of mystery around a supposed American being imprisoned in Stalin's Russia as long ago as the 1930s and by the aforementioned visit to Rawicz by U.S. Embassy personnel. Although they did not introduce themselves specifically as American intelligence officers or CIA agents (that would have been against embassy protocol, which never acknowledges intelligence personnel operating in another country), they communicated such an identity as they questioned Rawicz about Mr. Smith. Realistically, though, if Mr. Smith had, in fact, gone to Russia in the early 1930s with the other engineers of the Moscow Metro, he probably was an engineer and nothing else. American intelligence was in its infancy before World War II. Certainly there would not have been anything as organized as a web of infiltrators to the Soviet Union in the early 1930s, despite the fact the Soviets felt they were harboring spies of every nationality—not just Americans—in their midst; hence, the purges and trials throughout the mid- and late 1930s of hundreds of foreign workers.

The U.S. Embassy was interested in Mr. Smith, and the public at large was interested in anything to do with *The Long Walk*—when it was first published. To that end, Downing was interviewed on television in 1956 and, during the interview, made an appeal for anyone having information about the story to come forward. Alas, the tape of that interview could not be found five decades later. The people who did know something about the story, such as Rupert Mayne, were still overseas and never heard the television appeal requesting information from the public.

❧❧

Comments and criticisms about the book were reexamined while I reviewed the material I had uncovered so far. One of the most pronounced criticisms, aside from going without water while crossing the desert, was that there was no mention in the book about crossing the main east–west highway in China. This road runs, essentially, from the east coast of China to Urumchi in the far west of the country. It was already more or less in place as a caravan route centuries before and is perhaps more famously known as the Silk Road. By the 1930s, when motorized vehicles were becoming more widely used, the road was blacktopped and became the principal east–west artery for China. The highway was unavoidable to anyone traveling from north to south. So why hadn't Rawicz mentioned crossing it in the book?

This question was easy enough for me to answer because I had traveled extensively in China in the 1980s and 1990s as the country was opening up more and more to travelers. As recently as the mid-90s the highway was simply a single-lane road. I traveled along it by rail, by bus, and by hitchhiking. During those trips, there were periods of bad weather with the wind blowing at gale force, the sand so thick in the air that I had trouble seeing a few feet ahead, and the road disappeared from view. The narrow strip of tarmac was covered into the distance with several inches of fine sand, enough to make me realize that, unless there was prior knowledge about the existence of a highway, it could easily be missed under certain circumstances or if traveling at night.

While reflecting on my observations of the road in the 1990s, I began to wonder what the highway looked like in the 1940s when Rawicz and the others were escaping south. Reading books by Sven Hedin, Mildred Cable, Sir Aurel Stein, and many other travelers in pre–World War II China, and looking at the photos in their books, it became obvious that the east-west highway existed mainly in name only. Looking closely at those old black-and-white photos, I noticed that portions of the road were without any blacktop at all, only bits of gravel and sometimes only simple tracks in the sand. By the early 1940s, with civil war raging around China, the Japanese in Manchuria, and general chaos residing in the world, little attention was given to road maintenance—if at all—for long periods of time. Thus, I felt I had effectly addressed the question of the east–west highway.

The general chaos in China during the war years might also help in understanding another criticism, namely that the escapees from Siberia did not try to walk into China proper and seek help there; rather, they chose to walk around the Chinese heartland, all the way to India. As was stated in the book and by Rawicz during numerous interviews, the men on the walk had already learned of the chaotic conditions of war raging around the world. So, while there was some initial discussion about striking east, they talked themselves out of that path because of the unknown reaction by the Chinese toward them as escaped prisoners. They also perceived, during their southerly travel, that when mentioning any of the major names of cities in China to the few people they came across, they received negative reactions. Sign and body language denoting fighting and upheaval quickly deterred them from their idea of entering China. The one word that prompted a positive response from the few people whose paths crossed theirs was "Lhasa." Generally, the listeners pointed in the opposite direction of east when pronouncing that word; and the men of *The Long Walk* heeded their direction.

The escapees tried to maintain a south-by-southwest course so as not to find themselves drifting into China, but didn't want to stumble directly into Lhasa either. Keeping all this in mind, the description in the book concerning coming across a large body of water, almost an inland sea, and it taking them days to skirt the lake shore before continuing south, led to speculation about the location of such a large body of water. There are three choices for the lake's location: Manasarovar, in the west, near Mount Kailash; Namu, just north of Lhasa; and Qinghai, far to the north and east of Lhasa, at the outer boundary of greater Tibet. From Rawicz's description of an immense expanse of water with no horizon visible in the distance, the only possibility would be Qinghai Lake, also known as Koko Nor. Further speculation lead me to believe the escapees skirted the lake on its eastern shore before proceeding south. If so, their path would have taken them well to the east of Lhasa as they progressed in a southerly direction.

Another geographical criticism leveled at the time of the book's first printing and that continues today is the reference to having crossed an icebound river. With the escapees not having a map and not speaking local languages, they had no idea where they were when they got to this river. Rawicz later determined the river to have been the Brahmaputra or, as known in Tibet, the Yarlong Tsangpo.

By the time the book came out and the questions and criticisms began, Rawicz had only himself and his memory on which to fall back. During the interviews in 1956, he guessed that he and the others came down into India through Bhutan or Sikkim, based on a comment made to him by Mr. Smith. Peter Fleming and Eric Shipton, among other critics, immediately pounced on this by stating that Rawicz would then have needed to cross the mighty Tsangpo/Brahmaputra at some point. Rawicz replied that they had crossed a river by walking on the ice. However, it was pointed out by the well-seasoned explorers that the river does not ice over—it's a free-flowing river year-round. (I can personally attest to this as I was in Tibet in the spring of 1985, and the Tsangpo was moving very swiftly. It was deep enough that anyone attempting to cross it would remember the experience.)

It is odd to me, when thinking back to 1956, that there was no discussion of the possibility that, in fact, the Brahmaputra was not crossed. How could that be? The river runs from west to east across all of Tibet and then it suddenly turns back on itself before heading south into India, not quite reaching the border of the Chinese province of Yunnan. No critic ever seemed to suggest, or think it possible, that the men had walked much farther east than previously thought, that they had not only avoided Lhasa by doing so but they had also avoided crossing the Brahmaputra as well. In other words, their long walk quite possibly took them close to, if not definitely into, the Chinese border area along the western flank of Yunnan.

The betting is that whatever icebound river or stream they crossed was not the Tsangpo but some other smaller river or stream. Also, the trajectory of their southerly wanderings from Siberia could easily have put them in a longitudinal position to have passed east of Lhasa and closer to the Chinese border. This plausible route makes sense when, after roaming the shores of Qinghai Lake, they continued due south, trying not to swing too far either to the west or east in their wish to avoid populated centers and other trouble spots, such as military encampments.

The last critical comment dealing with the geographical accuracy of the walk originated with Shipton and others who were unable to grasp how it could have taken Rawicz and his party nearly two months to cross a part of Tibet which, under any circumstances at whatever time of year, could be crossed in a week's time. Shipton based his remarks on Rawicz's own comments of averaging a walking speed of approximately 20 miles per day. If, however, the group marched through Tibet much farther to the east, as I believe they did, and the river they crossed was some other than the Tsangpo, then the time frame could quite possibly fit.

Not only would the time frame fit but the description of stone houses and multi-story dwellings would also be plausible. These types of dwellings are still found in the eastern part of Tibet and also into Yunnan province, where Tibetan-speaking people live to this day. It is also striking that, in this eastern part of Tibet, *tsampa* is not normally eaten. For the uninitiated, *tsampa* is a roasted barley concoction that is a staple food in upland Tibet and, once tasted, is never forgotten. It was not mentioned in the book as Rawicz proclaimed he had never eaten it.

Having picked apart the thoughts and criticisms of fifty years ago I began to make a list of my own critical observations. Although the story and the book were riveting, there was something missing from the bigger picture, something that didn't add up in the overall series of events. A long period of pondering began in which I tried to think of another angle of attack, of another way to discover the real story.

Part III

THE WALK'S AFTERMATH

Chapter 9

INDIA AND BEYOND

It was time to take a different approach as 2001 came to an end. I had been busy concentrating on delving into names I already had. I browsed through genealogical Web sites looking into the names of the Moscow Metro engineers, of the men who had walked to India, and of the people who had contacted me with information or with offers of help. However, having reexamined a mounting pile of letters, e-mail messages, notes on the backs of envelopes and sales receipts, I decided to put aside these avenues of research and concentrate on another unexplained part of the story—the ship that supposedly took Rawicz to the Middle East. It later transpired during the recent interview with the scriptwriter and in letters to private individuals that Rawicz recognized the words *Empress of* . . . on the side of the ship that transported him half a world away.

As I began this stage in my research, I asked myself, "What did I know about ships?" It turned out I knew very little, although I had worked on fishing vessels during a particularly adventurous spell in my life. I knew nothing about ocean liners or troopships, though. The only starting point I had was *Empress of*. . . . Surely there were not many ships with names beginning like this and I believed it would not be difficult to track down the particular ship that had docked in Calcutta in 1942.

How wrong I was! There were Web sites and books about the *Empress* ships in World War II. Several very kind people, including Ron and Maureen Venzi and Billy McGee, were able to pull an amazing amount of data together about these ships and pass it on to me, including size, tonnage, trips to which port and when, how many passengers/troops were aboard, whether the ship made it to port, and so on. The wealth of information made for fascinating reading.

There were several ships beginning with *Empress of . . .* : *Empress of Japan, Empress of Scotland, Empress of Russia, Empress of Canada, Empress of Australia*—the list went on. The culmination of all this information, though, was to learn that by the summer of 1942 only the *Empress of Canada*, the *Empress of Russia*, and the *Empress of Japan* (renamed *Empress of Scotland* in October 1942) were still afloat; all the others were sunk or captured.

I eventually discovered the existence of passenger lists in the ships' logs housed at the Public Records Office outside London. This discovery drastically narrowed my search field. With the partial name of a ship, *Empress of . . .* , and a sailing date of late spring or early summer 1942, I was hoping to pinpoint which ship Rawicz boarded to the Middle East. From one of my contacts I learned that due to the Japanese bombing of Calcutta during that spring and summer, there was little to no Allied shipping calling in at Calcutta at that time.

Suggestions by the Venzis and Billy McGee were made that perhaps Rawicz had not left from Calcutta after all but from Bombay; however, despite his weakened condition, it seemed very likely that Rawicz would have remembered a multi-day trip across India to Bombay in order to board a ship. Nevertheless, I looked at various ships' logs and it appeared the *Empress of Canada* touched at Bombay in the spring of 1942. So, it is plausible that he left from Bombay; however, I soon learned that the *Empress of Canada* did not travel from Calcutta to the Middle East. Rather, it sailed to North Africa. The *Empress of Russia* also came into port at Bombay during 1942/1943 but turned around and went only as far as South Africa before docking again. I looked long and hard, but there were no *Empress* ships that touched port in India and then went to the Middle East during the late spring or early summer of 1942.

❧ ❧

Feeling at an impasse about which ship Rawicz may have taken out of India, I continued to receive dozens of e-mails and letters in response to queries sent to *The Statesman* and *Sainik Samachar* in India. Replies to other questions were coming in as well from my appeal in the Indian Army newsletter put out every spring by Patric Emerson in the U.K.

I decided to make appeals for information about Ronald Downing and Rupert Mayne in a similar manner. In the case of Downing, I contacted the *Press Gazette* and they offered to place a query on my behalf asking for people who had known or worked with Downing to contact me. I also contacted the Royal Naval Records Centre at Greenwich to find out more about Downing's wartime activities. Through this query I discovered that Downing was an ordinary seaman in March 1941 on HMS *Raleigh*; September 1941 saw him transfer to HMS *Drake*; he had a short stay on HMS *Beehive*; then a commission and a posting to HMS *King Alfred* in November 1942 followed. The list continued until Downing's decommissioning in February 1946.

As for Rupert Mayne, I posted his name, together with that of his longtime friend Boris Hembry of ISLD, on the Burma Star Association's Web site. That association had already placed a query on my behalf in their monthly newsletter, *Dekho*. I reached out to the author Terence O'Brien, with his myriad contacts, and he responded with an abundance of suggestions and names of publications to which I might write. There was certainly no shortage of avenues to pursue in my quest to discover the truth behind the story.

I probed into gulag sources, into Siberian labor camps and their names and numbers, their commandants, and whatever else I could think of. I began to write letters to "Memorial" in Russia asking if they had any documentation about World War II Siberian labor camps. I also asked if the Society had information about Rawicz. Ultimately, it took a long time to hear back from "Memorial" and the news was not encouraging. They had no specific information about the camps, and their records were based on personal names and not on locations. The Society recommended I contact Karta Indeks, the Polish affiliate to "Memorial." That organization also used a name-based system to identify the various labor camps, which did not help me to locate Camp 303.

Months went by while I waited for replies from these various organizations. Meanwhile, I contacted the Hoover Institution in California to ask whether they had any material on the American engineers who once worked on the Moscow Metro. They replied, stating they had letters, documents, and correspondence from Americans who had worked in the U.S.S.R.; and there were documents about the Moscow Metro and Amtorg, the company that did the recruiting for the Metro. The problem was that there was no cross-referencing between these entities. What was more disconcerting was that none of the dozen names of engineers I had already amassed appeared in the Hoover Institution records.

An interested employee at NARA replied to my questions about Coulter Huyler, the U.S. intelligence officer in India in early 1942, but had no information on a Mr. Smith. It also appeared there was no information about any of the names on my list of American engineers who worked on the Moscow Metro in the 1930s and 1940s.

So, decisions loomed. Was it worth a trip to California to dig around? Was it worth a trip to Washington, D.C., to wade through the National Archives? Should I consider a trip to England to visit the Public Records Office and the British Library's Oriental and India Office? It was becoming obvious that to get any closer to solving the mysteries behind *The Long Walk*, I'd have to make a trip somewhere.

Trying to keep a sense of direction while in the midst of grasping at straws, I began to formulate a letter to Slav Rawicz. I had put off writing him until I could collect my thoughts and gather as much information as possible about his story. I was partway through writing my first letter to him in 2002 when I suddenly made contact with the family of Ronald Downing.

The Downing family had been tracked down through various genealogical Web sites I had contacted. With their collective help, I was then able to contact friends and colleagues of Downing who knew him in the 1950s when he was actively involved with the great Yeti Expedition as well as with writing *The Long Walk*. Downing's friends, family, coworkers, and acquaintances all spoke highly of his integrity as a man and as a journalist. His work on the *Daily Mail* was considered an example of how journalism should be done. From all accounts, including those of Rawicz and his wife, Downing spent a year or so traveling to and from London interviewing Rawicz with patience and tact. He never pushed Rawicz when memories became painful, nor did he display boredom with the slow pace of the interview process. Downing did his own research, sent letters all over the world trying to find out more information about the story, and kept coming up empty-handed, though not without hope that the story was actually true and would be verified.

Once the book was published, Downing continued to try to authenticate the story. The only questionable comment I came across, and this was not about his efforts or his integrity, came from Noel Clark. Clark was mentioned in one of Downing's letters to his American publisher as a Washington-based correspondent. In his letter, Downing declared he had asked Clark to make inquiries, on his behalf, about how to approach Howard Donovan, the U.S. Consul General in Bombay during the War. When I contacted Clark, he said he knew Downing and knew he was writing a book in the mid-1950s but he had never been approached by Downing with a request for research assistance. There may be all sorts of reasons for Clark's refutation of Downing's request for his help, including errant letters and lost memories. Whatever the truth of the matter, Downing learned from Donovan that no trace of Smith was ever found in the consular records.

Downing's attempts at verification included being interviewed on television after the publication of the book when he made an appeal to viewers for any information about the story. (Rawicz later referred to that interview in a letter to me and went on to say that nothing ever came of it.) Downing was disappointed that his research was unable to authenticate the story.

Although Rawicz shared his disappointment, he was not overly perturbed by it as it was his story and he was sticking to it.

Over the years, there has been a tendency by some readers to blame Downing for errors, discrepancies, and misunderstandings surrounding passages in the book. Through my research, though, I've concluded that this was hardly the case. Judging from letters written by Downing and by Rawicz to a number of different people, Downing made great efforts to get the whole story of *The Long Walk* out of Rawicz and to then verify it. He concluded that the story was "sound." Rawicz, on his part, praised Downing in his prolific correspondence to readers over the years, stating his confidence in Downing, his respect for the man's honesty and patience, his admiration for his writing style, and so on.

The only point at which I could later question Downing's research involved Rupert Mayne. As the interviews with Rawicz progressed and Downing learned of the "British officer," why hadn't he attemped, through military channels, to identify the officer who interrogated the four survivors? Knowing that thousands of military men were still in far-flung parts of the British Empire, why hadn't he thought to appeal overseas? Although Mayne was still in India in 1956 and could not have seen or heard Downing's television interview, he willingly came forward in response to the appeal for more information in *The Statesman*.

There is no indication that Downing or Rawicz ever heard of Mayne at this time. The one possible link between these three men was the book reviewer, Shirleyanne Cumberledge. Neither Downing nor Rawicz knew of her efforts on the other side of the world to authenticate the facts of the story; and she knew nothing of their appeals for verifiable information. If Downing had heard of her efforts and learned the identity of Mayne, no doubt he would have corresponded with the latter. The fact that Mayne *did* come forward corroborated the existence of the "British officer" described in the book who came to interrogate Rawicz at the end of the walk. Regrettably, Downing was never to learn of Mayne, and Rawicz only learned about him some forty-five years later.

Chapter 10

RAWICZ AND DOWNING

Having spoken at length to Ronald Downing's family and associates, I sat down at the trusty computer and typed out a long letter to Slav Rawicz in the late summer of 2002. I introduced myself as someone who had read *The Long Walk*, was taken by the story, identified with the terrain, and was in contact with the TLW group, members of which were friends of his recent visitor, the scriptwriter from Hollywood. I finished up by passing on greetings from the Downing family. After a silence of nearly half a century from Downing or his family, Rawicz wrote a very long letter back to me expressing surprise. (Due to ill health, Rawicz dictated this particular letter to Marjorie, and she later wrote me another letter independent of the one dictated by her husband.)

It turned out that Rawicz had met Downing's brother, Kenneth, on a couple of trips to London while the interviewing and writing of the book were taking place and again at the book launch in 1956. Rawicz and Marjorie were aware that Kenneth had children and that Downing and his wife, Edna, were childless. They met Edna when she accompanied her husband on two of his interview sessions with Rawicz and again during the events surrounding the publication of the book in London. After Downing died, they had hardly any communication with Edna. Marjorie wrote that

Edna dropped out of sight and eventually died. (It was never made clear how she and Rawicz knew about Edna's decline and eventual death.)

At any rate, I outlined my recent contact with Kenneth's widow and his sons. Three of the nephews with whom I spoke centered their recollections on Downing's frustration at not being able to find hard evidence to support Rawicz's story and being unable to discover what happened to the other three escapees. One of the brothers observed that Downing's frustration was also focused on Rawicz's secretiveness: the latter's reluctance to divulge anything about Kristina (to the point where he would only speak about her in detail to Marjorie) and his furtiveness toward visitors—so much so that Downing had found it hard, at times, to gain entry into the Rawicz house on his monthly visits.

In my letter to Rawicz I included the thoughts and guesswork on the part of Downing's nephews as to what might have happened to Rawicz's companions, their surprise that Mr. Smith was actually Herbert Smith, and questions of my own that mirrored the questions of thousands of previous readers. I sent my letter and soon after received a reply from Marjorie.

In the first letter, Rawicz commented on the end of the walk and what had happened once he was in India. He recalled he left India by ship, naming the *Empress of India* as a possibility. As he spoke no English at the time, he only glimpsed the word *Empress* on the side of the ship and was later told there were three ships beginning with that word that were in service as troopships. He stated the ship was enormous and was a converted cruise liner. This ship took him to the Persian Gulf, where he noticed other ships unloading crates of American aid bound for the U.S.S.R. From the Persian Gulf he was taken to Tehran sometime in August 1942; from there he went to Iraq and Jordan, and then on to Palestine to join the Free Poles in November. In 1944, he was sent to England for pilot's training after having volunteered for the Polish Air Force. It was then that he settled down to a carefree life "with a loving family, doctors and the best human being, my English wife."

Rawicz then proceeded to answer my questions. He began with a comment regarding Mr. Smith. He was positive the American spoke fluent Russian without an accent. He stated that Mr. Smith reported he was from

Texas but gave no extra details about himself. (Rawicz emphasized, as he had done thousands of times before, that the escapees made a pact not to speak of personal matters in case they were captured; they were afraid repercussions would be meted out on their families.) He further stated that although he was in the worst shape of the four men who survived the walk to India, Mr. Smith seemed to have bounced back quickly, despite his age, and traveled to Bombay while the others remained convalescing in Calcutta.

The letter described feelings of remorse about the deaths of those men who had escaped from Siberia but who had not made it to India. The letter spoke of Rawicz's exhaustion and weight loss and implied that it was he who dragged the others along on their walk to freedom.

Rawicz's letter continued in this reminiscent vein when speaking of his three companions. Why hadn't they talked more about themselves once they were safe and sound in India? While in Calcutta, Rawicz indicated, he was suffering from such ill health that he did not have the strength or foresight to question the others. He supposed that his companions wished to remain in India for as long as possible as they wanted to keep away from countries under the sway of communism, fearing the communists would defeat Germany and take over Europe. He concluded that the other three escapees had no inclination to do as he did and join the Free Poles or any other military organization, to fight for the freedom of their respective homelands.

As to other memories at the end of the walk, he repeated that he had not recognized the photo of Rupert Mayne as the British intelligence officer who questioned him and that he had no clear recollection of any interviews. However, he did refer to people in uniform who came to speak wtih him including a translator, "a Polish Russian-speaking Jew from Calcutta." Rawicz said nothing about his time in Persia with General Anders's army but remarked on an occasion in Palestine when he came across lists of Polish names. On one of those lists he found the name of a distant cousin who was in the hospital with typhoid and who died two months later. Apparently, it was this cousin who gave him the news that his first wife, Vera, and the rest of his family had all perished in the War.

Towards the end of the letter, Rawicz addressed the question about going thirteen days without water while crossing the desert in Mongolia. He explained Downing "had not read the script properly" while praising his ghostwriter for not having dramatized the story but telling it in "clear impeccable English." (I was instantly curious as to what he meant by "script." After all, he and Marjorie often stated they had overall editorial rights. When I queried his statement in a subsequent letter, I never received a specific reply.)

So, after reading the letter more than once, pondering over the information contained therein, comparing it with copies of letters from Rawicz to other people (who shared their letters with me and the TLW group of enthusiasts researching the story), I put it aside and gave myself over to a reflection on its contents. The ending of the letter declared that Rawicz felt it his moral duty to tell his story: "It never was for material gain, but as a warning to those for whom freedom is the greatest love."

❧ ❧

Then there arrived a separate letter from Marjorie. She approached the subject of *The Long Walk* from a different angle. She wrote of Downing having initially come to interview her husband because of the latter's sighting of the abominable snowmen in Tibet. She recalled how difficult it was for Rawicz to open up and to overcome his nightmares and blackouts. It was their local doctor who advised Rawicz to speak to Downing and talk about his experiences as a form of therapy. (Downing referred to Rawicz's nightmares in a *Daily Mail* article from April 1956, which promoted *The Long Walk*. It seemed the nightmares were so intense that Rawicz would shout out in his sleep, reliving the tortures and hardships he endured years before.)

Marjorie praised Downing's patience and doggedness. He came to see them once a month and would "take down verbatim all that Slav had to say." Downing would then return to London, type out his notes, and send the script to Marjorie and Slav for editing. This continued for many months. There were delays while Downing peddled the manuscript to publishers. He finally found an editor at Constable who loved the story, and the book was published.

Judging from newspaper articles and memories, the contact between Rawicz and Downing took place from 1953 to 1956. Marjorie spoke of the difficulty those interviews with Downing sometimes caused her husband and "the effect those dreadful memories have on one's personality." She repeated her role in writing down the whole episode of Kristina after Downing threatened to finish the matter if Rawicz would not open up about this. (Rawicz dropped hints about Kristina during his interviews but never elaborated on the details. Then, one night, he awakened Marjorie and poured out the entire story to her in a long, agonizing recital.) As a result of Rawicz's opening up, the story of Kristina was included in *The Long Walk*, wholly written by his wife. Marjorie brushed aside criticism of the story at the time and later by declaring, "There had to be some editing, there is so much more that could be told. There is bound to be criticism." I never discovered what Marjorie meant when she alluded to "more that could be told."

In the last paragraphs of her letter, Marjorie again referred to having lost contact with Downing's wife and believing she had died in some obscurity; and she referred to HM Treasury having caused her husband so much trouble, heartache, and expense over the years that she sympathized with the Downing family's own dealings with the Treasury in attempting to establish proprietary rights over their uncle's estate. Neither she nor her husband had any idea what happened to Downing's original notes and subsequent papers. She reflected back to a time when Downing could not afford to buy a typewriter until he received the first advance of royalties on the book, and had had to do his typing at the *Daily Mail* after hours in order to complete the book.

I reread both letters more than once. I thought about their contents, considered their comments, reflected on their memories, and then began to compare what had been written to what I could read for myself in the book as well as in several newspaper articles. While reading these letters, I frequently glanced at photocopies of interviews with Rawicz in the *Daily Mail* and other British newspapers from 1954 and 1956. In the first interview, dated January 7, 1954, and written by Downing himself, the thrust of the story centered on abominable snowmen; however, in the summary of Rawicz's story, Downing noted the men had escaped from Camp 402, not Camp 303 as later stated in the book. Downing went on to quote Rawicz as saying, "Whether Smith was really his name I do not know . . . an engineer and sentenced to twenty-five year's imprisonment . . . had been working in gold mines south-west of Krasnoyarsk." (This was all very perplexing for me as, in the book, the mines were mentioned as being in the Urals, and Krasnoyarsk is not generally understood to be in that mountain group. The mines are also described as diamond mines, not gold mines, and Smith's sentence was only twenty years, according to Rawicz.) In the same article, as well as in another interview from 1956, Rawicz explained that while he was in Tehran during the summer of 1942 he joined General Anders's Polish Army, where he became a military instructor. I found this difficult to believe because of his reported ill health and weight loss. I just couldn't picture him in that capacity.

When Marjorie asserted in her letter that there was "bound to be criticism," I had to wonder whether she had these basic discrepancies I found through my research in mind. They were the kinds of discrepancies that were thought-provoking in more ways than one. It's natural that, when recounting a partial biography of real events some years after those events take place, there are bound to be erroneous statements, inaccurate names and dates, and forgotten incidents. The seemingly unnatural comment that leapt to my eye when reviewing the contents of the letters and comparing them with the book, its Afterword, and the newspaper interviews, centered on the disconnect between Rawicz claiming he was so malnourished and weak he had to be carried on board a ship leaving Calcutta, with his becoming a military instructor a short time later with General Anders's Army in Persia and during his time in Palestine. There is no mention of a lengthy recovery period that would be necessary to regain one's weight, let alone physical well being, before launching into the hectic and exhausting life of a military instructor.

Rawicz's remarks about the camp in Siberia and about Mr. Smith and his short biography were certainly confusing. Camp 402? Camp 303? Smith from Texas? His real name Herbert Smith? Was he sentenced to twenty-five years or twenty years? Was he sent to the Urals or to Krasnoyarsk before ending up in Siberia? Then there was the comment in the Afterword of the 1997 edition of the book alluding to the death of Rawicz's Polish wife, Vera, and the rest of his family in Poland (Belarus). Even though Rawicz's letter stated that his Polish family had perished, I continued to wonder if he ever truly tried to find out more about Vera and his family after the War.

I speculated on the practical side of things, namely, if one's first wife had died during the War, how was it possible to remarry years later in a foreign country without some kind of documentation stating the first wife was verifiably dead and not just missing? Obviously World War II tore families apart, and Rawicz's situation was not unique. Had Rawicz ever made any effort to find out exactly what had happened to Vera (and her family)? Had he tried to discover whether some of his own family members were still alive? Had he endeavored to track down the whereabouts of his companions on the long walk? Though lamenting the fact that he never learned what had happened to them each time the book was reprinted, surely after 1989 and the opening of Eastern Europe with its archives and Red Cross centers, natural curiosity, if nothing else, should have propelled him to make inquiries. After all, he had had no objection to Downing making inquiries at a time when it was much more difficult. This, apparently, did not happen, and Rawicz continued to proclaim his orphan status with regards to his Polish family and his Siberian companions.

Reflecting on what I knew so far about both Downing and Rawicz, I felt it was time to expand my research and come to terms with the various contradictions I had encountered. For that, I needed to be somewhere with access to archived material; and that meant a trip to England. I made a decision to fly to London in January 2003, determined to uncover the true facts behind *The Long Walk*.

Part IV

A NEW BEGINNING

Chapter 11

CRACKING THE NUT

In preparation for the trip to London, I organized materials and documents to take with me as research aids. Along with the Rawicz family letters, I also included material I received in reply to my various worldwide appeals. At the same time, I contacted people in England who had helped me get started and asked them for any research suggestions. My staunch supporter remained Patric Emerson of the Indian Army Association. His comments on the War and on military matters were invaluable to my research as his contacts ranged far and wide. With his help, I continued to make inquiries concerning events at the end of the walk, when Rawicz and his companions actually arrived in India.

It was at Emerson's suggestion to look into Rawicz's time in the Polish military that I contacted the Sikorski Museum/Polish Institute in London. Over the phone I listened to an interesting account by one of the retired military men working there. Upon telling him why I was phoning and asking whether anyone at the museum or within the general Polish community might have known Rawicz, he gave a deep sigh and then laughed, "Not that story again!" He muttered something in Polish that I didn't catch, then apologized and told me his tale.

Colonel Dembinski stated he had met Rawicz in 1956 when the latter came to London by invitation to speak about the book and about his life story. Rawicz stood in front of a group of Polish ex-servicemen and told them of his experiences. While addressing the crowd, several men jumped up and claimed they had known Rawicz before and during the War. One of them pointed out to the audience that Rawicz had not been in a cavalry unit as he claimed but in an infantry unit. Another man said he had met Rawicz in Persia and that Rawicz had either come from or had gone to Russia before going on to Palestine. Heated arguments and verbal abuse began; accusations and counteraccusations flew back and forth; shouts rang out; words such as "liar" and "communist agent" reverberated throughout the venue; and in the end, Rawicz stepped down from the stage and never again spoke in front of a crowd of his fellow countrymen.

What a phone call! My head was buzzing afterward and I wrote my thoughts down in a letter and mailed it to Dembinski, just for clarification. I followed up the mailing some time later by speaking to the colonel again. He stated that I understood what he said and that was exactly how he remembered Rawicz—standing up in front of a hostile audience of his own countrymen, being booed off the stage. (In my comments to Dembinski I questioned whether Rawicz had ever speculated that he would receive such a volatile reception. Dembinski replied that "he was either a fool or so full of himself he thought he could bluff his way through the talk.")

Rawicz's own observations about this episode, years later, were that the audience contained *agents provocateur*, meaning communists or communist sympathizers, who were trying to discredit him. His comments dwelt on the premise that he knew what he knew and he was sticking by it; others wondered who he thought he was. At a later date I was in touch with a Polish author who had been in the crowd on that particular occasion and who verified what had happened. He commented on the ugly atmosphere and the feeling that Rawicz had been lying about his life story. Although there might have been communists in the audience, there were also men who had been through the Russian camps, through the War, and were now settled in England, with similar stories to that of Rawicz. These were men who claimed to have known him in Persia and in Palestine, men who were emphatic that Rawicz had never escaped from Siberia and had never been in India.

Not long after hearing of Rawicz's connection with the Polish community, I had a letter from the Burma Star Association in which confirmation came from Viscount Slim that Rupert Mayne had indeed been on his father's staff as a G.2 intelligence officer during the retreat (from Burma) in 1942. They suggested I try to contact members of the Special Forces Club in London. So, I typed up letters and sent them around the world; and, once again, I received replies that stated the recipient of the letter had no information to impart.

⚬⚭⚬⚭

I finally headed to England to continue my research. I laid out a program of attack: where I wanted to go, what I wanted to look at, where I wanted to stay, how to get from A to B—and then I got stuck for twenty-four hours in a U.S. airport, waiting out the weather. All that planning was for naught.

I landed in a snowstorm and, moaning and slipping, I fumbled my way to Victoria Station, then out to Kew. I wanted to be as near as possible to the Public Records Office. Fortunately, there were several bed-and-breakfasts near the PRO, and, fortunately again, there was a single small vacancy in one of them.

I wasted no time in getting started at the PRO. I picked through file after file, spoke to one of the archivists, was directed to a higher authority, listened to how to go about requesting a "closed" file (in this case I would need to produce a death certificate to circumvent the hundred-year closure ban), and felt like a tired, soggy sponge by the end of the day. The rest of the week consisted of spending hour after hour looking at files from World War II. Whether I was at the PRO or at the British Library's Oriental & India Office, I remained focused, even if not much new was gleaned.

The only thing I really had to show for all my efforts in London was the unpublished memoir of Boris Hembry, close friend of Rupert Mayne, who had been in ISLD during the War. His son, John, kindly arranged for his father's memoir to find its way to me while I was in England, and I read it on the flight back to the United States. I had already been down to the Family Research Centre in London, where I had requested a copy of Hembry's death certificate. With that, I soon received documents labeled

Secret and Classified about Hembry's career. Regrettably, there was no mention of Rupert Mayne.

In fact, there appeared to be nothing on Mayne, Rawicz, or a host of other names I tried to feed through the system either at the PRO or at the British Library. All sorts of research suggestions were passed along to me by some of the members of the British Empire and Commonwealth Web site, by independent researcher Lance Visser—a contributor to the Burma Star Association Web site—by people at both the PRO and the BL and various others. And after all that work and those long hours, I found nothing that pertained to *The Long Walk*.

The only bright light while I was in London was establishing contact with the people who now lived at the same address as Downing when he was alive. Luckily, there was a young couple in the ground-floor flat, and they passed on some comments about the history of the building, mentioning that one of the owners of an upstairs flat had been living at that address for decades. That neighbor turned out to be a woman who had known Downing's wife, Edna, and remembered that she had a friend, Harold Ward, who lived around the corner. The neighbor never knew Ronald Downing, though. Through the course of our conversation, the woman helped me solve a small mystery. One of the reasons the Downing family could not locate Edna for some time was that all the renters were evicted while the building was being gutted and renovated in the mid-1970s. The previous tenants were not allowed back as renters; they could only return if they bought a flat, as this woman did. She further explained that Edna had had no choice but to leave when the renovations began and, because of Edna's financial situation, she continued to live with Ward until her death.

<hr>

So, my first effort at really investigating the validity of Rawicz's story came to naught. That's how I viewed my trip to England. However, I felt the experience had been worth the effort and I was already planning a future trip to England during my flight home.

While engaging in the gentle art of strategizing, I thought back on a comment that was made to me while still in England: to put an advertisement in the weekly Polish-language newspaper in London. Once I was home, I sat down and wrote out a simple appeal for information targeted at a Polish audience. I also decided to put that exact same appeal to a wider audience and so contacted several Polish Ex-Servicemen's Associations both in the United States and Canada. I wrote to White Eagle Associations and Sikorski Associations, asking for information and pleading that an appeal be included in their publications and/or on notice boards. Then, once again, I sat back and waited.

During this lull in my research, I continued to receive comments and suggestions from all over the globe. People were in touch with suggestions about the FANYs and the possibility that someone in their ranks might have been in Calcutta during 1942; information kept coming in about Rupert Mayne and his possible role in Force 136, ISLD, SOE, or a host of other organizations; labor camps in Siberia were suggested as possible locations for Camp 303; additional references to World War II gulags came through e-mail messages; genealogists got in touch with facts about Edna Downing's family—the inward flow of information was ceaseless.

With the influx of information I received, I wondered how to put all of these disparate parts to good use, especially since the majority of the information was of no use in answering my questions. I kept wondering when I would start to get some answers.

Chapter 12

~~~

GLINSKI

In the spring of 2003, I received a phone call from England. The caller had read my appeal in the Polish-language newspaper in London, and he was calling to ask why I was bothering to dredge up "that old story" again. His voice was that of a younger man, not a teenager but not elderly either. His accent was educated. He spoke very directly and definitely to me about the story and asked about my reasons for researching it.

I tried to get across to the caller that the book had made a profound impression on me. I pointed out that thousands of other readers obviously felt the same as there were references online to their interactions with Slav Rawicz, and I had copies of letters both from and to Rawicz spanning decades. I explained that living abroad for thirty years and traveling extensively in China, India, Nepal, and Tibet made the book even more captivating to me—that perhaps the story meant more to me as I had covered some of the same terrain. I mused that the sheer courage of the men and the hardships they endured evoked memories of some of my own difficult travel experiences in remote places. All these factors contributed to my desire to know more about the details of the trek and its participants.

(While speaking to a stranger on the phone, it's hard to infuse a lot of pathos into the word "research." On its own, "research" may not convey much. Taken in conjunction with vast geographical areas covering a good chunk of the world, a time in recent history when that world had been turned upside down, one's own past history and adventures, and the word does encompass a little more and begins to "flesh out," at least in the researcher's mind.)

I somehow made my case and asked if the caller knew of any information that would help me solve a couple of mysteries surrounding the story, especially the identity of Mr. Smith. There was a note of reluctance at first in his voice while I told him my reasons for researching the story. I was also slightly taken aback by the repeated comments about one of the survivors being "not a nice man." In fact, the word "murderer" was used. (My thoughts flew instantly back to one of the letters I had received from Rawicz in which his wife had stated, "There had to be some editing, there is so much more that could be told." Was that a reference to a murder [or murderer] that had been hushed up?)

By the end of our half-hour conversation it was revealed that the caller was phoning on behalf of an elderly gentleman who did, indeed, know something about the walk. We made arrangements for that gentleman to call me at a specific date and time, with the understanding that he wanted to remain anonymous. While stating that I would respect his privacy, I queried the reason for it. The caller stated that the elderly man felt he was protecting his life in the event Rawicz turned out to be a murderer, a man whom he had known as Batko. To say I was shocked by this is an understatement. At the end of our chat I was on tenterhooks anticipating that next call and what further surprises it might reveal.

Before the agreed call took place, however, there was e-mail traffic between the caller and myself, with me posing general questions and the caller writing them down, to be passed on to the elderly man who would contact me. In the blizzard of e-mails during the week or two that transpired between that first and subsequent phone call, I naturally asked about the "murderer." The reply came back that the man's name was Batko. This name was not mentioned in the book, and I could not see how or where it fit in with the story as I knew it—or thought I knew it. Nonetheless, I was intrigued to learn more, and more is what I got.

What I was to learn during the second call from England was that Batko was a cold-blooded murderer, and my contact was under the assumption that Rawicz was this man and had changed his name or adopted the name of Rawicz after the War to hide his identity. Talk about a revelation—I could hardly believe it! When I countered via e-mail that all of Rawicz's children were born with this name, my argument was brushed aside with citations of the chaos after the War and many people assuming new names and identities. Further, my contact added that the family of the Polish man I would soon be speaking to had been connected with the Polish cavalry at the beginning of the War, and that the name and biographical notes mentioned over the years about Rawicz were unknown to him.

Not only did the messages mention this man named Batko but they also mentioned Ronald Downing, once again the key name in this mystery. It appeared that Downing met my prospective caller soon after the War and tried to talk to him—without any luck. Downing was accompanied by a translator who was unknown to the elderly Polish man and did not inspire trust. Thus, the meeting was not a success.

The e-mails preceding the telephone call continued, touching upon the camp in Siberia; on the lack of personal information as a hedge against reprisals in the event of recapture; on Mr. Smith, who was described as a man in his late forties or early fifties, a technical advisor to the agricultural industry (rather than an engineer), and someone with an apparent military background; the yetis (rubbish!); Kristina (who had escaped from a farm after killing the foreman during his attempt to rape her and who had developed gangrene and died); and more comments about Batko. So much unexpected information was coming in that I found it hard to assimilate it with what I thought I already knew.

The real bombshell, however, was the remark concerning Batko. My contact wrote that Batko killed two men during the escape and long walk to China, and again at the end of the War. Apparently, during a robbery attempt in Antwerp, Belgium, in 1945, Batko killed a bank clerk and another man. Miraculously, he escaped by stealing a motorcycle, though he was later caught—but not for long.

Over the next week, as my thoughts somersaulted over one another while I waited for the arranged phone call to take place, I sent my mysterious contact a copy of the photo of Rawicz as he appeared on the dust jacket of an early edition of *The Long Walk*. At that time, I did not have a photo of Downing, but I did forward a photo of Rupert Mayne as well. I wondered at the chances of any or all three of these men being recognized by the Polish man with whom I would soon be in touch. I also wondered what new and startling revelations I would hear during that call.

❧❧

The day of the telephone interview dawned, the phone rang, and I found myself speaking to an elderly man with a decidedly Polish accent. After initial greetings and introductions, during which he asked me to simply call him "Witek" in compliance with his wish for privacy, he began to talk. I listened and took notes, jotting down question marks next to those comments I wanted to subsequently query. (Before beginning Witek's narrative, and in order to reduce confusion for the reader, it needs to be stated that eventually Witek came to trust me and made his full identity known: Witold Glinski, hereinafter referred to by his surname, Glinski.)

One of his first comments was to introduce Downing into the story. Glinski remarked that Downing, through his Polish translator, addressed him by name in Cadogan Square, London, sometime after the War, possibly in 1946 or '47. Glinski also stated that he had worked after the War at the office of the Polish Resettlement Corps near Cadogan Square, helping to establish documentation for Polish men at that time. He thought someone from that organization might have tipped off Downing to his story as he had been questioned about his past, along with thousands of other Polish ex-servicemen, before starting work. In the event, nothing came of that particular contact primarily because of the mistrust felt by Glinski toward the Polish translator who did not adequately introduce himself at the time, leaving room for suspicion as to whether the man might have been a communist. (While listening to Glinski I had to keep reminding myself how people felt about politics, communism, and leftists at that time. The War was over but the Iron Curtain was up; families were torn apart; countries no longer existed in their own right; and human feelings were exceptionally sensitive to political leanings.)

There were many random comments made by Glinski relating to his doubts and suspicions about the identity of Rawicz. He asserted he had only discovered the existence of *The Long Walk* in the 1970s when a family member read it and remarked on the similarity of names and events that Glinski had experienced himself. After he read the book, Glinski was convinced that Rawicz and Batko were one and the same person. Not wanting to go into the details of that particular allegation at the start of our phone call, I gently guided him to the beginning of his story, to his time in Poland in 1939 as a student. For my own sake I needed to fit his account of events into some kind of chronological time frame or I would end in a muddle. As it were, I had a hard time the first few minutes just keeping up with the bursts of information.

I learned that, at the beginning of 1939, Glinski had been a student. While we were speaking, he paused in his narrative long enough to backtrack further and state that he came from a mixed marriage: his father was Lithuanian and his mother was Russian but born in Poland. (This paralleled Rawicz's claims about his own family, in which he claimed his mother was Russian.) Glinski explained that his mother's family fled Russia in 1917 when the Bolsheviks murdered his grandfather because he was an Orthodox priest, and they had settled in northeastern Poland (today Belarus).

As a student, Glinski studied at a military academy and was there at the beginning of World War II. He had no great ambition to be a soldier but merely stated that at the time one could get a free education only through the military. There were about five hundred students in his group and they had no wish to compromise themselves with the Russians when the Red Army rolled over eastern Poland. Instead, the students were rounded up, interrogated, beaten, and herded into the U.S.S.R. to various prisons. This was Glinski's fate as well.

He spoke of being sent to a work camp in Archangel Province before embarking on the long train ride to Siberia, crammed into a cattle car. He replied to my question about the location of Camp 303 by stating that he never knew the camp number or name to which he was confined. He simply remembered the train arriving at Irkutsk, the forced walk north with thousands of other men, and, after weeks of exhausting struggle, arriving at what felt like a death camp. He referred to horse-drawn sleds; to men, women, and children struggling to keep up; to wood-fueled lorries carrying supplies; to chains from those lorries along which the prisoners were attached and pulled through the snow; to *treska* (fish soup) and 100 grams of bread per person daily.

Glinski described the place as a death camp, for being there meant just that—a place to die. As he was only a teenager he didn't want to think about dying. Instead, he slowly began to contemplate escape. He referred nostalgically to the wife of the commandant of the camp. I queried if her name was Madame Ushakov and he said he knew the book stated the commandant was called Ushakov but he was not sure if that was the man's actual name. On other points, however, his recollections matched the details given in the book: he was sent to repair the commandant's Telefunken radio that kept breaking down; the commandant's wife was sympathetic to him as a teenage Pole whose mother's family were Russian; and there had been a map in the commandant's quarters but with little notation on it so he never knew exactly where he was, only that the camp was north of Lake Baikal. He explained that, while the commandant's wife was helpful and sympathetic (she aided him with food and clothes), she never spoke outright of escape. In fact, from what Glinski related, very few outright comments were made by him or any of the other men about escape. Their communications were more on the order of murmured undertones rather than stated objectives. Long telepathic looks and hushed "when are we going to get out?" whispers were more the order of the day.

The day of the escape dawned with a severe change in the weather and prompted their determined will to be free. Those like Glinski whose minds were made up had already started saving food and clothing, and a small number of able men decided it was time to leave. They waited until dark, when the snowstorm was at its worst, crossed the stretches of barbed wire that surrounded the camp, and ran into the woods.

Although the book states that seven men originally fled the camp, Glinski suggested more had tried to escape with his group but had either turned back or were lost during the storm. He affirmed that he was the youngest, being sixteen at the time, and that his will to escape and survive was equal to, if not greater than, that of the other, older men. He felt his willpower served them all well in the end.

They walked, stumbled, pushed themselves to their respective limits during the first couple of days, not daring to take a break and hoping the ferocity of the storm would prevent the guards from following and capturing them. The snow was high and they crossed frozen rivers, finally coming to the northern tip of Lake Baikal, where they began their south-bound travel around its eastern shore. They kept their focus on the escape, trying not to think of what might happen to them if they were tracked down and captured.

I listened while Glinski spoke of the older men, especially the Polish soldiers, who were already suffering from the hardships of hunger, the weather, and the nonstop walking. There were complaints of bleeding gums and blood in their stool. Glinski speculated that these men were already manifesting symptoms of malnutrition.

And what about Mr. Smith? Glinski commented that he was definitely the oldest but very fit, with an air of authority and a military bearing. His Russian was very good, without accent and spoken like a native speaker. (He exchanged a few words of English with Glinski, who had learned the basics of that language at school; however, as neither Glinski nor any of the other men could speak English, they had no way to judge whether Mr. Smith was a native English speaker or not.) Although he did not talk about his background or family, Mr. Smith's demeanor was that of an educated man who had been involved with agricultural machinery in some capacity. Glinski was unable to deduce if he'd ever been an engineer. He also could not say for certain whether Mr. Smith had referred to being in Moscow and working on the Metro. He did state that on the occasions when Mr. Smith spoke, everyone listened and paid attention. Glinski described Mr. Smith as someone who kept very much to himself, a private person, albeit with a commanding presence.

The rest of the group was described cursorily, with Glinski commenting on Zora (possibly the same man as Rawicz's Zaro), who spoke only broken Polish and behaved like an animal at times. Whether Zora was a Yugoslav or from somewhere else in the Balkans, Glinski felt there was something "unwholesome" about him, something repugnant that Glinski was unable to define. I asked about Kolemenos. Glinski did not recognize the name but stated there had been a large Latvian on the walk who had died in the desert. He was a man of low cunning who portrayed himself as a simpleton most of the time but who could recite poetry and speak intelligently when he wanted.

And what about the menacing Batko, the unknown name from the story? Batko showed his mettle during the escape when the group came upon what Glinski could only guess was the Trans-Siberian Railway. While they were all hiding behind ramshackle buildings at a crossing, Batko stole around several railcars on a siding and killed two Russian guards. When the starving men broke open one of those cars, hoping to find food or clothing, they found tins of cocoa instead, which made them all sick. Glinski, especially, was upset by the way Batko had killed the guards and then cut off their heads, placing them on sticks. The latter mentioned this was a trick he had learned while in the French Foreign Legion. Placing heads on sticks made it look as if the guards were upright and on duty from a distance.

From annotating Batko's misdeeds, Glinski moved on to describe the last person who joined the band of escapees: Kristina Polanska. Glinski did not remember her name as Kristina but rather as something like Soba, Sasha, or some derivative of Sophia. Like Glinski, she was a teenager, seventeen or eighteen years old, and she'd run away from a *kolkhoz* after fending off a rape attempt and killing the foreman with a knife. When she joined the fleeing prisoners, she was already limping. To Glinski it appeared as if she had a blister that was infected, which ultimately led to gangrene. He explained that the escapees carried her for days on a makeshift stretcher of two poles and a coat after she begged them not to leave her when walking became impossible.

One by one, their numbers dwindled as the weeks rolled by and the fleeing men kept pushing themselves beyond their individual limits. On being asked how they survived crossing the desert and going nearly two weeks without water, Glinski scoffed. He stated the passage in the book that related the desert crossing and going without water was nonsense. He remarked that they collected water from frost at night that melted in the mornings; they sucked moisture from their clothes, which they used to mop up the frost; they licked stones; they dug holes in muddy areas, scooped up the liquid, and used their clothes as filters, squeezing water into their open mouths; and they did have a couple of tin cans with them that they used as scoops as well as drinking implements. Glinski also mentioned eating snakes and worms, which they grubbed for and ate as best they could, as well as mushrooms that he recognized as being harmless.

They may not have liked what they ate and drank, but survival was on everyone's mind, no matter what form it took. Their survival seemed more likely when they met a group of Mongolians—their first contact with people since leaving the camp. Glinski assumed they were Mongolians but had no clear idea of their exact ethnicity. The most promising part of this encounter was the fact that the caravan's leader could speak a little Russian. (Glinski speculated how their fate might have been different had the leader not shown some insight and compassion into their plight and had not been able to communicate with them.) In the event, the escaping men were shown kindness and were given food and water.

Glinski expounded upon the constant walking, the hunger, the fear, the arguments over which direction to take, the warnings given by the caravan leader not to veer too far to the east as there was fighting in China—all these aspects of the story dovetailed with those in *The Long Walk*. He described the deaths of the escapees as well as the endless trekking over high plateau country and into the Himalayas.

Once in the Himalayas, Glinski's narrative digressed from that of the book—the main point of contention being the purported yeti sighting. Whatever he and the others saw, he felt sure they were not inhabitants of Shangri-la. He surmised the "creatures," seen at a great distance in the clear air of the mountains through extremely tired and sore eyes, were men wearing sheepskin or fur coats. (I sent Glinski copies of drawings of the yetis as detailed by Rawicz in 1956. He laughed at the sketches.) Whoever or whatever the "creatures" were, they marked a milestone of sorts as, at the time of their sighting, the last man to die during the escape fell to his death.

From that point in his tale, Glinski began to wind up our ninety-minute phone call by mentioning the hospitality of a Tibetan village into which they stumbled, the barely concealed hostility of a German-speaking missionary who was passing through the community, and the ultimate kindness shown to them upon leaving the place—they were given a guide who walked with them for a few days to make sure they stayed on the path to India. Once on that path, and with the same advice given by the Mongolian caravan leader to be careful not to stray too far east and get caught up in the fighting in China, they kept walking, gradually descending paths that veered south by west, until they looked down into the astonished faces of a Gurkha patrol on the slopes below them.

⌒∽⌒∽

Glinski ended his story by describing the kindness of the soldiers upon whom they came, the compassion shown to the escapees when they were taken to what was most likely a casualty clearing station and were attended to by medical personnel, and the care received once they arrived at a transit camp with medical facilities outside Calcutta. Glinski explained that he last saw Mr. Smith between their initial encounter with the Gurkha patrol and their arrival outside Calcutta. He remembered Mr. Smith talking to the British officer leading the patrol, and then later, when they were all in trucks and being taken to the field hospital, Mr. Smith asked where and how to contact Glinski at a future date. Regretably, Glinski did not ask for a contact address from Mr. Smith.

Once he arrived at the transit camp, Glinski collapsed and had little memory of what he did or what happened to the other men during that time. He did remember being told by the Indian nurses, who giggled a lot, that he hid food, that he wandered about, that he didn't know where he was, and that they had to keep putting him back into his bed, urging him to rest. Although he was the youngest of the men who had escaped from Siberia, the endless walking and hardship took its toll on him. He remembered Mr. Smith, the eldest, being the one who held up the best.

When I questioned him on these last events, he declared he had been in a shack-like facility on a military base outside Calcutta. He had a memory of people (medical and military personnel) coming and going, of being questioned and interrogated, and of hearing people make references to Calcutta as if it were not far away. I then asked if he recognized the photo of Rupert Mayne as being one of his interrogators; regrettably, he said, he did not recognize the man and went on to say he had memories of being questioned many times by dozens of people during his stay in the medical facility. He stated there were Red Cross representatives at the military base and he received travel documents from them to leave. I inquired about the other survivors, and Glinski, disappointingly, stated that he had no idea what had happened to them. He had no memory of being with them while convalescing or of seeing them before he left India.

After resting for a few weeks, he found himself on a military transport convoying west across India in the company of other East Europeans (I wondered if they were displaced persons or even refugees). The transport consisted of several lorries driven by Sikhs, with their distinctive turbans and beards. After what felt like endless traveling in the back of the army lorries, with long benches running down both sides and holding perhaps two dozen people in each vehicle, they came to the Caspian Sea. From a small port on the eastern side of the sea, the convoy took boats at night and landed at Camp Pahlevi, Persia, the next day. There, Glinski was deloused and given better clothes. He was more or less signed over to the Free Poles who comprised General Anders's army in Persia. He was transported over the mountains from the Caspian to a camp outside Tehran. Later, he was put on a ship leaving from the Persian Gulf port of Ahvaz.

This was not the end of Glinski's story, though. The ship he boarded in Ahvaz zigged and zagged to Egypt, Palestine, then back to the Red Sea, and finally landed at Durban, South Africa. Along with a few thousand men, Glinski was taken inland from Durban to camps near Pietermaritzburg: Camp Oribi and Camp Hay. This sojourn started as a restful existence at the camps but that was not to last for long. Eventually, Glinski and his many companions marched back to Durban and sailed for Cape Town, where they waited several weeks for an escort before heading into the Atlantic, destined for Europe. Luck was not on their side as their ship was promptly sunk by German U-boats off the northwestern coast of Africa. Although many people died, Glinski and others were picked up by a British submarine and taken to Casablanca before being transported on to Glasgow, Scotland.

❧❧

As I became aware of silence on the other end of the phone, I realized I had been waiting for *more*. What a story! It was almost unbelievable. Then I remembered how many other stories I had come across that seemed equally unbelievable while researching *The Long Walk*. Unbelievable, yes—but not unimaginable. The dry, pedantic tone of Glinski's voice rambling on from one event to another for nearly two hours struck me as authentic and truthful. I found myself believing every word of it. How could I not? There had been no prevarication, no blame, no accusations, no theories or speculation—just facts, one after the other.

As a parting shot, Glinski brought up Batko the murderer once more. After last seeing him in India, Batko reappeared at the end of the War in Meppen, Germany, where Glinski was stationed with his unit of the Free Poles. He learned that Batko had robbed a bank in Antwerp, Belgium, and killed a bank clerk and another man during the robbery. Incredibly, Batko managed to flee the scene of the crime on a stolen motorcycle but he was caught and turned over to the nearest Polish unit: Glinski's unit. Then Batko confounded everyone by escaping *again!*

Miraculously, Batko reappeared in Glinski's life a couple of years later, in 1948. While working for the Polish Resettlement people in London, Glinski managed to find work in Cornwall on the Clowance estate near Camborne. There, with other Polish ex-servicemen working on the estate, who should appear one day but Batko. As soon as the two laid eyes on one another, Batko made a sign for Glinski to keep his mouth shut while using his forefinger to draw a line across his own throat as a warning. Glinski was alarmed but immediately left the estate and reported Batko to the police.

Although that incident occurred in the late 1940s, Glinski continued to live in fear since that last encounter, believing Batko had become Rawicz, written a book about his escape from Siberia, and might reappear at any time to settle old scores. Once he saw the photo of Rawicz (whom he did not recognize), Glinski knew his worries were over.

Our phone conversation ended with assurances on both sides that we would be in touch again soon. I felt this initial contact with Glinski had laid a solid foundation on which to base future exchanges of information. Although most of the information had been one way, from Glinski to me, the photo of Rawicz I sent had a dramatic impact. It demonstrated to him that Rawicz and Batko were two different people, as the latter looked nothing like the former. The photo, then, put Glinski's mind to rest after all these years. He expressed his gratitude as we thanked one another at the end of our phone call.

Chapter 13

BATKO, ZORA, AND MR. SMITH

Afer that mindboggling conversation with Glinski, it took some time for me to regain my equilibrium. My contact, Glinski's son as it turned out, didn't miss a beat and immediately sent me an e-mail message the next day with further details. As I suspected, the message concentrated on Batko. He described Batko as an evil man who had plagued Glinski's thoughts for decades.

Now that it seemed certain Rawicz and Batko were two separate people (thanks to the photo of Rawicz that demonstrated a lack of resemblance between the two men), Glinski's son asked me to pass on any information that might crop up later in my research with regards to Batko and what happened to him. He also speculated on Downing as well as Rawicz and wondered which one had misled the other. Had Downing been told or heard about Glinski's story right after the War and kept it under his hat all those years? Had he only looked at that story again once the Yeti Expedition was off the ground and being sponsored by the *Daily Mail*? Had he heard something about Rawicz and suggested they cook up some kind of story between them with a view to cashing in on "yeti mania" in the mid-1950s? Or, had Rawicz somehow heard about the story and adopted it as his own? It was hard to determine where he would have gotten all the details: from Downing, from Mr. Smith, or from someone he met in Persia or Palestine. The mystery thickened.

I was fairly certain there was more than one mystery involved, and this prompted a considerable amount of reflection on my part. Whether one mystery or many, it seemed they all revolved around one central figure: Ronald Downing. Was he the weaver of the tale? Even though the initial contact with Glinski after the War had been a damp squib from his viewpoint, perhaps Downing kept notes of that brief encounter; perhaps he tucked away a note to himself in relation to some story he heard or was told, to use at a later time. If so, then at what point would Downing have considered using a surrogate to tell someone else's story? Speculating further, I asked myself how he could have convinced such a person, in this case Rawicz, to be that surrogate. I felt I needed to ask these questions even though, from what I had learned of Downing's character, this avenue of conjecture didn't seem plausible.

I then asked myself whether Rawicz heard something about Glinski's story while in the Middle East. Perhaps Mr. Smith or one of the other men who had survived the walk told Rawicz Glinski's tale. For reasons unknown, could Rawicz have prompted the contact with Downing during the excitement over the Yeti Expedition to see where it would lead? Had he known Downing (or the *Daily Mail*) might have been interested in his story? Had he stated at the beginning of his relationship with Downing that it was the story of other men, not his own, and he was the mere teller of the tale (or had he convinced Downing that it was, indeed, his story)?

The speculation continued throughout several e-mails until it boiled down to the basics: either Downing convinced Rawicz to pretend the story was his; they collaborated on a composite story hoping to make money out of it while the glow of "yeti mania" was still strong; or Rawicz pulled the wool over Downing's eyes. Whichever section of the board one squinted at, the dart was likely to hit just one of those three choices. There really weren't any others—if I believed Glinski's story wholeheartedly.

I had listened to Glinski's recitation of events during our phone call with a very open mind. My initial hope was that he had known or met one of the escapees and would tell me of that encounter. I had no inkling that Glinski would proclaim *himself* as one of the actual escapees. So, instead of getting details to corroborate the story behind the walk, I found myself listening to a new version of events. Later, I asked myself whether

Glinski's version could be true. If so, in what light should I view Rawicz's story as embodied in *The Long Walk*? I realized I now had two accounts of the same story that would have to be investigated for comparisons and contrasts. Both versions would call for an open mind on my part while I sifted through details to get to the truth.

As I sat back and thought about Rawicz and Glinski, one of Glinski's last comments from our phone call struck me. He and his wife (who had been on the other line listening and contributing comments) declared that Rawicz had stolen his identity in 1956; and not only stolen his identity but made money off it. I reread Rawicz's letter from the previous year, in which Rawicz stated, in the final paragraph, that he felt writing *The Long Walk* had been a moral right and duty; it hadn't been for material gain.

This sentiment seemed extremely honest. On the other hand, in letters over many years, Rawicz intimated that his financial base was greatly enhanced by the royalties received from the publication of the book and the sale of the film rights. In fact, with the proceeds from the book, he had been able to buy not only a big house for his wife and children but also a couple of acres of land to go with it. It was also a big enough house to allow him to rent rooms so that the house became a self-sustaining invest-ment. While he might have espoused fine moral sentiments, both he and his wife referred more than once to their battles with HM Treasury over a variety of rights—all with the purpose of garnering material gain.

※※※

In the midst of guesswork concerning identitites and intentions of people fifty years ago, more detail came to light regarding Glinski's story. In a follow-up phone conversation, Glinski was sure the patrol he and his fellow escapees encountered in the foothills of the Himalayas was comprised of Gurkhas rather than Indian soldiers. Glinski described the Gurkhas' uniforms as being dark green and adorned with their distinctive knives, known as *kukris*. Their appearance was neat, not travel-stained, and they had not been on patrol for long when the two groups encountered one another. He also emphasized that at no time did the group cross a major river, such as the Tsangpo/Brahmaputra. I had already mentioned to him that the Tsangpo was a free-flowing river year-round, and he persisted in having no knowledge or memory of having tried to cross something like that.

Glinski continued to go over the highlights of his story during the phone call, concentrating on his arrival in India and its aftermath. When I asked about his time spent in India, he continually mentioned ramshackle huts used as medical facilities, both at the casualty clearing station where he and the other men were taken when they first encountered the Gurkha patrol and, later, when they were outside Calcutta. He repeated several times that they were never in a "hospital" as such. Glinski was also quite insistent on the blur of faces, both medical and military, that passed before his eyes, but he could supply no definite details about these people due to his state of health.

Glinski emphasized that he was alone after reaching India. He wanted to distance himself from the other men as much as he could. With the exception of Mr. Smith, he wanted nothing more to do with his fellow escapees. He stated more than once that, as convicts, they had thrown in their lot together for the sole purpose of escape and survival. At sixteen, he felt he had nothing in common with these much older men. He also scoffed at the romanticized ending of Rawicz's book, when they wished each other farewell and there were hugs and tears all round. It was rather the opposite—he couldn't wait to get away from his comrades of the road.

(Downing and Rawicz wrote *The Long Walk* as an adventure—a romance of the road—depicting the escapees as men [and one woman] of goodwill, as ordinary human beings caught up in the maelstrom of World War II. There runs a thread of camaraderie à la *The Three Muske-teers* throughout the narrative: the valiant struggles against injustice; the bonding of the group members; and the ultimate attainment of freedom. In the 1997 Afterword, Rawicz emphasized the good nature of the band by lamenting his loss of contact with them after their arrival in India. The four survivors of the walk were depicted as having become close friends with unforeseen events keeping them from ever reuniting and renewing their friendship. By contrast, Glinski's attitude toward his fellow escapees couldn't have been more contrary.)

I collected all my notes on both Rawicz and Glinski and started sifting through them. In the end, I found myself with two similar stories about the same event. In their basic ingredients, the two stories were identical. Each man was young and Polish, with a Russian-speaking mother; each one went through military training before the War and was subsequently caught up by events and taken prisoner by the Soviets; each experienced prison treatment and injustice, and reflected upon the hand Fate had dealt him as he was propelled eastward to a Siberian labor camp, where thought of escape became reality.

The similarities continued from the time each man arrived in the labor camp until the end of the book. Rawicz and Glinski both laid claim to being the youngest member of a group contemplating escape. Rawicz declared he was befriended by the camp commandant's wife; Glinski made the same declaration. Rawicz recounted the names of all the escapees; Glinski only knew the surnames of the other three survivors who, like him, made it to India. Their separate accounts of Mr. Smith matched, both describing him as a "mystery man." The escape from the camp in atrocious weather, the endless walking over unknown terrain, the uncertainty of where they were and where they should be going, all tallied, as did the separate accounts of the encounter with Kristina and the deaths of three of the escapees.

Each man's story wrapped up with descriptions of being welcomed by local people along their escape route, of being pushed to their physical and mental limits, and of finally arriving in a land where they could once again be free men. A major difference appeared right at the end of the story, though. Rawicz tearfully described his time convalescing near Calcutta and saying good-bye to his comrades before boarding a troopship to join the Polish Army in the Middle East; but Glinski barely remembered his convalescence and never saw the other escapees again before being put on a convoy headed for Persia.

Once the similarities were noted, then the discrepancies came, mainly relating to the escape and the walk. Rawicz spoke throughout the book as if his fellow escapees had become boon companions. He briefly described their personalities and quirks, and the fact there were occasional disagreements, but the book conveys an impression of acceptance of one another, of helping each other overcome adversity, and of a genial camaraderie developing during the course of the walk. Glinski spoke with no such feelings. He related a mutual distrust and suspicion they all felt toward one another and that fate had thrown them together and they just had to make the best of it—they didn't have to like the situation or each other.

Details such as Kristina's actual name, the sequence of encounters with Mongolians, Chinese, or Tibetans, and the order in which half the group died were minor variations. After all, both men had retold their stories long after the events took place. The one glaring difference in the two stories was the existence of Batko and the murder of the train guards. On the other hand, the one point on which the stories agreed unequivocally centered on Mr. Smith. Rawicz thought of him as a friend and mentor, and lamented the fact he had lost touch with the older man after leaving India. Glinski was under no illusion he had been friends with any of the men; however, he voiced friendly remarks about Mr. Smith—a figure of authority and a silent, intense man who generally kept his own counsel. To a sixteen-year-old teenager, Mr. Smith was a man who inspired confidence and respect, not friendship and affection.

In contemplating two versions of the same story, I found myself in a true dilemma: who to believe? I had wholeheartedly accepted Rawicz's account when I first read *The Long Walk*. If Rawicz agonized in the Afterward of the book about the loss of contact with his fellow escapees, the reading public certainly did the same. The incompleteness of the story drew readers to wonder what happened to Zaro, Kolemenos, and Mr. Smith. With the collapse of the Soviet Union and the advent of Internet communication, it became possible to pry open once closed archives and ask for data. Readers around the world were asking each other why research into the book wasn't being done. Surely someone, somewhere, might still be alive who remembered something about the story.

Downing undertook research before and after 1956; Rawicz never did; and Glinski had been so frightened at the thought of Batko enacting revenge on him that he kept silent for decades . . . until he saw my plea in a Polish-language newspaper. I had to ask myself why I believed Glinski's account over Rawicz's. I had only spoken to the man once, but his story had the ring of authenticity to it. He had only heard about *The Long Walk* and read it in the 1970s when a family member commented on its contents being coincidental to Glinski's own personal history. Not only were the stories almost the same but so were the subsequent lives of the two men. Rawicz settled in England after the War, married an English woman, had a family, worked at odd jobs, and battled health problems and nightmares before meeting Downing and co-authoring the book that would change his life. Glinski also settled in England after the War, married an English woman, had a family, worked as a heavy machine operator, and tried to keep his own nightmares at bay.

My instinct to believe Glinski's account, while not wholly discounting that of Rawicz's, had to do with Glinski's willingness to ask questions and help with my research, a fact that was slow in coming. It took some time for Glinski to overcome his fear of Batko, to realize that Rawicz and Batko were not one and the same person and that in all probability Batko was dead, having been many years older than Glinski in the early 1940s. Glinski's trust in me—and mine in him—slowly grew, and I found myself having to make a conscious effort not to push him for information but to allow him to reveal details at his own pace. Concurrently with investigating Glinski's memories, I was juggling thoughts of how to learn more about the exact details of Rawicz's account. Was there any way to rationalize, I wondered, the two individual accounts of the same event? Either the one man or the other had been on that walk, had known Mr. Smith and the other escapees, and had experienced the adventure of a lifetime—but it clearly had not been both.

Chapter 14

THE BIT PLAYERS

During the time I was busy learning all the new developments in the story from Glinski, more information started coming in from other sources. I began to get e-mails and letters from the Mayne family, from friends of the Mayne family, from retired policemen in Camborne, from the PRO in London, from the Polish Institute, from the Cornish Studies Library, from a contact at Harper & Co., from the Burma Star Association, from the Home Office, from genealogical Web sites and other places.

Frustratingly, though, not much in the realm of solid fact came to the surface. Then I looked again and thought I noticed something important. It was a short e-mail from someone in the British Intelligence Corps Section. The Intelligence Corps wanted to know what I had discovered about Rupert Mayne and his intelligence activities during the War. I wrote back, providing him with what little information I did know about Mayne, his family, his career, and his connection with my research. What I had missed the first time I read the reply was that my connection there was willing to check for more information on Mayne the next time he visited the Intelligence Corps Museum.

"Intelligence Corps Museum?" I asked my friend Patric Emerson of the Indian Army Association. He had never heard of it. After our conversation, Emerson contacted a friend of his at the National Army Museum in

London and was informed that, indeed, there was a Museum of Defense Intelligence at Chicksands, Bedfordshire. Upon learning of that fact, and looking at a map, I phoned the Mayne family, got the names of relatives who had lived in the same village as Mayne when he died and learned from them that Mayne had stated his intention years before to donate his wartime memorabilia to a local archive. The only archive in that area turned out to be part of the Museum of Defense Intelligence. For once, I felt I was on the right track. Then, as matters transpired, I received a very nice letter from the Museum stating they had found a 3 x 5 index card noting Mayne's name and nothing else. They had no idea if he had donated something, arrived for an appointment, or simply dropped by. Whom he saw and when he paid his visit were mysteries.

Though disappointed at my findings, I was quickly distracted by more e-mails coming in from people who had been in Calcutta and Assam in 1942.

Len Thornton, the author of *Another Brummie in Burma*, was in touch with me through his granddaughter. His memories of being a surgeon's assistant at Imphal were fascinating. Although he had never heard of *The Long Walk* or of the men on it, he put me in touch with hordes of people who were nurses or who drove ambulances and who knew the eastern side of India very well. From these various contacts, I learned about the FANYs and the Chinthe Women's Auxiliary Corps, about the Queen Alexandra's Imperial Military Nursing Service and the Lady Minto Nursing Association, about the Friends' Ambulance Unit drivers; I heard about the tea planters and their collective function during the war years as intelligence gatherers.

While I was deep in the Assam of half a century ago, listening with bated breath to tales of heroism against the advancing Japanese who had overrun Burma, I was also receiving data about the refugee camps in Persia. Ever since Glinski mentioned his exit from India via a military convoy to the Caspian Sea, I tried to find out more about the transit point in Persia where people (refugees, displaced persons, etc.) were sent. Camp Pahlevi on the southwest shore of the Caspian Sea was that transit point—the place where the refugees were welcomed ashore, given clean clothes, had their papers checked, and were given medical treatment before being moved farther into Persia.

From Pahlevi, various nationalities of European refugees were dispersed to camps nearer to Tehran. Beyond that, as in Glinski's case, the mainly Polish refugees were scattered to the four winds. There were those who went to South Africa, others to Europe, more to Palestine, a few to Kenya, Tanganyika, or Uganda, some to Mexico, and still more to India, where they congregated into a few large camps near Bombay while the War proceeded. Glinski bounced from Persia to Palestine to South Africa to Scotland before ending back in Europe, fighting with a Polish unit for the continent's freedom.

⁕⁕⁕

During this hectic last quarter of 2003, a Web site devoted to World War II Polish refugees from Kresy-Siberia came to my attention. I found myself immersed in the history of these valiant people, reading one true survival story after another. The amazing content, the vigorous research efforts, and the suggestions and willingness to help one another have made this Web site a particular favorite of mine. More importantly, the contacts made through the Web site were extremely helpful in assisting me to understand what the refugees went through, how they managed to survive from Kresy (eastern Poland) to Siberia to Central Asia to Persia. The survivors and their descendants have gone out of their way to delve into, explain, share, and propagate the history of these refugees, which was most helpful in my research.

My contact with this group of people gave me a clearer insight into the possibilities of what might have happened to the men of *The Long Walk* once they left India. In Glinski's case, his path led him into the military to fight on European soil until the end of the War. Might not that have been the path for the other three survivors? Would they have chosen the military path when it came time to leave India? These were avenues I needed to explore.

While contemplating which avenue to investigate, I was contacted by someone who had information about General Stilwell's march out of Burma in early 1942. General Joseph Stilwell, Commanding General of U.S. Armed Forces, CBI Theater, led a ragtag host of nearly 200 people on a nightmarish "long walk" from Burma into India during the spring of 1942, with the Japanese in close pursuit. One of the people on that infamous walk was Dr. Gordon Seagrave. He came from a line of missionary doctors who had devoted their lives to the service of the Burmese people. It was pointed out to me that, perhaps, Dr. Seagrave may have had some knowledge of the story behind The Long Walk.

I found a copy of Seagrave's book Burma Surgeon, as well as its sequel, but there was no reference in either to the adventures of the men who escaped from Siberia. Seagrave's books were adventurous and good reads. As always, many names and details were mentioned, including those of the Friends' Ambulance Unit. With Google well out of its infancy by 2003, I typed in the name of the World War II unit and up came some biographical information. With a little more searching, I made contact with some of the actual drivers who saved lives in faraway Assam during the War.

Through my connection with the ambulance drivers, I heard of Pete Lutken. When we first made contact, I politely listened to his recollection of being a young man bound for India in early 1942. The more I listened, however, the more my interest was piqued by his life story. Lutken, an American, was sent out earlier than most GIs because he went as a member of the Office of Strategic Services (OSS). His unit was known as Detachment 101, and he was seconded to a British intelligence group in the far north of Assam, along the Burmese border. His commanding officer was British Colonel J. R. "Reggie" Wilson of V-Force.

What came to light partway through our conversation was the surprising fact that Lutken had never heard of The Long Walk, but he knew the story. Instantly I experienced one of those moments that rarely comes in a person's life, a moment when time slows down and words become crystal clear. Lutken repeated, "I never knew about any book, but I did hear about those men who made that walk." Lutken went on to elaborate.

Sometime in the winter months of 1943, after he returned from being upcountry for a time with Wilson and his crew (Vincent Curl, Dr. John Grindlay, and a few others), they were sitting around a campfire at Tagap Ga, just inside Burma, swapping stories. At one point, Grindlay entered the conversation and remarked on the deplorable condition of men who made a grueling walk from Siberia. He stated they were in appalling condition when they reached India.

As soon as I found my tongue, I began to pepper Lutken with questions. He was not a man who kept a diary or journals, but he was sure Grindlay had. He also mentioned that Grindlay had died sometime in the 1960s but that his children were all still alive. While I was noting down this information, I returned to what Lutken had just said and began to elicit as much detail as possible from him about what he remembered hearing in 1943. He thought he remembered hearing Grindlay say that the men were picked up in the Brahmaputra valley—on the south side of the Himalayas where the river seems to turn back on itself. He had the impression that Grindlay did not actually give medical treatment to the men but either heard about them or saw them at some point once he had left Burma and arrived in India in the spring of 1942. Grindlay initially went with Seagrave to Imphal, then accompanied Gen. Stilwell to New Delhi before traveling to different spots around India and eventually passing through Tagap Ga, where Lutken was based.

While listening to Lutken, I formulated a mental picture of field hospitals and casualty clearing stations that corresponded with Glinski's description of the thatched medical facility where he and the other escapees were brought for treatment upon reaching India. Medical facilities of this type were prevalent throughout the CBI theater.

After our conversation, I took to the computer to search for more information about Dr. John Grindlay. I stumbled upon a contact at Dartmouth College, Grindlay's alma mater, who referred me to one of his daughters. Soon after, I made contact with Grindlay's two daughters, one son, and elderly widow, plus some old family friends as well. One of his daughters kindly pointed me in yet another direction, that of Alan Lathrop at the University of Minnesota, to whom the Grindlay family had lent Dr. Grindlay's diary for research purposes. Upon reaching Alan and unwinding my story to date, he had a look through the journal and photocopied some pages, but there was no written mention of the men of *The Long Walk*, though there was a reference to a "campfire chat" as described by Lutken.

Looking for Mr. Smith

Despite all the goodwill and the multiple phone calls, e-mails, and letters, no new, relevant facts were collected. Regrettably, Grindlay died young in the 1960s, his widow had trouble remembering details from the past, and his children had been too young to take in many details of what he might have said in regarding to the escapees. Yet, one of his daughters thought she remembered something, perhaps a spoken reference, pointing to the men who walked from Siberia. She rather thought that on a hiking trip with her father, when she was a teenager, he had talked about these men. Later, though, she admitted her uncertainty as to whether she had mixed up some comments of his about fleeing Burma on his own "long walk" with the adventures of the escaping men.

My overall impression, once the dust settled on this little byway of research, was that, indeed, Grindlay either played an active role of some sort with the escaped men or had a passive role as listener to some other medical man who treated the survivors. Whatever the case may be, the fact that people remembered his remarks, the time and location of which could be pinpointed, lent further credence to the tale.

One very good thing came of this delving into Grindlay's story, namely, that I established a rapport with Pete Lutken and with Alan Lathrop. They have both continued to this day to be helpful and inspiring, whether suggesting additional leads to explore or being willing to share information they possess that would help my research. Lutken, with his exceptional memory, continues to reel off name after name every time we talk. My envy of the man's memory knows no bounds.

He encouraged me to contact the family of Dr. Gordon Seagrave, a missionary doctor, and Troy Sacquety, who was working on a history of Detachment 101 and who hosts an OSS Web site. Sterling Seagrave, the doctor's son and a famous author in his field, did not remember anything about men escaping from Siberia and ending up in India, because he had left Burma with his mother as a very young child on one of the last boats out of Rangoon. Sacquety did quite a bit of digging in OSS archives but came up with nothing. No one in the OSS reported the incident or commented on it. Sacquety posted my query on the OSS Web site but no one with any information replied.

At Lutken's behest, I also contacted the widow of his wartime British V-Force commander, Nancy Wilson. She spent quite some time with her husband in India during the War, and she was full of memories from that period—and had even more names for me to contact. The remarkable thing about Nancy was that, during our first conversation, she mentioned she would be one hundred years old the following year. Yet, she was sharp as a tack with a memory like Lutken's. However, she had never heard her husband nor anyone else mention *The Long Walk* or the escapees from Siberia.

One of the contacts she recalled, the sister of a man who had been a district officer in far-off Assam, remembered the presence of American GIs in that part of the world and wondered if it would be worth tracking any of them down. I replied that I had, citing Lutken and others. At the same time, I had been directed to a CBI Web site in which quite a bit of material was laid out about the American presence in Assam, complete with names, locations, and so on.

An embodiment of that American presence was Francis "Brad" Obradovich. He and his wife, Elaine, met at one of those locations: the 20th General Hospital in the Ledo Road area. Another American, Bob Younger, was also there with the 27th Engineers at Lakopani. My contact with these people, and especially with Younger, opened yet another field of inquiry. Younger knew of Drs. Grindlay and Seagrave, and in 2004 he asked me, "Were those walkouts Russians?" I stated that the escapees were of various nationalities but spoke Russian among themselves as a common language. He caught my attention when he responded, "There were Russians living in the Ledo area in World War II."

This mention triggered something Lutken once told me—that I passed on to Younger—about a Russian living in Assam during the War. He was a "White Russian," a leftover from Russia's civil wars. His name was Basil Alexandrovitch, last name unknown. Lutken met him and a friend of his, George, in 1943 when Basil was working with American medical outfits in the Assam/Burma area. Younger responded, stating he had met *two* Russians at the home of a Mr. Lehaney. Lehaney was in charge of the telephones in the Ledo area and lived across the road from the 20th General Hospital.

Younger's outfit purchased and supplied building materials in the area for the entire Ledo Road. He met Lehaney through Colonel Sultano, who was in charge of the native labor camp nearby.

This all sounded quite promising to my research, but I should have known better. Sadly, no new information came to the fore pertaining to the identities of the escapees. And it transpired that the two Russians were actually the Johannes brothers who had walked from Armenia to India before the War. No further mystery there.

⁂

I felt at an impasse as 2003 drew to a close, overwhelmed with all the information I'd gathered that hadn't led to any definitive answers. I continued to receive many e-mails from Web sites, contacts, and fellow researchers. But no new information surfaced. The main topic of inquiry continued to be the identification of Mr. Smith.

In the midst of all the e-mails, I received some startling and sad news—Marjorie, Slav Rawicz's wife, had died in January 2004. It spurred me on to greater efforts in solving the mysteries behind the book, as the realization that the people with whom I was dealing were well into their eighties, and the answers I sought would soon be forever lost to the past.

Part V

RESEARCH RENEWED

Chapter 15

CHINA TO BURMA TO INDIA

Before taking a step away from searching for more information about Russia, I was contacted by a Mr. Russell, who had heard about my research. Russell wrote that his father was a missionary surgeon in Shillong, Assam, until the end of the War and was friends with a Russian there. He added that his father kept a diary and mentioned a Major Dorofeef (*sic*), who was a Russian officer who gave Russell's father a radio. Russell doubted the information would be of any use, and with that I had to agree, as it was obvious Major Dorofeef was not Mr. Smith.

During the hectic start of 2004, Alan Lathrop came up with more suggestions of avenues to persue. Following his advice, I contacted the American Society of Civil Engineers (ASCE), wondering if Mr. Smith had been a "real" engineer rather than, say, a glorified mechanic. The ASCE had records that went back decades, but I had no luck in locating a Mr. Smith who disappeared in the U.S.S.R. in the 1930s.

Lathrop's second suggestion did bear a little fruit. He came across the mention of another American company specializing in building subways that had had an interest in participating in the construction of the Moscow Metro. The owner of the company in the 1920s and 1930s was Samuel Rosoff. His company was also prominent in constructing the New York subway. With little effort on my part, I tracked down Rosoff's son, still alive and in possession of a very good memory, even though he was ninety-three. Rosoff spoke of being a young man, just starting university in 1929, when he accompanied his father and a delegation of engineers to Moscow. Included in that delegation was a representative of Amtorg, Mr. Polia-koff, and there were members of the J. Henry Shroeder Company that represented the London Banking Company. They were wined and dined, taken on tours, visited the nascent construction site for the Moscow Metro, and came home without a contract. He told me that two of the engineers who worked for his father and who had experience constructing the New York subway returned to Moscow to work on the Metro in the 1930s: Mr. Sanford and Mr. Olmstead. Later, in a letter to me, he said he was sorry that no records of his father's business had survived over the years.

Correspondence at this time was proving frustrating, with promising leads that were of no real value. For instance, names of people in British intelligence who corresponded with Mayne in 1942–43 (such as Brian Hammond Whitehorn and Alexander Boyes-Cooper) led nowhere; and when I tried to uncover facts about Gurkha patrols within India during the war years, I discovered there was little information. Not only was the information limited but it was also confusing. Although Glinski stated the patrol he and the other men encountered was comprised of Gurkhas, there was not an actual Gurkha Rifles patrol assigned to the mountainous border area of northern India in early 1942. There were, however, patrols comprised of Gurkhas who were members of the Assam Rifles at that time. There were also references to internal patrols of the Eastern Frontier Rifles.

Earlier in my research, the members of the British Empire and Common-wealth (BEC) Web site stated the patrol that picked up the survivors might have been some kind of police or constabulary patrol. This supposition was also suggested in letters from people who were tea planters in Assam and who volunteered their services as intelligence officers during the War. They agreed with a comment made by Ronnie McAlister of the 3rd Queen Alexandra's Own Gurkha Rifles who pointed out the likelihood that the patrol mentioned in *The Long Walk* was one of those consisting of domi-ciled Gurkhas that abounded in the North-East Frontier Agency (NEFA) at that time. These Gurkha patrols were employed in local security units with a British officer in charge of each patrol. It was further suggested that the British officer leading the patrol would have also been in the Indian Army or the Indian Police. The next step was to find documentation about these patrols, but there appeared to be nothing in the British Library's India Office archives or at the PRO; the Gurkha Museum had archives but were doubtful they had information on NEFA patrols; and another member of the BEC Web site informed me that there had been a distribution of police records after 1947 and any paperwork concerning the wartime patrols might be anywhere—another dead end to contend with.

Lance Visser, a contributor to the Burma Star Association's Web site, came to my rescue with precise details on where to look for information regarding Gurkha patrols and many of my other questions. He was very good at sending me the volume and page number for items of interest residing in multiple archives in the U.K. He thought that the Gurkha patrol in *The Long Walk* might have been a small detachment of the Assam Rifles. The bottom line, as I was to learn, was that this specific information would be very difficult to track down.

As if to verify the difficulty of finding such information, I began receiving a stream of reminiscences from the Koi-Hai Web site, from retired tea planters who raised regiments for the Assam Rifles and fought at places such as Imphal and Kohima. Many of them did remember Dr. Gordon Seagrave's and Stilwell's walk out of Burma; some sent me addresses of Burmese nurses who married and settled in the West after the War. One point of interest included details about the possible location of the casualty clearing station or field hospital where it is probable the escaped prisoners from Siberia were initially treated. By process of elimination, and considering there were not very many of them functioning in the first few months of 1942, Panitola was pinpointed as a strong possibility for the location of the clearing station.

Panitola turned out to be near Dibrugarh and the Dinjan airfield in northern Assam and, before the War, was used as a tea plantation hospital. Despite unearthing quite a lot of material on Panitola, I could never verify whether it was truly the initial first stop in India for the escapees.

Through the continued inundation of e-mails and correspondence revolving around various facets of my search, one illuminating letter arrived. Mrs. Alison Ross, whose husband had been in the 7th Gurkhas and later in the 8th Gurkhas during the War, wrote to say that during the mid-1950s, when she and her husband were stationed in Malaya, she recalled that an official request from the British government had been circulated. The request wondered if anyone having been attached to a Gurkha unit in India during the War remembered anything about a group of men who escaped from Siberia. This request was put out at the same time the book was published. I spoke to Mrs. Ross and subsequently exchanged letters with her and her husband. Although they had nothing more to add other than to remark on the coincidence of the publication of the book and the official inquiry into its contents, they suggested possible people to contact and query further.

One of those on their list was Col. J. P. Cross, who was involved with the Gurkha Welfare Trust and who currently lived in Pokhara, Nepal. Cross responded to my query, stating that he had read it in a regimental newsletter but had never heard anything about *The Long Walk*. He did, however, add more names to my never-ending list.

In the midst of all this digging, my attention was turned away from India for a while due to new lists of names coming in from the Kresy-Siberia Web site that identified Poles arriving at Camp Pahlevi (Persia) during the War. I became actively engaged in locating people on the lists who, like Glinski and Rawicz, had survived the ordeal of leaving the U.S.S.R. to join the Free Poles in Persia and Palestine and were posting their own histories on the Web site. There was a good possibility that the names Rawicz or Glinski might appear on one of the lists or in someone's family history.

Polish refugees confirmed what Glinski had related, namely, that transport from Camp Pahlevi to the camps outside Tehran was manned by Sikh drivers from diverse detachments of the British Indian Army. The unit that built and supervised the maintenance of Camp Pahlevi was the Royal Mechanical and Electrical Engineers, a part of the Royal Corps of Signals. (When I inquired why that particular group of engineers were in Persia as early as the end of 1941, building a camp on the shores of the Caspian Sea to welcome Polish refugees from the Soviet Union during March 1942, I was informed that the British units involved were part of the PAI Force [Persian and Iraqi Force] posted to that area to protect the oil fields from a possible Nazi invasion.)

As I tried to extricate my thoughts from both India and Persia, and concentrate again on pursuing leads regarding Ronald Downing and his colleagues from their far-off days on the *Daily Mail*, I received sad news: Slavomir Rawicz was dead.

Chapter 16

RAWICZ AND GLINSKI

The news of Rawicz's death caught me by surprise, as it did innumerable readers of his book. Despite the fact that he had not been in good health for some time and that Marjorie had passed away at the beginning of the year, it was still difficult to think of Rawicz suddenly not being there. I had planned to pull my thoughts together and get another letter off to him with the information I uncovered since we had last corresponded—and now it was too late.

Before contacting Rawicz, I wanted to try to formulate a way of introducing Glinski and his story in a letter and then ask Rawicz what he thought of someone else claiming to have made the same escape and having known the same Mr. Smith. I had a pretty good idea that any such claim by someone not named in *The Long Walk* would bring a storm of protest from Rawicz.

Another reason why I put off writing such a letter was that I was waiting for a reply to a query I sent to "Memorial" several weeks earlier to try to authenticate the story. However, it took until 2005 before I got a response from the Society.

When I passed on news of Rawicz's death to Glinski, there was a momentary regret that the two men had never met and confronted one another. If Glinski's story were true, how had Rawicz heard of it and why had he appropriated it as his own story? If Rawicz's story were true, why had he not been able to substantiate it—why had he not made any effort to verify the story and help others find the three escapees lost to history?

Glinski, it seemed, was inspired by my questions and started his own search to verify the facts of the story. I told him that his military records might provide information concerning his whereabouts in India, which would then lead to the exact location of the medical facility near Calcutta where he and the other escapees were treated, and where he enlisted with the Free Poles. A definite location would provide a jump-off point for researching what became of his fellow escapees. He contacted the Polish Office of the Ministry of Defence and asked for a copy of his records—if, indeed, his records were even held by the MOD. By the beginning of 2004, he had received a reply.

Stripped to a bare synopsis of his military career, the MOD noted their paperwork showed that Glinski had enlisted in the Polish Army, 1st Reconnaissance Squadron, 1st Armoured Division, 1st Polish Corps on March 7, 1942. The record also showed Glinski being in the Reconnaissance Squadron of the 8th Infantry Division, but this was changed to the above 1st Armoured Division on November 27, 1942 when he arrived in England. The typed extract of his record went on to state that Glinski was evacuated to Iran (Persia) and came under British command on April 1, 1942. Disappointingly, there was no mention of *where* he was when he enlisted in March. Also, it came to light that the 8th Infantry Division was comprised of those Poles who had fled the U.S.S.R. via the Caspian Sea to Camp Pahlevi—there was nothing in the Polish Army records about military men coming from India. Glinski thought mention of the 8th Infantry Division was an error—he was sure he had been in the 1st Reconnaissance Squadron; instead, it was very possibly a reference to him being one of the thousands of Poles entering Persia to join the Free Poles.

My contact with Glinski became more frequent as I learned more of the details about his experience once he had arrived in India. He reaffirmed that the patrol on which he and the other escapees had stumbled was definitely comprised of Gurkhas. They wore the renowned curved knives (*kukris*) as part of their kit, and their uniforms were dark green; their appearance was Asian, not Indian. He referred again to his memories from that point on as being hazy because he had been in such bad shape. He had only vague memories of medical personnel, mostly Indian, taking care of him. He did recall being questioned by several people, all British military men with translators. We continued back and forth in this fashion, trying to dredge up additional memories and focus on particulars.

I sent Glinski copies of Rawicz's newspaper interviews in the 1950s. In some of the interviews were references to Rawicz having been on the staff of General Anders in Tehran. Did Glinski know of or remember anyone who might have been on General Anders's staff? He said no one came to mind, and he did not recognize any of the photographs of Rawicz taken in the mid-1950s either. Glinski just could not fathom who Rawicz was and why the latter had seemingly stolen a chapter out of his own life.

It was during this time, while prodding Glinski's memory, that I began to question who Rawicz actually was. It had only been on the occasion of his wife's death earlier in the year that I had come across his full name: Rusiecki-Rawicz. While Rawicz, during early interviews, referred to writing under a pseudonym to "protect his privacy," Marjorie's full married name was printed in her obituary: Marjorie Rusiecka-Rawicz (the final "a" instead of "i" in Rusiecki denoting female gender). For whatever reason, she used that particular surname until the end of her life. That being the case, and knowing the ease with which I was able to track down the Rawicz family's vital records, Rawicz's decision to shorten his name would not have been an effective way to protect his privacy or his family back in Poland (from communist reprisals after the War) while his wife and children used their full family name in England.

About this time, Glinski announced that he felt confident to return to Eastern Europe and visit his birthplace. He confided in me that it was due to my research, questions, openness in sharing information about Rawicz, and the possibility that Batko was truly dead that he was able to think of the future. He had had no contact with his Polish family since the 1950s and now, in his later years, he felt a real desire to find out what happened to those family members he left behind.

He, his wife, and a son and his family, all traveled to Belarus (western Belarus had been eastern Poland before the War). Glinski and his family returned to the village of his birth, wandering around and learning that buildings had been destroyed or torn down during and after the War, when they came across someone who knew his family. They were eventually hailed by a distant cousin who remembered and recognized Glinski after so many years. Shock, amazement, tears, and a babble of languages ensued as Glinski had to dredge up memories of Polish and Russian vernacular while translating everything into English for the benefit of his family.

The greatest shock came as the afternoon wore on and his cousin brought Glinski over to a telephone, dialed a number in Warsaw, and said to the woman on the other end, "There's someone here who would like to speak to you." When Glinski spoke to the woman, she promptly hung up, thinking someone was playing a horrible joke on her. Glinski dialed again, kept her on the line long enough to explain, then listened to a torrent of sobs that had been kept in check since 1939, when he had last seen and spoken to his sister.

Needless to say, travel plans were amended, Glinski and his family flew to Warsaw, and the reunion was memorable and bittersweet. There was a lot of lost time to be made up. Each member of the family believed the other to be dead, and many members of Glinski's family had died in the interim without ever knowing Glinski had survived the labor camps and the War.

Glinski's sudden reunion with his family did not stifle his research into *The Long Walk*. He asked, but none of his family had ever heard of Rawicz or the story; his birthplace was far north of Pinsk, Rawicz's birthplace; and there did not appear to be any kind of familial or geographic connection. Yet, their two lives were seemingly intertwined. How had that happened?

❦❧

Although hundreds of people were interested in my search for the truth behind the story, no one I contacted had definite documentation that would further my understanding of these events and people. Throughout 2004 I continued to receive negative replies to my queries about gulags. The POW/MIA group that constructed a Web site and did a lot of spadework in Russian archives came up empty-handed when asked about the camp mentioned in the book. At the beginning of 2005, I finally received a reply from "Memorial," but it contained no substantial documentation regarding either Rawicz or Glinski. Around this same time I received confirmation of Glinski's story through the Karta Indeks Web site. Glinski's name did appear within its files, as did the name of his father; but the information was only rudimentary and did not include anything about his "consignment" to Siberia. Although frustrating, this little bit of data provided me with the first glimmer of hope that something more would be forthcoming—and that, perhaps, 2005 would be the year of revelations.

Chapter 17

∽

DOCUMENTATION SURPRISES

The new year saw my research start off strong. I felt I was now in contact with major organizations with millions of records at their disposal and there might be a chance that some bit of knowledge would float to the surface in time—and that's precisely what happened.

Having attempted on numerous occasions to find out about Rawicz using his shortened last name, I next tried using his full name: Rusiecki-Rawicz. Now different replies came in. Suddenly, in the spring of 2005, letters began to arrive at a rapid rate. Stamped and certified copies of sixty-year-old documents rested in my mailbox after long journeys from Russia. Some came direct from Moscow; others came by way of Khrasnoyarsk and its archives—all thanks to "Memorial."

I also had to thank the Hoover Institution, in the guise of Lora Soroka and Irena Czernichowska, for responding to my query concerning Glinski. It came to my attention during 2004, via the Kresy-Siberia group, that papers from General Anders's army were housed at the Hoover. Although Glinski was not part of that army, he once passed through Persia on his way to join the Free Poles in England and, I reasoned, the collection might have information on him. When I opened the envelope and read an aging document from the Ministerstwo Obrony Narodowej, dated September 1944, I quickly discovered Glinski's name on page 2. His name and the names of his family members were listed. At the same time, I pulled out another sheaf of documents that I couldn't make heads or tails of at first. The documents were handwritten, in Polish and Russian, and I could not figure out how they connected with Glinski. In fact, they did not.

When I had originally contacted the Hoover Institution, I added Rawicz's full name to the end of my query. What I was looking at were documents pertaining to Rawicz who, as Rusiecki-Rawicz, patronym Feodor, had indeed been a prisoner in Siberia. I felt that at long last I had stumbled onto the right trail, though that feeling did not last for long.

Once the documents were translated into English, my feelings of progress came to an abrupt halt. The smallest of the documents was a half sheet of paper, a form of some sort, with numbers down the left side of the page and short designations next to those numbers, such as Name, Age, Profession, and so on. "Roscilaw Slawomir Rusiecki-Rawicz" was written at the top of the page. His birth year was 1915. Next to Profession was written construction (technical) engineer. His last address was simply given as Pinsk, Poland. He left Poland as a prisoner. His time and term of imprisonment was from November 27, 1939, to April 29, 1940. Under the heading of Prison, there was a list of places including Pinsk, Kharkov, and Sverdlovsk; under the heading of Labor Camp, *camp "105" Irkutsk, 800 km. north east from Irkutsk* was written. Lastly, the form noted Rawicz's dates of release: April 15, 1940, and March 1, 1942. (I reminded myself that right in the middle of these dates was August 14, 1941, the day a formal military agreement or "amnesty" was signed by Stalin and General Sikorski, leader of the Polish government-in-exile in London, pinpointing a release date of September 1, 1941, for all Polish citizens held in Soviet labor camps.)

I read and reread the form. I especially noted that last date, March 1, 1942. Hadn't the book stated the escape from Camp 303 took place in 1941? Why did this form show March 1942 as Rawicz's release date? Why were there *two* release dates? One of the members of the Kresy-Siberia group who was a prisoner in Siberia during this time and had benefited from the above-mentioned amnesty to exit the U.S.S.R. via Camp Pahlevi in March 1942 explained that each time there was a transfer to a new prison, or new charges were trumped up to lay on a prisoner, imprisonment and release dates were listed. Did that mean Rawicz was arrested more than once? What about March 1942? Fortunately, a reply was quick in coming. The man from the Kresy-Siberia group immediately stated that March 1942 would stick in his memory forever: that was the month of the first mass exodus of Poles from the U.S.S.R. They began in March 1942 and continued throughout that year at sporadic intervals, with tens of thousands of Poles (and others) leaving the U.S.S.R. as fast as they could.

Though still trying to gather as much as I could from the sparse information on the small form, I turned my attention to the much longer document comprising two legal-sized pages. This document was written by Rawicz while serving in General Anders's army in Persia. Right at the top of the page, in flowing copperplate handwriting, was the word for "Questionnaire." The document began as the form had, with Rawicz's full name, his military rank of private, his date of birth—1915—his profession as a technical engineer, and his marital status as married. Then the details began.

His date of arrest was shown as November 27, 1939, when he was imprisoned in Pinsk until April 15, 1940, including twenty-seven days in solitary confinement. On April 27, 1940, he was formally arrested again for killing an NKVD man and was taken with a group of other prisoners to a prison in Minsk. (Before I read further, my mind stuck on the words *killing an NKVD man*. What did *that* mean? Was it a murder or an accident? An NKVD man meant an officer in the secret police. Did someone who killed an NKVD man simply get sent to prison? Weren't they tortured and killed themselves? I couldn't find anyone to shed light on those speculations. I asked three different people to translate that paragraph, and every one of them came to a halt when they read those words. I finally decided to take the words at face value for the time being.

Tearing my attention away from that particular phrase, the details on the form continued. Apparently Rawicz was in Minsk from May 3, 1940, to September 11, 1940. He then went to a prison in Kharkov from September 16, 1940, to December 21, 1940, and later was transferred to another prison in Sverdlovsk, where he remained from December 25, 1940, to March 4, 1941. While in prison in Sverdlovsk, he spent seventy-four days in solitary confinement. (Although my mind and eyes kept drifting back to the line about killing an NKVD man, I continued wondering why the interminable transfers from prison to prison, ever eastward, and why the solitary confinements. What exactly had Rawicz done?)

The specifics continued. During the period March 7, 1941, to March 1, 1942, Rawicz was sentenced and exiled for twenty-five years of forced labor to Camp 105, Irkutsk, approximately 800 kilometers northeast of the city of Irkutsk. From that jump-off point there was a description of the long trek to the camp that was made on foot, without food, in -85°F weather. The camp itself was gloomy and dark, with dilapidated buildings full of small compartments, meant for fifteen to twenty people, wherein fifty to sixty people were crammed.

Although I diligently read every line, I kept glancing back not only at the word NKVD but also at the March 1941 to March 1942 dates. Wasn't that the time period in which Rawicz and the other escapees were legging it to India across China and Tibet? Were the above dates just that, merely dates written on a piece of paper that had little meaning because the person about whom they were written had gone under the wire fence and fled? I kept reading.

The next few paragraphs in the questionnaire focused on profiles of prisoners, including nationality, levels of education, and so on. Polish prisoners who were in the camps and prisons were there for insignificant incidents, Rawicz wrote on the questionnaire. They were people with a high moral and intellectual background; good mutual relationships helped them to survive. Each day in camp or prison began with an examination (roll call?). The diet was horrible and not sufficient. In the labor camps, the assignment of labor was based on personal strength. Clothes were very basic. The prisoners were isolated and lacked information from the outside world.

There was an additional reference to the NKVD included in Rawicz's observations of the relationship between NKVD officers and the Polish prisoners. Terrible treatment was meted out to the Poles during examinations (interrogations?). There was interrupted sleep; sitting on the edge of chairs for twenty-four to forty-eight hours during interrogations; hitting of the prisoner's head with a stick; threats with weapons to the temple and head; threats to cut off noses and ears, or gouge out eyes; threats of hanging, of being left in a cold cell—the descriptions went on and on. After detailing such tortures in the questionnaire, Rawicz added that medical assistance was rare. During the time Rawicz was in Camp 105, sixty-four people died (twenty-six women and thirty-eight men) between the ages of sixteen and sixty-five years old, mostly from exhaustion and hunger. There was absolutely no communication with Poland or their families.

Toward the end of the questionnaire more baffling information surfaced. The last question dealt with release dates and how Rawicz entered the Polish army. He wrote that he was released March 1, 1942, to go to Khrasnoyarsk. From Camp 105 to Irkutsk he traveled approximately 500 kilometers in some kind of cart and 300 kilometers on foot. On March 14, 1942, he went by train from Irkutsk to Khrasnoyarsk; then from Novosibirsk to Lugovoj (a transit point mentioned by many of the members of the Kresy-Siberia group, very near to a major train junction, Dzamboul, in present-day Kazakhstan), arriving on March 25, 1942. He was inducted into the Polish army on March 26, 1942, having already learned while in Khrasnoyarsk on March 20, 1942, about the amnesty and the creation of a Polish Army in the territory of the U.S.S.R.

At the bottom of the second page was a beautifully written signature, Rusiecki-Rawicz Roscislaw Slawomir, and a date of March 23, 1943. This was one of the thousands of documents within the General Anders collection housed at the Hoover Institution—and it took my breath away. For my purposes of better understanding Rawicz, it appeared that instead of trekking across Asia worrying about recapture between March 1941 and March 1942, Rawicz was in a labor camp in Siberia, and released because of a general amnesty signed the year before. It was baffling and difficult to comprehend.

There was also a disconnection with the distances quoted and the amount of time it took to cover those distances. In the book, Rawicz stated it took the prisoners weeks to slog through the snow to reach their camp; in the handwritten record, it appeared that the 800 kilometers from the camp back to Irkutsk took barely two weeks, albeit with the help of riding in some kind of cart. Horse-drawn carts would not have been much faster than walking in the snow, however. Perhaps it seemed like weeks instead of several days when he marched out of Irkutsk the year before.

As I tried to wrap my head around what I read, the speculation started to mount: "Could these documents mean . . ."; "Maybe there's some explanation . . ."; "Why didn't these organizations answer my letters last year, when Rawicz was still alive . . ."; "How am I going to track down this information?"; "Who to write to next?"

My immediate response to the questions I posed was to begin writing letters to the Hoover Institution, Karta Indeks, and "Memorial" once again, keeping my fingers crossed that replies might be forthcoming in less than six months. My next task was to contact Glinski and fill him in on the content of the questionnaire, asking if any of the information contained therein sounded familiar. In other words, was there any point of reference upon which his path might have unwittingly crossed that of Rawicz? The reply came back as a singular "No." Nothing contained in the questionnaire rang any bells, with the exception of the similarity in geography; for example, both Rawicz and Glinski were in labor camps several hundred kilometers north of Irkutsk. It appeared that Rawicz only arrived in Siberia in March 1941, at which time Glinski and the other escapees were under the wire and on their way to India.

Both Rawicz and Glinski were hazy about dates in their various correspondences with me. Considering their circumstances, the starvation and sleeplessness, not to mention the beatings they endured, it was no wonder their memories were not infallible. Other survivors of the labor camps with whom I spoke also said they were never sure what month it was, let alone the day. They realized when the seasons changed and passed, and perhaps someone had kept note of a major holiday such as Christmas or Easter but, otherwise, millions of people plodded through a timeless murk all during the war years. It was incredible, then, to come across a document with specific dates and locations, with specific information about a person's progress through the gulag.

(This vagueness on the part of gulag survivors is described by Alexander Dolgun in *An American in the Gulag*. Dolgun referred to actual memory and "what must have been" to fill in the blank spaces of time he experienced while moving from one prison to another, from one interrogation session to another. He subsequently tried to reconstruct his past by piecing together those portions he remembered and then talking to other gulag survivors who helped him construct bridges linking his islands of memory. He needed the real memories as well as the supposed memories to build up a more comprehensive picture of what had happened to him. He also wondered why certain events or people stood out so clearly in his mind years later but others didn't. This vagueness versus vividness bothered Dolgun, and he referred to memory blanks and the distress they caused him throughout his story.)

In Glinski's case, there was documentation both from the Hoover Institution and from Karta Indeks. The information from the Hoover Institution was part of General Anders's collection encompassing just about any and every Polish citizen who passed through Persia during the War. Karta was another matter. Within a few months, the information I originally discovered about Glinski had changed and was "updated." When I inquired about the update, I was told that Karta was still in the process of patching bits of information together to form a whole picture. Apparently the people at Karta were gathering material from a variety of sources and trying to make sense of what they had.

Verification of Glinski and of his family was available. He had indeed been rounded up and deported, initially to Archangelsk *oblast* (province) in 1940 and later sent to a "special type settlement" in Gorkowska *oblast* in 1941. (I asked one of the Kresy-Siberia Web site members if he could tell me what such a settlement was. He explained it was for political prisoners rather than for ordinary criminals.) Many of the Karta Indeks cards showed a "release" date of September 2, 1941. In fact, that was the date of amnesty to release all Polish prisoners, the amnesty that was signed by Stalin and his Polish counterpart on August 14, 1941. This left a large hole in the appropriate time frame—a hole that could have been filled in with a stint of hard labor in Siberia and a subsequent escape.

While Rawicz's document clearly stated that he had not even arrived in Siberia until March 1941, and that he benefited from the amnesty the following year, was it possible that, like Glinski, he did escape, had some kind of adventure, and then found himself in Persia? When I looked further into Glinski's story, I learned that the information sent to him by the MOD was, indeed, equivocal. History buffs answered my online inquiries to say there was no record of any kind of squadron, division, corps, and so on, of Poles having been organized in India during the War. The information Glinski was given simply mentioned that he had arrived in Persia in April 1942. It appeared that, like thousands of other Poles, he was listed as being part of the 8th Infantry Division that was specifically formed in March 1942 in the U.S.S.R. That particular division left Persia and made its way to the U.K. via South Africa later in 1942; Glinski happened to be part of it. Upon arriving in Scotland toward the end of the year, Glinski was put into what he always thought of as "his" unit, the 1st Reconnaissance Squadron of the 1st Armoured Division; and that part of his story was substantiated.

❧ ❧

The flipping and flopping between the two versions of the same story caused me a lot of headaches. It was difficult to accept that Rawicz's story was made up, or rather, that the story was true but his part in it was not. On the other hand, could I wholly accept Glinski's story? I kept in mind that Glinski had never publicized his experiences and hardly ever spoke of them except to his family. He was convinced that Rawicz was a murderer using an alias and, therefore, had kept quiet about his own past for decades. At this point in time, six decades after the escape and walk, what had he to gain by talking about his wartime experiences? Nothing. He simply answered my query in a Polish-language newspaper in a moment of irritation—a moment of wanting to correct the record, thinking Rawicz and Batko were the same man, and wanting me to know it. It thus came as a surprise to Glinski when he realized we were discussing two different men, and Rawicz was no longer a threat to him.

That still left Glinski wondering about Batko. At this time I received news from Cornwall, England, about the mysterious figure of Batko. His true existence added *another* element of perplexity to the tale, as if there weren't already plenty of unsolved mysteries to investigate.

In mid-2005, an e-mail arrived from the archives of the Cornwall Record Office in southern England stating that someone had taken an interest in my request regarding Batko and, voilà, had found an old record. That record went a long way in corroborating the existence of Batko—the man who was a murderer and whose presence and subsequent memory had terrorized Glinski for years. As it turned out, Jan Batko had in fact existed: He was arrested in Redruth, Cornwall, on June 19, 1948, and was found guilty and fined for taking and driving a lorry without the owner's knowledge or consent, said lorry being uninsured and said driver (Batko) not having an operator's license. He appeared in court on June 22, 1948—and that was the last anyone knew or heard of him. Still, it confirmed his existence and added further believability to Glinski's story.

Hot on the heels of this proof of Batko's existence was additional information pertaining to Rawicz. Photocopies arrived from Russia of official documents with many rubber-stamp imprints. The smaller of the two new documents was a typed certificate in Russian stating that Rawicz was amnestied and allowed to move around and leave Russia. This document was dated September 1, 1941 (the official amnesty date for Poles as designated in the treaty signed between Stalin and Sikorski on that date). The second new document was longer and was a certificate with an expiry date: April 1, 1942. This document certified that Mr. Rusiecki-Rawicz, patronym Feodor, currently living in Taseevo region, may depart from Khrasnoyarsk to Dzhambul for the purpose of joining the Polish Army. It ended with a flourish, stating that the representative of the (Polish) Delegatura Ambasady R. P. in Krasnojarsk region, Irkutsk province, was honored to ask the government of the U.S.S.R. to provide Mr. Rusiecki-Rawicz help with transportation! This was dated March 20, 1942—in time for Rawicz to join the first trainload of Poles leaving the Soviet Union for Persia.

Chapter 18

∽

DOCUMENTATION DISCOVERIES

After the excitement of discovery, I took time to have a long, hard look at all the documents and bits of paper in my possession. I needed to examine all the incoming data with fresh eyes and, perhaps, a fresh mind. My feeling was that I was missing a link somewhere. There had to be one bit of information in the jumble that would shed light on all the rest and provide some logical connection between the documents, the story, the book, everything.

One comment made to me about the sixty-five-year-old paperwork was that, although Stalin and Sikorski had signed an agreement to pardon Polish prisoners and release them from prison or labor camps, there had been no "blanket" amnesty. Members of the Kresy-Siberia group, who had been through this process themselves, stated that one did not simply show up at the Polish Delegation in Krasnoyarsk, state one's name and—*abracadabra*—receive an amnesty and travel permit. The amnesty document and the travel permit to leave the Soviet Union were made on the spot for each individual Polish citizen who appeared at the Delegation. Apparently most, if not all of them, had some kind of documentation they were given upon release from their respective prisons or camps, which verified their identity as amnestied prisoners. So, with proof in hand, one appeared before the Polish authorities, stated one's name and history, passed over one's prison documents, and on that basis an individual amnesty and a separate travel pass were issued to that particular person. (The reader needs to keep in mind that the Polish Delegation was manned by Poles helping their fellow citizens leave the Soviet Union in order to join the Free Polish military and fight for the liberation of their homeland from the Nazis.)

Digesting that tidbit, it became clear that Rawicz could not have argued his way out of all this paperwork. In other words, he was very clearly on the spot in Krasnoyarsk in March 1942 to request and receive his amnesty and his travel pass, which were not prefabricated or mass-produced; therefore, he could not have been in India after a year's trudging across desert and mountains. There was no other way to look at the documentation and make sense of it. Had he still been alive when I finally received these documents, what would his comments have been? How would he have rebutted the documentation that stated he was in one place at a particular time when he had definitely stated to the world—in the pages of *The Long Walk*—that he was somewhere else at that same time? How would he react to all these documents had he still been alive—that was the question; and perhaps there was an answer.

❧❧

An argument was put forward by people who were interested in the story and in my research. They were trying to help me figure out why all roads leading to verification of Rawicz's story seemed to lead away from it. The only possibility we could deduce, after having gone round and round with the dates and the knowledge that amnesty/travel pass documents were not mass-made, was mistaken identity. Could a relative of Rawicz's have been sent to Siberia at more or less the same time as he was, with a similar or near identical name and birth date/place? Knowing a little about genealogy and the propensity of some families, in Europe and elsewhere, to name their children after themselves or other family members, it became a real possibility in my mind. Was it possible that Rosieslaw Slawomir was a family name? Was his father's name Feodor as described by the patronym in the documents? How many Rosieslaw Slawomirs with the father Feodor were born in Pinsk in 1915? Was the family of Rusiecki-Rawicz large or spread out? Clawing through genealogy records meant keeping a sharp eye out for distinctions in date, place, and parents' names—and where was I to begin? At the beginning, of course.

Once again, letters of inquiry and e-mail requests went out to the same institutes I had previously contacted. This time, I wanted to find out just how prevalent a surname Rusiecki-Rawicz was. People at genealogy sites, surname sites, family research sites, Polish sites, and the like, replied politely that they had either never heard of these names or they were rare, especially for the time period and place (the era between World War I and World War II, and Pinsk, Poland).

At the same time, I also inquired about information concerning Camp 105. Did anyone out in cyberspace have any knowledge of such a camp? The response was negative and, because of the secretiveness of the current Russian government, never mind the old Soviet regime, records were scarce, hard to come by, or nonexistent.

Nevertheless, and with the above negative responses in mind, I set out to write again to "Memorial," knowing in advance that I would wait many months for a reply—and that's just what happened. During this time, however, I did receive a reply from the POW/MIA group concerning gulag sites; but the reply was in the negative. The group stated they had never heard of a Camp 105, and they could not place it using the facts they had. So, I was stranded once again with information I couldn't authenticate.

It was during the summer and autumn of 2005 that research into *The Long Walk* really became bogged down. I felt I was treading water, feebly chasing after leads and information about various aspects of the story but without getting anywhere. As always, there were lots of suggestions, tentative byways, and possibilities, but nothing much seemed to be happening. The next thing I knew, it was 2006. It was obviously time for a change; and, before long, change stood up on its hind legs and roared. It certainly caught my attention.

⚜⚜

This change came from the BBC. I had tried to get in touch with a granddaughter of Rawicz's who had contacted me back in 2004 asking for information. This time, I was the one with questions for her about her family history, hoping she might know something about her great grandparents, such as whether Rawicz's father was named Feodor. Her e-mail bounced back, however. I was then able to locate an e-mail for another member of Rawicz's family only to be told I needed to put my queries to the executor of his estate. While trying to second-guess the dynamics of the Rawicz family after Slav's death, I soon learned what was happening on the other side of the Atlantic.

A BBC producer, Hugh Levinson, who works on documentaries for Radio 4, came across some of my cyberspace queries relating to *The Long Walk*. He had recently read the book and was captivated by the story. His e-mail was very straightforward, asking me about my research and what results I had obtained. For my part, I was a little distant, not wanting to be drawn into something about which I knew nothing, and not wanting to part with any of my hard-won information without getting anything in exchange.

Before I became too involved with the BBC, letters arrived (at long last) from "Memorial." It had taken several months of turnaround time for my query to arrive and for a reply to be forwarded my way, but someone at "Memorial" took a minute to really look at their records and get back to me with details.

This time "Memorial" outdid itself. Not only did I receive letters from Moscow, which were registered and had to be signed for at the post office, but additional letters came from another "Memorial," the Krasnoyarsk branch. (This was my first appreciation of just how far-reaching "Memorial" had become in its service to the worldwide community. Volunteers were apparently working diligently not only in Krasnoyarsk but in branches elsewhere in Russia as well as in many locations in Eastern Europe. I can only offer my sincerest thanks to those faceless volunteers, but it is a "thanks" with deepest gratitude from someone who knows how much work and dedication are involved in shedding light on lost or forbidden knowledge.)

The first letter came from the Polish section of "Memorial" in Moscow. It referred to my request regarding information about Rosieslaw Rusiecki.

Apparently, there were documents from the Bureau of Internal Affairs in Khrasnoyarsk region concerning Rawicz. One of the documents was a directive stating that, according to the NKVD of the Baranowiczeska region (in Belarus) in June 1941, Rawicz had been exiled and sent to a special forced labor camp because he was considered a "socially dangerous element." His property was confiscated and he was shipped from the Baranowiczeska region farther east to the Tasijewskim region in Krasnoyarsk province. (I later discovered that Tasijew and Taseevo were one and the same place in Siberia—but it was still not a camp 800 kilometers north east of Irkutsk.)

The letter went on to state that, because of the amnesty in August/September 1941, Rawicz was freed at that time—although according to his aforementioned questionnaire he only became aware of the amnesty several months later. The writer of the letter apologized for the long delay in replying. She also added that "as citizens of the country that committed crimes against Poles, we offer our apologies for all the suffering." (The reader should be aware that documents and correspondence about Polish prisoners were written or typed in both Polish and Russian. When I requested copies of documents, the accompanying letters were typed in both languages. The apology only appeared in the letter written in Russian, not in the Polish letter.)

While mulling over the comment and wondering about its inclusion in this particular letter, I did not want to lose sight of the content of the letter itself. The gist of it gave more details about Rawicz's time in Siberia. I thought back to the March 1941 to March 1942 dates in the sixty-five-year-old questionnaire and wondered about this new information. According to NKVD records from June 1941 Rawicz was in the Taseevo region of Krasnoyarsk province. No mention was made of a camp northeast of Irkutsk. Why then was it mentioned in the questionnaire? Had Rawicz moved around between the March to March dates and not thought it significant enough to detail on his questionnaire? Was there another reason? One word, however, did stand out among all the others: freed. I had different people translate the letters, wondering if the Russian and the Polish versions were compatible. I also wondered if there was another, perhaps equivocal, word used other than "freed." I was wondering if there was any mention of "escape." There wasn't. In matter-of-fact style, Rawicz was sentenced to years in a labor camp, was sent to Siberia, and was amnestied in 1941. (One has to keep in mind that, according to his questionnaire and to the experiences of thousands of Polish prisoners, he was kept in Siberia for several months after the amnesty date, only exiting the Soviet Union in March 1942.)

Within a month of receiving the letters, another letter arrived in a fat envelope. This had come all the way from Krasnoyarsk, from the Ministry of Culture. The letters within the envelope came from the Ministry and were accompanied by others from the Federal Archival Agency in Moscow.

These letters began by stating that in documents held at the Krasnoyarsk Regional State Archive there was information about Rusiecki-Rawicz, patronym Feodor, born in 1915 in Pinsk. Rawicz was identified as an inhabitant of Pinsk who had been sent to a special camp, a forced (labor) settlement, and was released in 1941. The letter stated the information came from the State Archives and that Rawicz was released in 1941 by decision of the U.S.S.R. Further, there was no information about the camp he was in (another dead end for Camp 105).

By the time these letters were translated and retranslated, looking for discrepancies, I felt it was time to face facts: Rawicz might have been in a camp in Siberia, but he had never *escaped* from one. He was freed, amnestied, but did not escape. Now what to do? I didn't have long to think about my next step; it was taken for me, thanks to the BBC.

Part VI

REVELATIONS AND CONFIRMATIONS

Chapter 19

THE BBC

K nowing nothing about the inner workings of the legendary organization known as the BBC, and being cautious in my initial contact
with Levinson, I eventually concluded that his interest was genuine: He
wanted to make a documentary about Rawicz and *The Long Walk* in as
factual a manner as possible. When he first contacted me, it was the result
of having interviewed three of Rawicz's five children for the documentary.
They stated (I assume from something Rawicz and his wife said) that I
had done a considerable amount of research into the story, and Levinson
should contact me. Somehow or other the Rawicz family was under the
misconception that I was part of the Hollywood scene and worked with
the scriptwriter who had flown over to England to interview Rawicz in
2002. I had to inform Levinson that there was a misunderstanding, as I
had never been to Hollywood, never met the scriptwriter, and was only
a fan of the book who was researching the true story and doing a lot of
archival digging as well.

I was a listener to the World Service for many years and to be contacted
by BBC Radio 4 was a bit amazing. At the same time as Levinson contacted
me, word leaked out to the general public about the forthcoming documentary. The next thing I knew e-mail messages were stacking up in my
in-box, asking if I had heard that a radio documentary about Rawicz was

planned for later in 2006. One of the e-mails was from a member of the Kresy-Siberia group. Among all the people slated to be interviewed for the program was a man who had survived the Siberian camps and lived to write his own book: Aleksander Topolski, author of *Without Vodka*.

Topolski had been a member of the audience when Rawicz was invited to speak about his life and experiences in 1956. Having been familiar with conditions inside prisons and camps in the Soviet Union during the 1940s, Topolski felt Rawicz's descriptions of that aspect of his life were accurate. In agreement with several members of the audience, including the afore-mentioned Colonel Dembinski, he felt something didn't ring true about Rawicz's account. He also suggested that Rawicz's responses to questions from the audience were evasive and less than satisfactory. Topolski put this down to a certain amount of embellishment on the part of the ghost-writer of the book, Ronald Downing, rather than on Rawicz. (For some reason, Topolski was under the impression that Downing was Rawicz's landlord as well as his ghostwriter, not realizing that Downing lived in London while Rawicz and his family lived in Nottingham.) Even at that early stage, Downing came in for more than his fair share of criticism. Little could he have guessed that his name would be under attack as questions arose about the veracity of the story. Rawicz, when being interviewed or questioned about the facts in the book, kept up his self-effacing image by shrugging his shoulders, sticking to his story, and stating his wish that his long-ago companions had stayed in touch with him.

Some of the members of the TLW forum chimed in with thoughts of their own about Topolski, Rawicz, and the BBC. One of the members spoke to Topolski some years before and listened to the latter describe his reaction to Rawicz's comments in 1956. The gist of that reaction was a feeling that Rawicz had been defensive and his story was full of questionable accounts; and that Rawicz disassociated himself from the Polish community at that time. Ultimately, members of the Kresy-Siberia forum, the TLW forum, and others were looking forward to the airing of the documentary. They hoped new information might come to light, authenticating Rawicz's story.

At this juncture, the documentary was scheduled to be broadcast on BBC Radio 4 on September 18, 2006. As previously stated, the BBC was active in contacting anyone with an interest in or knowledge of *The Long Walk*, Slavomir Rawicz, Ronald Downing, and the like. Once I was contacted, I got in touch with the scriptwriter from Hollywood. Having learned that the members of the TLW forum had moved on to other interests and become involved in other things, I also learned that the scriptwriter had moved on to other projects. He had written a film script, it had been accepted by the studio, and, predictably, it had been shelved for later reference. This was the outcome forecast by Rawicz, who had experienced many disappointments with regard to filming *The Long Walk*. Speaking of disappointments, I began to wonder how disappointed people around the world would be if the story was found to be true but that Rawicz had played no part in it.

Along with the sentiment for authentication came a wish to learn more about the events in the story and to speculate on what might have happened to Rawicz's companions. To that end, and after having been in contact with Levinson for some time, I put him in touch with the children and associates of Rupert Mayne, the family of Ronald Downing, and any other people I thought might add substance to the documentary. Personally, I was hoping this overall collaboration would bring forth a mountain of further data, including the identities of the other escapees—especially Mr. Smith—and what happened to them after the War.

Although I had been in touch with the Mayne and Downing families on an ongoing basis, I had not had any contact with the scriptwriter since 2002. When we did make contact, it took him a little time to jog his memory and think back to his visit with Rawicz. I filled him in on my research to date. The documents that came from archives around the world pointing to Rawicz as an amnestied prisoner, not an escapee, took his breath away. He felt that Rawicz was the genuine article during the few days he had spent in the latter's company.

I brought him up to speed on what had recently transpired, the BBC's interest in making a radio documentary, and passed on comments I received from Levinson's interview with the Rawicz children. I mentioned that my contacting him after so many years was by way of breaking the ice to discover whether he would be amenable to speaking to Levinson.

His reply was gracious, even though he felt that he could contribute little, having been busy with other projects over the past four years.

I also asked whether, during his interviews with Rawicz, the latter ever mentioned his full name and when/why it had been changed. The scriptwriter said he didn't recall any reference to the name change. He did state that Rawicz had detailed the dreadful physical condition he was in while in Palestine and, later, in England. Rawicz referred to having been under a doctor's care for years with regard to seeking treatment for blackouts and depression; he also spoke of wandering away from his home and family, sometimes for days, and not remembering where he had been. (These comments coincided with those in letters to me from his wife.) The scriptwriter also stated that he felt Rawicz had been honest with him, that he came across as a charming, emotional man. He also stated he was satisfied with the script he wrote for a future film and could only hope that, one day, the film would be produced.

Rather than harp on his impressions of Rawicz, I asked for his impressions of the Rawicz family. He had no comment on Rawicz's children as, during his stay, he had not met them; of Marjorie, he found her very kind and supportive of her husband. He was surprised, therefore, when I relayed the impressions made on Levinson and a Polish translator by the Rawicz family during their interview session.

When Levinson first contacted me, he stated that three of the Rawicz children were recently interviewed. It was during the interview that they mentioned Levinson should contact me because of the amount of research I had done. When Levinson repeated their sentiment, I found the remark strange: it struck me as odd coming from people who had never corresponded with me (except on one halfhearted occasion) and who knew nothing about me. I could only assume their parents told them about my research and our subsequent correspondence.

In summarizing the Rawicz family visit, Levinson focused on the apparent lack of curiosity felt by the children toward their father and his life's history. Did they feel they had lived under his shadow? The impression Levinson got was of middle-aged siblings who looked back at their father and mother with puzzlement. They told stories of their parents but the stories came across as rather bizarre, especially when they referred to their father's periods of depression. As Rawicz had declared to the scriptwriter and in letters to me, he had spells when he roamed, away from home, and came back days later with no memory of where he had been Unbeknownst to the general public, however, were those times when the black moods would descend upon him and, reportedly, he would pick up his shotgun, stalk out of the house into the nearby woods, and shout to everyone within hearing distance that he was going to "end it all."

The Rawicz family then produced bags of letters, postcards, and correspondence of all sorts for Levinson to peruse, stating that no one in the family could read or speak Polish or Russian. Levinson anticipated this fact and had a translator on hand. While foraging through the bags and boxes, the translator came across letters and postcards signed by Rawicz's mother, postmarked 1948. When questioned, none of the children had any idea what the cards said or who they were from, although the universal word for "Mama" should have provided a helpful hint. Once again, the family appeared apathetic to their father's past and his fame. When questioned about their mother's attitude toward the family history, the collective reply almost knocked the interviewers off their feet: Marjorie was sick of *The Long Walk*.

At the end of the interview, Levinson asked if any of the siblings had ever attempted to investigate their own history; had they done the kind of research that I and others had or were doing? Replies were vague, however, and the seeming lack of curiosity shone through. Later, after mulling over what I had been told, I wondered if their attitude reflected a lack of curiosity or of fear—fear of what they might discover once they began investigating on their own. Perhaps the truth of the family's lethargy in looking into its past was somewhere in between apathy and fear. I considered this possibility. After all, the book had helped feed, clothe, and house the family of seven for decades. How devastating would it be to learn that it was all a lie?

Despite the financial security that came with the book's publication, Marjorie was allegedly fed up with *The Long Walk*. I wondered why, and when, the apathy set in for her. Had she felt she was living in her husband's shadow? Both Marjorie and Slav were in poor health by the end of their lives. According to Rawicz's literary agents, for several decades before their deaths Marjorie had been the one to shoulder much of the business side of Rawicz's affairs of responding to queries, answering well-wishers' notes, dealing with publishers and agents, and arranging for talks and interviews. It was she who appeared to be the mainstay of the Rawicz family and on whom Rawicz leaned.

The culmination of declining health and dealing with the less glamorous business side of The Long Walk since the mid-1950s might have made Marjorie feel as if she were going mad. What, however, was the basis for her exasperation? Rawicz's story made headlines around the world; a veritable cottage industry grew up around the book and gradually moved from the realm of pen and ink to the Internet; book/film rights were sold, and the proceeds were used to set the family up. If one thing was certain, Marjorie's exasperation was hidden from visitors and fans. Did Rawicz feel the same exasperation as did his wife? It seemed as if he did not. Although the Rawicz children remarked on their mother's boredom with the topic, Rawicz seemed to have basked in the memory of his life story.

As a possible memorial to their father, Rawicz's children became active on the allreaders.com Web site and had their own Rawicz family Web site for a short period of time after Slav and Marjorie died in 2004. It seemed they had overcome or shaken off any indifference or apathy their mother might have felt. Yet, while fielding questions and inquiries, asking for information about the story, and generally keeping interest alive in The Long Walk, they did little or nothing in terms of researching their family's history. They ostensibly divided up the correspondence they inherited without ever asking someone to translate the earlier papers so they could learn their contents.

While the BBC representatives tried to gauge and understand the mood swings of the family, they were also tuned in to the family's skepticism about the story. The family expressed doubts about the yeti sightings and suggested Downing (because of his connection with the Yeti Expedition) was very keen to incorporate that part of the tale into the book, while Rawicz had felt less inclined to do so. There were doubts based on the impossibility of walking across the Gobi Desert without water, even though Rawicz told his family, and a wider audience, privately, that he and the others had survived on earthworms and occasional rain storms—why had those references been left out of the book? I found it intriguing that the family still had doubts about their father's story, never mind the book, after all this time.

Although the children of Rawicz and Marjorie were given the surname of Rusiecki-Rawicz at birth, they were told later in life by their father that the Rusiecki part of the name swas "borrowed." When pressed, apparently Rawicz declined to go into detail. (Naturally such a declaration would prompt anyone to ask when it was that Rawicz "borrowed" the name because it appears on his military records with the Anders army as early as 1943—as well as on his amnesty and travel documents in 1941 and 1942.)

Family histories, yeti sightings, borrowed names—all these intriguing elements in Rawicz's personal history needed clarification. With that in mind I planned my forthcoming trip to England in the summer of 2006.

Chapter 20

INTELLIGENCE OFFICERS AND MISSIONARIES

With e-mail messages traveling between me, the BBC, the Maynes, the Downings, and everyone else with an interest in *The Long Walk*, word came during the summer of 2006 that the documentary had been moved to another time slot. Instead of being aired in September, it would now be aired on October 30. This meant a little more time for digging.

During that summer, I planned a trip to England, with visions of spending long days at the British Library, the PRO, Kew Gardens Archives, the BBC, the Museum of Military Intelligence, and points in between. The plan was to search for anyone who might have been in the Himalayan area of India/Tibet in early 1942 and anyone who might have been with military intelligence at that time and place. While laying my plans, I received a message from the Mayne family. Mayne's son was recently in London and was interviewed by the BBC for the documentary. He felt he had not been able to contribute much, as he recalled little of what his father told him in 1956. All he knew was that his father claimed the men who reached India had been in appalling condition but seemed harmless, in the context of British intelligence gathering at that time.

His comments led me to wonder about contacting Charles Allen, the author of *Plain Tales of the Raj*, who had extensively interviewed Mayne while he was writing the book. Levinson notified me that he had already listened to the original tapes of the interviews with Mayne and there was nothing on them concerning *The Long Walk*. My curiosity was piqued by what the tapes did *not* contain. When taping another person, or being taped, there is a great amount of extraneous chitchat before, during, and after the interview that is usually edited out. The only person who might remember any off-the-cuff remarks would be Charles Allen, but Levinson (and I) had no luck in contacting him firsthand.

Still on Mayne's track, I once more contacted Shirleyanne Cumberledge, the book reviewer who spoke to Mayne in 1956. Her memories coincided with those of Mayne's son. I also contacted the Downing family and we went over the comments, thoughts, and observations of what they knew and remembered about their uncle. They were hoping, as was I, that the broadcast would shed more light on the story and perhaps give a greater recognition to Downing's role in co-authoring the book. In fact, I hoped that a great deal of light would be shed upon a variety of topics relating to *The Long Walk*.

One of those topics I hoped to see illuminated was the actual role of Rupert Mayne in British intelligence. People from around the world were in touch with me stating that Mayne was quite a character—a real raconteur—but they knew very little about his wartime activities. I hoped that something in the Museum of Military Intelligence at Chicksands might shed light on his activities.

I had the same hopes for gathering more information on the interest expressed by the U.S. Embassy in London at the time of the book's publication. To that end, during the summer months of 2006, I went on a short trip to NARA in Washington, D.C. I anticipated finding information about Neil Ruge, the U.S. vice-consul in London, who, according to Downing and Rawicz, took an interest in the story and obviously made other people at the embassy interested as well, hence the visit to Rawicz by two embassy staff members who questioned him about Mr. Smith. My efforts proved fruitless, though, as I found nothing on Ruge or any U.S. interest in Mr. Smith.

By contrast, the trip to England proved quite fruitful, although instead of unraveling any mysteries, I added more. The archival work proceeded rapidly. Trips were made to Cambridge, to the Churchill Archives, to Chicksands, to London, to Kew, and to the BBC. I also squeezed in a visit with old and new friends, namely, with Glinski and his family.

My first stop in Great Britain was at Cambridge, from where I launched a research effort at the Museum of Military Intelligence. I contacted Major Edwards at the Museum beforehand so I was able to breeze through the preliminaries and get right down to work—only to discover that no one could place their hand on Mayne's files. With a bit of crawling around and digging in stacks of folders, the long-lost files Mayne had donated years before were in my hands—and so were a host of other, very relevant files.

Mayne had donated a total of four file folders back in the early 1980s. Almost every scrap of paper in them was marked Classified or Top Secret. Although the rule was that files such as these should have been turned over to the proper authorities at the end of the War, and Mayne was a stickler for proper procedure and hid behind the Official Secrets Act for decades, on this occasion he went against all the rules and kept those files in his possession for nearly forty years. Be that as it may, he contacted someone at the Special Forces Club to ask if anyone would be interested in his wartime work. One thing led to another and he donated the files, approximately four to five inches thick, to the museum.

In a separate stack, which I placed next to Mayne's, were letters and notes from people who had known him through the Special Forces Club. The intriguing point was, at last, to actually see, in writing, that Mayne was the person he had always said he was, namely an officer in British Intelligence. Letter after letter in his files, either addressed to him or written by him on official letterhead (showing an address at 235/2 Lower Circular Road, Calcutta), referred to interrogations, interviews, meetings, conferences, and so forth, all pertaining to intelligence work in the CBI theater during the War. All of the work had to do with either Japanese military men who were picked up as prisoners (suspected of stirring up trouble with the native Indian population) or with Indian nationals themselves who were using the cooperation extended by the Japanese to further their cause for Indian independence.

In the stack adjacent to Mayne's files were comments between various people about Mayne, both when he was alive and after his death. The majority of the comments had to do with Mayne's authenticity as an intelligence officer. Several people questioned whether he had ever been in intelligence and essentially wondered how he came to be in the Special Forces Club. The correspondence made for interesting reading and a quiet chuckle. Reports surfaced, however, that were serious and incorporated lists of intelligence officers, where they studied, which units they were with, and so on. This was an invaluable bit of paper because of the names on it, including that of Mayne himself: "Roaring" Rupert Mayne! (The names of Boyes-Cooper and Whitehorn, mentioned earlier, were also on the list.)

At the end of a long day of reading, I could honestly say I had laid one little mystery to rest: Mayne had indeed been a British intelligence officer in World War II. The disappointment I encountered, however, was that the papers in the files he had donated only began in mid-1942. Any interviews or interrogations of the men of *The Long Walk* would have taken place earlier, but there were no reports from an earlier time.

Undaunted, the search for information moved to London. I tackled the Kew Gardens Archives immediately. With the list of names unearthed at Chicksands still on my mind, I turned my thoughts to other avenues of research, namely, finding out who might have been in Assam during early 1942. Word of four white men wandering over the Himalayas in late winter or early spring most certainly would have spread among the colonial population at that time. In fact, with censorship in the press, the only way people might have heard about this incident would be through word of mouth. Having already been in touch with the nephew of Francis Kingdon Ward, a renowned pre–World War II explorer and botanist, I planned to take a look at his journals, hoping to find some comment about the sudden appearance of the survivors from Siberia.

In the event, his microfilmed journals made very interesting reading, but there was not a peep about any escapees walking into Assam. There were kernels of interest in the many names he mentioned, though. Two of those names sparked an inquiry when I next visited the British

Library. The inquiry led to a "hit," and eventually I was looking at a real report made by two British officers undertaking survey work in the border area between Assam and Tibet from December 1941 to mid-February 1942, the details of which will be elaborated upon in the following chapters.

I began to feel as though I were wasting my time by reading Ward's journals. There was nothing in the journals for my purposes, I believed, until something prompted me to back up and reread one of the pages, noting the many and varied comments, all steeped with gratitude, concerning the French and Swiss fathers of the Missions Étrangères. From what I read, the Catholic fathers of the Missions Étrangères had established a series of missions and outlying churches up and down the Chinese/Tibetan border, having been prohibited from entering or proselytizing in Tibet. The report expressed thanks for the generous hospitality of the fathers in allowing travelers to stop and refresh themselves at the missions.

Mention of the Catholic fathers of the Missions Étrangères set me thinking about the possibility that someone within that organization could have been the German-speaking missionary described in *The Long Walk*. I concentrated my efforts on scanning the Internet, looking at Web sites regarding the Missions Étrangères, reviewing their contents, following leads, poring through reference materials, grappling with names of mission stations such as Bahang and Tat-sien-lu, and trying to understand the connection between the Mission based in Paris and the Order of St. Bernard in Martigny, Switzerland, which had sent Catholic priests out to China in the 1930s and had effectively taken over missionary activities from the Missions Étrangères at that time.

Fortunately, I made contact with Father Jean Charbonnier at the Missions Étrangères, who filled me in on the history of the organization and suggested I contact Father Savioz, a Swiss missionary, who had been in China fifty years ago and who would have known Father Georges André, the principal priest at the Bahang mission on the Tibet/Yunnan border. By an unbelievable coincidence, I had met Father Savioz many years ago while living in Taiwan. (After the War, he was sent to Taiwan and remained there until very recently when he returned to Switzerland due to a decline in his mental and physical health. In fact, I was told he had very little memory of past events.)

Realizing that contacting the elderly Father Savioz would be pointless due to his diminished memory, I tried to find out about Father André. I knew he had died many years ago as I had recently come across a book about him, detailing his life story. I tracked down the author of the book, hoping he might have additional information, only to learn that *he* had recently died. It was disheartening to feel I was so close to real, solid information only to have it disappear when it was almost within reach.

What I did learn, however, was that several Catholic priests were stationed in the Tibetan Marshes—the border area between Tibet and the Yunnan province in China, running right down into Northern Burma, in the years between the world wars. Of the many orders of priests and nuns, I learned that the French and Swiss were most active in the mountainous areas of Yunnan province. Through arduous searching at the British Library and the PRO, I also discovered that foreigners, especially missionaries, were forbidden to enter Tibet during this period unless granted special permission. There had been riots, murders, arson, and general mayhem against foreigners, and against Tibetans who showed any interest in Christianity. Therefore, the Chinese government, in collaboration with the British, the Indians, the Tibetans, and anyone else with an interest in political stability, put Tibet off-limits to all foreigners, except to those with the chutzpah to sneak in or those who had no choice.

After wading through many documents pertaining to foreigners and their activities in and around Tibet during the War, I realized the group of prisoners who walked across China could not have stumbled into a village in Tibet proper where they met the German-speaking missionary mentioned in the book. The consequences, if caught, would have been painful. Even though borders are sometimes hard to define, it became apparent that missionaries were not freely roaming across Tibet at this time. The only place the escapees could have come into contact with a Catholic priest would have been in a border area.

My original thinking about where the men of *The Long Walk* had stumbled into India pinpointed the Sikkim/Bhutan area. Articles and interviews in 1956 referred to Downing and Rawicz both speculating about the possibility of entry through either of the little Himalayan kingdoms. In letters and subsequent interviews, Rawicz always stated he had no idea where he was when he and the others were picked up by the Gurkha patrol. In my long conversations with Glinski, he also could not pinpoint where, exactly, he entered into India.

Knowing the restrictions placed on missionary activity in Tibet before and during the War reinforced my thoughts that the escapees entered India through some other route. As referred to earlier, my thoughts already dwelt on the far eastern section of Tibet/Assam as the probable entry point, only because of the placement of the Brahmaputra River. This river would have been a major undertaking and, therefore, memorable. Coming into India via Sikkim/Bhutan would have meant crossing this mighty river.

In commentaries and articles concerning *The Long Walk*, questions are repeatedly raised as to why there was no description of crossing the Brahmaputra—a major geological divide running west to east across practically the entire length of Tibet—and it was a question that was difficult to answer, unless India was reached way to the east along the Chinese border, that same border coincidentally being a hive of missionary activity.

Also puzzling was the list of names that gradually came my way of all the many Catholic priests who had been assigned to mission stations in the Tibetan borderlands in the 1930s. I received, by mail, a photocopy of a list of priests who served in Yunnan province and not infrequently ministered to Tibetans during that time, and eventually I discovered more details about those priests. In reports and correspondence it appeared the fathers traveled up and down the border areas on a regular basis. I kept reading through the lists and pondering on which of the names might correspond with that of the German-speaking missionary. There were a few possibilities: Father Nussbaum, Father Burdin, and Father Gore. However, I was looking for an elderly, German-speaking priest who had already been in the region for many years: a priest who was tall, thin, and clean shaven, and who traveled with a mule. The more I read, though, the more possibilities appeared. Although Rawicz thought the missionary might have been German or Austrian and described him as a non-conformist,

Glinski remembered the man as being a Catholic priest who stated he was Austrian. Rawicz's account in the book and Glinski's firsthand memory both coincided in describing the missionary as wary and unfriendly.

As I thought about the priest and who he was, I suddenly realized he absolutely could not have been either German or Austrian for the simple reason that, in India and China, nationals of both countries were interned in camps for the duration of the War. But what about a Swiss national— someone who came from the Austrian-Swiss border area, spoke German, and who would have been considered Swiss by virtue of having spent most of his adult life as a missionary from a Swiss order? That was a much more realistic approach than, say, trying to guess whether any of the Moravian missionaries, who were busy proselytizing in the northwest of India, might have wandered halfway across the subcontinent to be in the same village at the same time as the escapees, or that the priest was possibly affiliated with any of the China Inland Mission stations that were populated by Scandi-navians as well as English-speaking missionaries. No matter who he was, he would have needed to be based somewhere, funded by someone, and would have reported to some religious order. Again, both the Chinese and the British Indian governments kept tabs on missionaries and, during the war years, made sure they knew where everyone was.

Alas, this vein of speculation petered out. Information from Switzerland showed that most of the missionaries stationed in Yunnan were evacuated during the War. Those who remained were younger or middle-aged men in 1942. I was looking for someone already on the other side of fifty; and, by the German-speaking missionary's own account, someone who had been in China for decades. Those few who fit the age bracket didn't fit the description. I also learned that no annual reports from the mission-aries in China were received in Europe, due to the general wartime chaos, after 1941. Thus, no records were submitted for 1942. This puzzle is still waiting to be solved.

Chapter 21

GLINSKI'S WALK

While my time in the U.K. continued in research frenzy, I managed to squeeze in a visit with Glinski. This visit was eagerly awaited on my part, and my list of questions was very long. Before we met, I acquainted myself with the Polish Institute and Sikorski Museum in London. The building was a treasure trove of documents, many still waiting to be cataloged, with hardly a computer in sight. Index cards and the staff's impeccable memory led me to the appropriate drawer, shelf, or box. In my case, the staff was very helpful and rounded up as much material as they could find, perplexed as to what I was going to do with it, not being a Polish speaker.

It was true that most of the material in the Institute was in Polish, but, because I was focusing on Poles in India during the War, there was a lot of information to glean in English. In fact, there was a large folder of uncataloged material pertaining to the Banasinski family. Mr. Eugeniusz Banasinski was the head of the Polish consulate in India before the War. When hostilities broke out in Europe, and Poland was overrun by Germany, Mr. Banasinkski continued to act on behalf of the Free Poles, representing not only Poland but also the Polish Red Cross. He and his wife, Kira, were very active in the latter organization. Mrs. Banasinski became quite a leading light in organizing subsequent arrangements for Polish orphans, and then Polish families, fleeing the U.S.S.R. in 1941–42 to come to India via Persia, where they were housed near Bombay at Balachadi, Kolhapur, and Valivade.

Going through file after file in the Banasinski collection took some time but made for very interesting research. Old newspaper stories, letters, contracts, brochures, lists, and forms all spilled out of these files. The materials were in Polish as well as in English. Then there were the photographs: convoys of lorries leaving India with Red Cross supplies piled high, making the vehicles top heavy and clumsy, with a caption in one instance stating that a convoy left Bombay in December 1941. The supplies were heading *west* from India to the Soviet Union via Persia. The route went via Mashad in eastern Persia before turning north-northwest toward the border with the Soviet Union.

This was the first instance of real, solid information stating that, indeed, convoys did go from India to Persia, rather than the other way around. Later, of course, as the numbers of Polish refugees swelled and plans were made to bring them to India, there was no great need to send supplies to Persia, so almost all of the traffic was from that country to India. That was the mantra I had been hearing ever since I began researching *The Long Walk*. Now, I had come across evidence that there had been traffic the other way. This was very important, because it meshed with Glinski's story of having been in a convoy of lorries as early as the spring of 1942 going *out* of India to Persia.

There were innumerable other bits of information in the Banasinski files, but nothing that connected with the story of the escapees coming to India and then leaving at some point in time. Rather, there were lists of Polish refugees trapped in India, who were being helped by the Polish Red Cross—refugees who requested permission to travel on to a third country, and those who begged for work. Many of these refugees eventually left India.

❦❦

Before I left London to meet Glinski, I made a quick afternoon stop at the legendary Special Forces Club to meet Rupert Mayne's son. He was one of many people who was collaborating with the BBC on their forth-coming documentary, and the two of us got together to go over our notes and thoughts one more time. He pointed to framed photos of his father on the walls of the club and told stories of his father's frequent visits to the club while he was an active member. I outlined the information I had received regarding his father's career as a British intelligence officer during the War. My revelation that Mayne had donated thick files of Top Secret documents to the Museum of Military Intelligence was a surprise. I had already learned through his children that Mayne had always been a little bit of a "surprise" to his family. He did not frequently talk outright about his time in intelligence; instead, he threw out hints and suggestions. The most notable example of this was his interaction with Cumberledge, the book reviewer, when he avoided answering specific questions by hiding behind the Official Secrets Act while simultaneously admitting to having been in British intelligence and knowing about the escapees from Siberia. Mayne, I concluded, was not only a man of mystery in regards to *The Long Walk* but also an enigma to his own family.

The meeting with Mayne's son did not add any new information about what was already known regarding *The Long Walk*. Mayne's family had always stated that their father had seemed pleased to be mentioned obliquely in the book and that he commented on his "role" in the story whenever the book was reprinted and someone brought it up in conversation. Mayne's son repeated his father's comments to Shirleyanne Cumberledge, namely, that the men had been in appalling condition when he had interviewed them, that they had very possibly escaped from Siberia and walked to India, that it was difficult to actually verify their story while at the same time believing they had made their epic walk, and that they hadn't appeared to be a security risk. In the event, Mayne was the officer who interviewed them, declared them to be harmless, and never forgot their story.

At the beginning of my second week in England, in mid-September 2006, I traveled to Cornwall for a meeting with Glinski and his wife. They invited me to spend a few days with them while I was in England. It was an encounter I had long ancitipated, and one that was not disappointing.

During my visit, I asked questions and listened while Glinski repeated his life's story to me. He went over many of the same points we had previously discussed but with more elaboration. At times, the flow of memories became a flood. He had been through so much in his young life and now, more than sixty-five years later, the retelling of it caused him no outward pain or sorrow—he seemed complacent about those life events.

As I listened to him speak of the ordeals in his life, it struck me that, even as a teenager, Glinski had a will to live and a determined approach to life. His resolve and his youth became powerful motivators and propelled him southward from Siberia to India. My objective was to probe for details that might establish where he was at any given time during the walk and after, and what he might have seen that was in any way unusual and could serve as a geographical marker.

As near as possible, Glinski traced his steps from the time he left Poland for Russia and Siberia in 1939 till his feet carried him to India in 1942. He spoke of his family, mentioning that he followed them in 1940 when they were sent to a "special location" in Archangel Province and later, in 1941, when they moved to Shakhunya region between Gorki and Kotlas. (Trying to find these places later with their transliterated spellings proved to be a feat in itself. The many members of the Kresy-Siberia group were able to lend a hand and point to places on a map that corresponded to the above spellings.)

While Glinski was not arrested for anything specific (he was all of fifteen years old in 1940), he was not sentenced to a labor camp—but his father was. When the family moved to Shakhunya in 1941, his father urged Glinski to leave the area and head east to Irkutsk. The idea was to try to get out of Russia by traveling east; and, with his father's advice in mind, Glinski did just that. Unfortunately for him, and hundreds of other passengers on the train, he was rounded up upon arrival in Irkutsk, kept in a separate area from actual prisoners who had been sentenced to the labor camps, and was forced to march off with the condemned to increase prisoner numbers. Glinski shrugged six decades later and alluded to the lack of travel or identity papers at that time, so he and everyone else on the train were, technically, traveling illegally and were, therefore, "fair game."

(I stopped to reflect that if I were telling his story as my own, I would have thrown back my head and howled over the injustice of the situation; instead, Glinski simply shrugged, taking his life as it had happened.)

The walk from Irkutsk in a northerly direction took weeks. (Glinski's wife, Joyce, brought out an atlas to help me visualize his route.) Glinski remembered walking around the southern end of Lake Baikal before marching north along the eastern side of the lake. It was very cold, the snow was piled high, and the gang of prisoners (with an accompaniment of vehicles, horse-drawn and motor) followed a primitive track that ran under a telegraph line. Occasionally they came across native peoples using reindeer sleighs, and from time to time they caught glimpses of Lake Baikal in the distance—just a vast sheet of ice that stretched to the horizon. During the memorable march, all of the prisoners were tied with ropes to a long chain from the back of a lorry. This action was not meant to drag the prisoners along but to keep them from falling down and becoming lost in the snow. At one point, though, Glinski fell and was dragged some distance before the rope could be cut away. (He showed me the scar that wound completely around his ankle as well as similar damage to his wrist.)

Glinski described the tall watchtowers and barbed-wire fencing the group of prisoners saw as they approached the camp. The camp was not an old, established site but relatively new, and Glinski and the other prisoners had to walk through more than one perimeter fence complete with guards and dogs. The inhabitants of the labor camp spent their time cutting timber and making skis, as well as making tools and other metal works in the blacksmith's shop: the metal forged in the shop was used for clamps for skis and rims for sleds. Food was on the order of stacks of dried fish, *treska*, and very large tins of beans. The prisoners all saved the tins and used them to contain their soup. (Glinski stated that during his time in the camp, he never saw any supplies being delivered and, so, assumed that supplies had been brought in earlier in the year to last until spring.)

While working in the blacksmith's shop and the ski-making area, Glinski heard some of the other prisoners comment on the commandant's annoyance that his radio wouldn't work properly. Glinski had some little knowledge of how a radio worked, offered his services, and was taken to the commandant's quarters, where he met Number One and the latter's wife. "Number One" was the euphemism given by the prisoners to the top brass in the camp. Glinski never knew the man's name, nor that of his wife, save that her Christian name was Maria, the same as Glinski's mother. Rumor had it that the commandant had somehow disgraced himself because of alcoholism while he was in Poland, and he and his wife were in exile in Siberia—marking time so to speak—until he had rehabilitated himself.

For whatever reason, the commandant's wife was sympathetic to Glinski. Glinski commented that he had long pondered the reason for her kindness. Although she never discussed with him the actual act of escaping, she made encouraging observations about when a good time to try to escape might be. She was also aware of the logistics, such as the need to hoard food and clothing before the escape, as well as the need to keep an eye on the weather and wait for a particularly bad spell in order to thwart any attempts at tracking by the guards and their dogs.

Escape from the camp was one thing; which direction to take afterward was another. While there was a very large map in the quarters where the commandant and his wife lived, which Glinski saw whenever he was called to repair the radio, the map was oddly devoid of detail. Glinski remembered a vast expanse of blank space with a few major cities noted. He did hear, however, that Yakutsk was about 1,000 kilometers to the north, and he already knew that Lake Baikal lay to the south.

Despite all the blank spaces on the map and around the camp, Glinski was already dreaming of escape. He stated again that, although no one spoke outright of escape, it was on the minds of most of the prisoners. So, on a day when one of the Poles in his work group asked whether he wanted to live the rest of his life in the camp, Glinski's reply was just one word, "No." From casual comments, winks, nods, innuendo, long looks, and even silences, three of the prisoners knew they all wanted to escape. Little by little, the threesome became a group. There was no plan as such; in fact, there was no verbally stated goal. There was simply an "understanding," a silent communique with the common aim of getting out of the camp.

The casual and very loose plan to escape moved along at a rapid pace. One thing led to another. Food was tucked away for future use; metal wire cutters were made in the blacksmith's shop to cut the perimeter fence; rope was made so that weights could be attached and heaved over the taller portions of the fence, allowing the prisoners to pull themselves up and over the barbed wire; blankets or pieces of blanket were salvaged to drape over the vicious barbs. Although everyone remained casual and quiet about the forthcoming escape, quite a bit of planning went into the enterprise, and it proved a success. With help from atrocious weather conditions, the escapees cut the wire, scaled the fences, and ran off into the white Siberian night.

During the escape, Glinski was surprised at how many people showed up. He speculated that perhaps nine or more people attempted to get out of the camp. At least one man turned back very soon after they got through the fences, and another man was lost in the severe weather and never seen again. Once day had dawned, Glinski counted seven escapees, including himself. This little band kept on the move for some days before sighting the north end of Lake Baikal and beginning their travels south, along the eastern shore of that vast body of water.

During the scramble to cover as much distance as possible while the bad weather lasted, Glinski mentioned the group came across what appeared to be an abandoned camp where they found axes and other tools. Not long after passing the camp, the escapees came across a deer whose antlers were trapped by a tree branch. As odd as this sounded, Glinski said it was not an unusual occurrence that trees would split in the winter from the extreme cold and the sound was like an explosion or gunshot. Possibly the deer was rubbing its antlers against the tree and had inextricably become caught by a branch. At any rate, the encounter with the deer provided them with food at a crucial moment.

The group of escapees saw no one on the way south nor did they look for anyone. In the distance they would occasionally see smoke from factories. Glinski repeated reaching what they took to be the Trans-Siberian Railway, how Batko killed the guards, how they opened one of the boxcars to find tins of cocoa, and how they all became sick trying to eat the stuff.

He also detailed how they covered their tracks to avoid discovery when they fled the scene.

With no calendar, just the sun rising and setting each day, Glinski had no real idea of how long it took the group to escape the camp, reach Lake Baikal, race down its eastern shore, and cross the Trans-Siberian Railway. On reflection, he thought it took between four and six weeks to reach the rail line. Initially, they were racing for their lives to put as much distance as possible between themselves and the camp. Glinski said the trek was brutal, with the bad weather and high snowbanks slowing their progress. Once at the lake, and rounding its northern tip, they then slowed their pace to make better use of their energy. As Lake Baikal is a little over 600 kilometers from north to south, and the rail line on the eastern side of the lake is approximately 100 kilometers north of the southern tip of the lake, it is possible that the escapees covered at least 500 kilometers or more in six weeks, keeping in mind the uncertainty of their actual starting point Their rate of travel would have been about 12–14 kilometers/day and, considering the weather conditions as well as the terrain, it would have been possible for them to cover that distance within the allotted time.

⬳⬳

They continued walking once they left the rail line, with the addition of a fugitive Polish girl, named Kristina in the book and remembered by Glinski as having been called by a diminutive of Sophia. Evidently the girl, whom Glinski thought was in her late teens, had been watching the group, as one fugitive might watch another, for some days before gathering the courage to approach them. What tipped the scales was her hearing Glinski and the two other Poles speaking her native language. She claimed that she killed a *kolkhoz* manager for attempting to rape her and was able to escape by hitching lifts on trucks and then walking. Her parents were well-off peasants, *kulaks*, in Poland and were murdered; she was put on a transport vehicle and shipped off to work on a *kolkhoz* in Siberia. By the time she and the group encountered one another, she had been on her own for quite some time, walking south. Glinski remembered noticing how she limped when he first saw her. He thought it was possible her socks or shoes had rubbed against her feet, causing blisters, and they had become septic, which ultimately led to gangrene. (At this point, Glinski digressed to mention the general lack of hygiene among all of them and how exceptionally dirty some of the men in the group were, with no sense of keeping themselves clean.)

The Polish girl was not with them for long, perhaps just a week or two, before her limp became so pronounced that she could hardly walk. When she took off her shoe and the men saw her leg, they noticed it was black and blue, and extremely gangrenous. She insisted on continuing with them, begging them not to leave her, and they made a travois of poles and shirts, dragging her along as best they could until she died. As they were somewhere where the soil was sandy, possibly Mongolia, they were able to dig a shallow grave and bury her. Looking back, Glinski remembered she was with them for a short time, measured in weeks, not months.

Not many weeks after the girl's death came two more deaths. One of the Poles in the group and the Latvian, the man described by Glinski as playing the village idiot most of the time but who could recite long lines of poetry, died from the effects of malnutrition, possibly of scurvy or pellagra. (Glinski called their illness *tzinga* and stated both men began to bleed from their mouths and rear ends, and they both lost all their teeth.)

While one escapee after the other died off, the group itself was pushing across Mongolia with as much speed as possible. During this harrowing period, the escapees came across a caravan led by an old man who could speak Russian and had a good idea who they were—namely, escaped prisoners. He was kind to them and gave them food. It was he who mentioned the word Lhasa and pointed them in that direction. (It's possible they were well into Mongolia or even into the western provinces of China by the time they crossed paths with the caravan. Many Mongolians are Buddhists and would know the direction for Lhasa; they would also know that India lay beyond Lhasa.)

Despite the kindness of strangers and the directions given, Glinski remembered arguments erupting nearly every day concerning which direction to take. It seems that Mr. Smith, being the eldest, tried to keep out of the arguments; however, when he had something to say, he said it quietly and with authority, and the rest listened to him. Glinski described Batko as a braggart as well as a murderer, and stated that Zora identified himself as a businessman who ran a café or restaurant somewhere in the Balkans before his arrest, possibly in Slovakia or Serbia. Zora was a bit of a comedian, and he was very obese. Glinski always thought there was something unwholesome about him. He also thought Zora was crazy, as the latter would bite a stick or chew grass, and Glinski described him as eating like a dog, gulping his food rather than chewing it. Be these differences as they may, the members of the group tolerated one another for the sole purpose of escape; no fast friendships were ever made.

Glinski backtracked a little when he thought about Mr. Smith. There was nothing friendly about the man: he was very quiet and kept to himself. On the other hand, he was not unfriendly to Glinski. He was a puzzle for Glinski. Although Glinski didn't trust any of his comrades, he felt Mr. Smith was not an evil man. He also felt Mr. Smith was an educated man. (When the group finally stumbled down a hillside in India, into the arms of a British patrol, Mr. Smith did all the talking and appeared, to Glinski, as if he were fairly fluent in English.)

Once the group of escapees was reduced to five, Glinski remembered walking for weeks on end. They came across different small settlements and were treated with kindness by the nomads. On one occasion they came across an old man herding goats and sheep who invited them to partake of milk and cheese with him. He was kind and offered to share what little he had in exchange for their company. Glinski remembered being surprised that the old man didn't wear trousers but rather a kind of skirt made of a stiff canvas-like material. It was not long after parting company with the old man that the escapees came to a village and met a schoolteacher who could speak Russian. For whatever reason, the schoolteacher had been to Russia but had not been smitten with the country or with its people. Nonetheless, he welcomed the stragglers into his home and fed them: another stranger bestowing kindness on this group of unkempt, obvious fugitives. (Glinski remarked they had a knife with them and, from time to time, would sharpen it and cut each other's hair and beards. Despite the attempts at trying to look civilized, Glinski was pretty certain anyone encountering the group would have known instantly that they were escaped prisoners.)

During their brief stay in the village, the teacher arranged for a guide to take them along pathways that kept them from straying into China to the east or population centers in Tibet to the west. From what they could understand, there was serious unrest of some kind in both areas. This comment caused them to think back to the earlier warnings from the caravan leader about unrest all across China and its many provinces. While they talked to the teacher and looked over the village, the German-speaking missionary mentioned in Rawicz's book arrived, leading a mule. The man wore a long cassock tied at the waist, as priests used to do, and wore trousers underneath. Glinski surmised the priest was already past middle age and was possibly in his seventies. At some point in the conversation, which was carried out in a variety of languages, the priest mentioned he was Austrian and had been a missionary in the region for many years. The schoolteacher did not appear to like him much, as he stated the missionary was always asking for money from the villagers.

Before leaving the village after a day or two, they witnessed a celebration of some kind. Glinski remembered watching the villagers dance and noted that the women wore blouses with puffy sleeves and long, layered skirts with flounces that swirled out when they danced. They didn't wear any special hats or headgear but had something colorful tied around their heads. (Glinski made gestures with his hands while he recited his memories, and the gestures made me think of braided strips of silk or cotton that are woven into the plaits of Tibetan women in certain regions and are then wound around their heads with the tasselled ends hanging down onto their shoulders.) Glinski stated the women had colorful belts that hung down their sides with tassels on the ends, and the men wore long, tan-colored skirts over their trousers and flattish hats on their heads with rounded flaps—a description that anyone who has visited Tibet would recognize. He also noted that some men wore fur hats.

When asked what people in the village ate during this celebration, Glinski said he remembered some kind of meat stew and said he and the others were offered a type of rice wine, possibly *chang*. He had no memory of either *tsampa* or buttered tea—and these items of Tibetan cuisine are most certainly memorable.

Once on their way out of the village, the guide stayed with them for three or four days before turning back. He left them at the apex of a mountain ridge. Glinski remembered both the village and the ridge as being in high, open country without many trees: no jungle, just bushes and shrubs in open land on which grazed goats, sheep, yak, and donkeys. After another couple of weeks walking through this terrain, gradually going downhill, they spotted a dirt and gravel road in the distance. They then realized Gurkhas were on that road and were watching them come closer. Glinski remarked that the British officer with the patrol was somewhere in his thirties with no distinguishing marks on his face. The officer and Mr. Smith spoke together, the group was put on a lorry, stops were made, and eventually Glinski found himself somewhere in a camp near Calcutta. Once in that camp, he didn't remember ever seeing any of the others again. He did remember the Indian and British staff, doctors and nurses, and he remembered hearing people use the word "Calcutta" in the sense of it being nearby, within a short traveling distance. He also remembered hearing the word "transit" and associated that word with "camp."

Glinski later added his memory of being interviewed and questioned but had no idea who conducted the interviews, save that more than one British officer, with translators, came to question him. Glinski's time recuperating in the camp was a series of blurry memories. He did have memories of being given papers that allowed him to join the Free Poles, memories of people in Red Cross uniforms, and memories of joining dozens of other displaced persons on lorries with long benches against the sides for the seemingly endless ride across India to the Caspian Sea. If not sitting on the benches, the travelers were able to stretch out on the floor and attempt to sleep. Glinski had little memory of that trip, what they ate, or where they stopped. He simply knew the convoy was heading west; he was in a lorry with about twenty people (all men, some Russian-speaking); and he was aware that in some of the other lorries there were women and children. The traveling was almost nonstop with the drivers, whom he judged to be Sikhs by the size of their turbans, taking turns to keep the convoy in motion.

The end of the journey came when the lorries reached the Caspian Sea—not at a large port, but at some small place—and everyone was put into what seemed to Glinski as large fishing boats, not ferries. The trip to the other side of the sea, to the port near Camp Pahlevi, was just an overnight journey. Upon landing, he and everyone else were deloused, given new clothes, warm food, a couple of days' rest, and then they joined another convoy that took them to camps outside Tehran, set up for Poles leaving the Soviet Union.

✧✧

By the time this part of our conversation came to an end, we were both worn out: he from retelling a long story of the most memorable moment of his teenage life and me from listening to it. Although Glinski detailed his subsequent adventures in reaching England via South Africa, we kept coming back to his exploits as one of the four survivors of that incredible walk from Siberia to India. There were definitely differences from what was recorded in the book and what he remembered. I had to keep in mind, though, that the book was written a mere fourteen years after the events took place; Glinski was recounting his escape and subsequent walk after more than sixty-five years.

We backtracked, and Glinski tried to remember who had died first during the escape. Although the book mentions people by name, Glinski stated that he hadn't known the names of the men who died early on, just the last names of the three who, with him, reached India. So, the sequence of deaths varied from the narrative in the book. What about the Mongolian chief with the Pavel Bure watch? Readers of *The Long Walk* may remember mention of an old-fashioned pocket watch on a silver chain that was inscribed in Russian with the name of a famous nineteenth-century watchmaker, Pavel Bure. Glinski remembered the watch and stated the Mongolian chief said it came into his possession during the Russian civil war, when the Reds fought the Whites from one end of Russia to the other.

We discussed Batko and his killing of the two guards on the railroad during the robbery of one of the freight cars. We both pondered why that incident was left out of the book. Had it been deemed too hideous? Had Rawicz even known about the incident? Crossing the Gobi without water was scoffed at by Glinski, as stated earlier, and he spoke at length about how the small group found water, mainly from dew that gathered on their clothes and from eating such delicacies as earthworms. Rawicz had spoken privately of using clothing to catch moisture to slake thirst and also of eating earthworms. Why had those details not been included in the book as well?

I asked Glinski about the Circassian chief or headman mentioned in the book. He remembered someone who might have fit that description but wasn't sure the man was actually from Circassia. Nor was he sure of the time frame in which he met him. In the book, it described the encounter with the Circassian as taking place after traveling through Mongolia but before entering Tibet. What Glinski did remember was staying in a village where there was a church and school, and where he and the others met the German-speaking missionary. This village was memorable because of the celebration going on during their brief stay and the fact that the headman directed someone to guide them for the next couple of days to make sure they were on the right path to reach India without venturing either into China or toward Lhasa.

When we reviewed Glinski's memories of his stay in the village and his observations of the surrounding area, I asked whether the vegetation had been lush and tropical. I did this because Rawicz alleged, in consultation with Eric Shipton and others in 1956, that he and the other escapees entered India somewhere in the Bhutan/Sikkim area where there were thick, semitropical forests. In trying to find mention of tropical forests in the book, however, all I came across were comments about trees, flowers, and birds at one point and then, at the time of the encounter with the Gurkhas, there was further mention of "scrubby" country. Did Glinski remember tropical forests?

For some reason my question bothered him as he had *no* memory of tropical forests. The terrain he described was high, windblown plateau most of the time and then, after leaving the hospitable village and beginning to descend off the plateau into India, he remembered the countryside as having sparse vegetation with some trees but by no means tropical forests. There were trees and shrubs and tall grasses, and he remembered charred hillsides where fires had recently burned. I had to assure him that his memory was fine; that my own research corroborated what he remembered; and that when rereading the book, there was a passage describing the countryside similar to his memory—rough and scrubby.

The one episode we had *not* touched upon so far was the encounter with the yetis. When the subject of abominable snowmen was broached, it was greeted with derision. Glinski explained that he and the others had seen something and, at the time, they put it down to men in sheepskin coats in the far distance. At no time did any one of them think they had seen something out of the ordinary, something supernatural. As exhausted as they were, with wind and dirt constantly blowing in their eyes, with malnutrition wearing them down, Glinski mentioned there were times when his eyes were so sore he could hardly see out of them; and the others were in a like predicament. In looking back, however, did he think he might have seen yetis? He really didn't think so.

Part VII

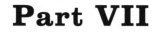

LOOSE ENDS

Chapter 22

Expeditions and Memories

I stayed with Glinski and his wife for two days, and during that time his story remained consistent. There were few other details he could dredge up. He kept coming back to the fact that he was frightened of running into Batko again after their last encounter in 1948; and since he learned of the *The Long Walk* in the 1970s, he always assumed that Rawicz and Batko were one and the same person. It now bemused him to think he had been afraid of someone who was not the person he thought him to be. We discussed the probability that Batko would now be nearly one hundred years old, if alive, and would be of no threat to anyone.

This helped Glinski overcome his longstanding fears, but it only added to my burden of tracking down the proof of who escaped from where and at what time. The ultimate question, of course, was what happened to the other three men, especially to Mr. Smith. Going back over my notes and rereading the book, it struck me there was no actual description of Mr. Smith beyond the words "quiet," "well-built," and "gray-streaked beard." When I presented the question to Glinski, he paused for a while and described him in a similar fashion, noting that Mr. Smith had a military bearing, seemed very intelligent and thoughtful, and spoke in an educated manner without any noticeable accent. Glinski considered that Smith might have been either Jewish or from the Middle East, stating that he had brown hair mixed with gray, while his eyebrows were still very dark, and he had eyes that were rather deep set and piercing, with blue irises that appeared almost black at times when the pupils were dilated. He also noted that Mr. Smith had a darkish complexion, what Glinski thought of as Mediterranean, and was well-built, though shorter than average. And the scar mentioned in the book from his accident while working on the Moscow Metro? Glinski had no memory of a scar nor did he remember Mr. Smith ever talking about the Moscow Metro, despite mention of it in the book. He did remember allusions to working with machinery on *kolkhozes* and in mining: Mr. Smith worked with his hands, either as a mechanic or an engineer, and was familiar with farm machinery, mining machinery, and the like. All in all, he was as much of an enigma to Glinski as he became to countless thousands of people who read *The Long Walk*.

This conversation reminded me of Rawicz's comments regarding not calling Mr. Smith "Herb" because of the connotations with grass, even though Rawicz didn't speak or understand English. Reflecting on Glinski's account of Mr. Smith reminded me that Glinski, like Rawicz, grew up speaking both Polish and Russian, the latter being spoken at home with his mother and her relatives. At sixteen, though, would he have had the knowledge to remark on accents in Russian? In other words, would he have known if someone were a native speaker of Russian as opposed to someone who had studied the language and could speak it fluently? I alluded to Rawicz's comment that Mr. Smith spoke Russian like a native. When I asked, Glinski replied that after having been in Mr. Smith's company for months, he was sure the man was a Russian speaker and not a foreigner who learned the language.

Following up on this remark, Glinski reiterated that Mr. Smith had a Mediterranean look about him but reflected that he could have been from an ethnic background wherein he spoke Russian as a family language. I then asked if he had noticed any distinguishing marks on Mr. Smith, such as scars or birthmarks. I referred to the passage in the book stating that Mr. Smith had a scar on his neck resulting from an accident while working on the Metro; but Glinski didn't remember any particular marks. Instead, he described how filthy and ragged they were, with long hair and beards they periodically hacked at with a knife they found. His description reminded me of the dreadful condition the escapees were in when they reached India.

≈≈≈

When my visit with Glinski and his wife ended, I returned to London, visiting the British Library and the PRO once again, spending as much time as possible ferreting in the archives. On my last day in the British Library I came across a reference to an expedition to reconnoiter the Sadiya Frontier Track, Assam, spanning December 1941 to February 1942. This was the record mentioned previously by Francis Kingdon Ward of Lt. Col. W. E. Cross, R. E., and Major J. W. V. Sadleir of the 7th Gurkhas, with the latter as commanding officer of what was known as the Menal Krai column.

Lt. Col. Walter E. Cross, Royal Engineer, FRIBA, FRSA, and Maj. James W. V. Sadleir, 7th Gurkha Rifles of the Lohit Valley Reconnaissance of 1941–42, left Sadiya, northern Assam, in mid-December 1941 and traveled northeast along the Menal Krai plateau to Tibet, ostensibly gauging the feasibility of a more northerly supply route than the Ledo Road between India and Burma, and the subsequent Burma Road to China. Their primary conclusion was that the route was not feasible for development; and their secondary conclusion was that this remote route was also not being used by infiltrators.

The account of the expedition made for fascinating reading, more so as the time and place coincided with the time and place of the escapees from Siberia entering into India—according to my calculations. I had high hopes of tracking down more information about these two people through their respective family members. Little did I know what a task that was to be.

Trying to find out more about these two men and their careers during World War II proved to be extremely time consuming; it took many months of investigation. Tracking down their families caused me to remember how long and hard it had been to find the families of Boyes-Cooper and Whitehorn, British intelligence officers with whom Mayne corresponded. The end results in this case were better, although not apparent at first.

After many frustrating months, I dropped the search for Sadleir and Cross. I began to wonder if either man had ever existed, as there was such a shortage of information about them; and my suspicions were aroused by this lack. Their names meant nothing to either the 7th Gurkhas or the Royal Engineers. Either these men were completely faceless or someone at these organizations just wasn't looking in the right file.

Fortunately, there were the initials FRIBA and FRSA after Cross's name, which would lead me to find out who Cross was and how to contact his family. FRIBA (referring to the Royal Institute of British Architects) was not helpful for my purposes; however, FRSA (representing the Royal Society of Architects) looked through an aging file and passed on information about Cross. (I later learned that Cross was very active in the Burma Star Association for many years before his death.) With a great deal of sifting through information and making telephone calls, I tracked down neighbors of his, who then passed me on to his family.

I later spoke to Cross's widow, daughter, and one of his sons. The trouble I went through to track them down proved worthwhile as the Cross family very patiently searched through correspondence and materials they had, as well as a copy of the report their father lodged with the British Library.

During the time I spent tracking down the Cross family, I was also in touch with several Gurkha organizations that still published annual newsletters. I asked if they would put in a request for information about Major Sadleir. At first, I had difficulty finding information on Sadleir. By coincidence, though, while I was corresponding with the Cross family, a surprise e-mail arrived stating the writer was a granddaughter of J. W. V. Sadleir. She stated that she lived in Australia and had come across a query I had placed on a genealogical Web site. She noted the family had very little solid information about Sadleir in the way of journals or diaries. They knew, of course, that he was once a military man, stationed in India during the War, and that he and his family then migrated to Australia once the War was over. The information drought was alleviated somewhat by the abundance of photos the family shared with me.

Thus began several weeks of e-mail exchanges with information and photos passing between three continents. I put the families of Cross and Sadleir in touch with each other so they could help identify who was who in several old photos from both families. It was one of those moments that made all the effort worthwhile, even though nothing came out of all my investigative efforts that related to the men of *The Long Walk*. Bringing these families together after so many years, enabling them to share memories and photos of their fathers, made me feel that the time spent researching these men was worth the effort.

Having tracked down information about Cross and Sadleir, I came across the names of two other explorers who were in northern Assam, northern Burma, and southeastern Tibet in the late 1930s and who worked for British intelligence in that area during the War: John Hanbury-Tracy and Ronald Kaulback. They were contemporaries of Kingdon Ward and referred to him in their respective books, but they never mentioned knowing or hearing about the Menal Krai column headed by Cross and Sadleir. I, of course, was hoping they had kept private journals of their travels and might have possibly heard of and written about the escapees from Siberia.

I was able to track down Hanbury-Tracy's daughter in the U.K. with the help of the Jacques Marchais Museum of Tibetan Art in New York. His daughter was interested in my quest and told me stories of her family and their long association with India. Regrettably, there was no memory or mention of *The Long Walk*. On the other hand, there was mention of the Kaulback family, and I eventually made contact with his daughters in the U.K. as well as his nephew in New Zealand. I listened to lots of family history via the telephone and e-mail, tales of divorces and remarriages, stories of house fires having destroyed papers and artifacts years ago, the possibility that some items might have gone to the Royal Geographical Society, the questions as to which sibling or cousin might have kept a photo or memento—the list went on. Ultimately, however, there was no memory or mention of the men who walked to India.

Dredging up old memories of India kept me probing for information on that continent, and I continued tracking down family members of people who were in Assam before, during, or after the War. One of the most prominent families before and during the War was that of the Governor of Assam, Sir Robert Reid. Even though I was unable to contact anyone in his immediate family, I managed to locate and talk to the family of his secretary, James Phillip Mills. They suggested I contact another family that had spent decades in India, that of Ursula Betts. Her daughters followed the family pattern and were involved in anthropological research in India for many years. Again, however, no one in any of these families remembered mention of scraggly survivors of a labor camp in Siberia.

Regardless of the fact that most of the people I contacted had never heard of *The Long Walk*, they unfailingly tried to be helpful by suggesting names of other people who had an affiliation of some sort with Assam. Pete Lutken, my faithful guide to all things OSS in the CBI theater, added yet more names of people who came to mind during one of our many conversations. Koi-Hai, another dependable source of information, made further suggestions. At each turn it seemed a name would pop up, and I would add it to my list to investigate.

While all these suggestions did not lead to additional knowledge pertaining to my quest, they did allow me to introduce families who only knew about each other through rumor or old photos. Once Lutken mentioned the names of two brothers, the Meston brothers, and a Colonel Pizey, I was off and running. I managed to track down the descendants of the Meston family as well as those of the Pizey family, thanks to the help of genealogical Web sites and entries I located on the Burma Star Association Web site. The two families were intrigued by my queries and wanted to learn more. I put them in touch with Lutken, who could tell tales of their fathers. These were families that had moved around throughout the British Empire after the War. They were grateful for my effort in connecting them with a part of their past.

Exhaustion, however, crept in after all of the name chasing. Once the rush of names slowed down I took time to breathe and refocus my efforts. I felt, at this point, that I needed to step away from the entanglements of family histories and think about my next move—to contact Kazimierz Zuzmak (Kazik), who had been a close friend of Rawicz's.

With our first conversation, Kazik made me feel as if we had known each other for years. (I experienced the same feeling with Glinski—a profound empathy and understanding that allowed us to talk and listen to each other on a personal level while feeling completely at ease, despite the fact we had never met.) In Kazik's case, I never did meet him in person; our contact was only via the telephone.

Young Kazik was a teenager in 1939. (Already his story had a familiar ring as Glinski had also been a teenager in that fateful year.) Kazik's father was arrested at that time and no one in the family ever saw or heard from him again. Kazik and his mother were deported to Siberia along with hundreds of thousands of other Poles in 1940. They barely survived the journey and the life of exiles. They were first in western Siberia doing forestry work, then moved to what is known today as Kyrgyzstan. After the amnesty in 1941, they managed to leave the U.S.S.R. in February 1942 and arrived in one of the first waves of Polish refugees to enter Camp Pahlevi during April 1942.

Kazik and his mother came a long way from their village of Luninic (pronounced Wuninitz), approximately 30 kilometers east of Pinsk in what is now Belarus. Following a brief stay in Persia, Kazik was first sent to Iraq, where he worked as a Polish-French translator. During the summer of 1942, he became ill with jaundice and was sent on to Palestine, where he initially worked as a driving instructor. He later joined the Polish cadet corps (Junacja Szkola Kadetow) and continued his education while training for the Polish air force; his mother, meanwhile, was sent to a refugee camp in Uganda. They met up again in England in 1944.

Between August 1942 and early 1944, Kazik moved around a few different camps in Palestine, including Camp Qastina, Camp Barbera, and a camp at Gederah. In speaking to me on several different occasions, he was fairly sure he first met Rawicz soon after he had arrived in Palestine but they did not become acquainted at that time—nor was it an instant friend- ship at first sight. Although Kazik remarked that he and Rawicz recognized each other's regional accents and, in talking about their families, they realized they had mutual acquaintances, Kazik was some years younger than Rawicz and that age gap did not initially inspire a close friendship. Over time, however, the age gap became less of a handicap, and a friendship began that lasted until Rawicz's death in 2004.

Despite the fact that Kazik moved around to several camps while a cadet, he and Rawicz kept in touch during their eighteen months in Palestine. They both trained for the Polish air force and they were both sent to England via Port Said in 1944 on board the SS *Franconia*. What I really wanted to know from Kazik was just how Rawicz appeared to him in 1942. Taking a deep breath, Kazik began to reminisce and immediately stated that his first sight of Rawicz was during a parade-ground exercise. What was Rawicz doing on a parade ground when he had repeatedly stated that he was a walking skeleton when he arrived in Palestine? I asked Kazik if he had met or heard of Rawicz during his short time in Persia, as Rawicz had spent some time in that country with General Anders's army before going on to Palestine. Kazik replied that his first encounter with Rawicz was definitely on a parade ground far removed from Persia.

(The BBC was unable to delve very far into Rawicz's time with Gen. Anders's army in Persia before he went to Palestine. I had already come across interviews dating from 1956 in which Rawicz stated he was a military instructor at Camp Barbera after having been with General Anders and his army in Tehran as a translator. The Ministry of Defence records showed Rawicz to have been a cadet officer, not a lieutenant, during his time in the military. In 1944, Rawicz was in England with the Polish air force on one of the RAF bases, furthering his military training. While doing that, he also found time to meet Marjorie, court her, get married, and start a family—and then the War ended and he settled down. Where in all this nonstop activity on Rawicz's part did he have time to recuperate from his walk to India? By his own account, repeated during many interviews, he weighed only 7 or 8 stone (approximately 112 pounds) when he left India. How was it possible that a few months later, in late 1942 or early 1943, he had recovered his health to the extent that he was able to carry out the duties of a military instructor?)

Kazik stated that he saw Rawicz off and on during their time in Palestine but never remembered seeing him emaciated. In fact, he described his first impression of Rawicz as a very tall, physically fit military man in charge of exercises, leading cadets in parade-ground maneuvers. Eventually, they both went to England. During 1944, Rawicz met Marjorie, his future wife, and introduced her to Kazik. Marjorie, a widow, was apparently bowled over by the attentive and courtly Pole. Kazik found her to be very intelligent and quite conservative in her views. While attending college in Nottingham after the War, in 1946, Kazik rented a room from Rawicz and Majorie in the house she inherited from her first husband. He was the best man at their wedding in 1947.

The Rawicz family grew in size; Kazik married and began a family of his own; the two families saw each other from time to time, each family busy with its own affairs. The years marched on, 1956 came and went, and Kazik had no idea his friend had written a book—no idea, that is, until Rawicz and Marjorie sold their first house and bought what became known as Cloud House in Sandiacre, where they lived until their deaths in 2004. From 1947 until 1956, Kazik knew nothing about Rawicz's "adventures." It was many years later that Kazik read the book. Being a man with limited curiosity (developed from a sense of not bothering other people by asking personal questions), Kazik never asked Rawicz about his life prior to meeting him in Palestine. In his turn, Rawicz never mentioned his past to Kazik apart from the usual desultory comments one makes from time to time. They knew they had mutual acquaintances from the Pinsk area, they had a vague idea about each other's backgrounds, and it didn't seem necessary to probe further—until the book came out.

In reviewing past memories and thoughts, trying to understand who Rawicz really was, Kazik remarked that Slav had been a bit of a mystery to him as well. He knew Rawicz had been arrested, and Kazik felt that the time spent in prison certainly affected him. He also commented on his friend's penchant for having loaded firearms in the house, both for hunting and for self-defense. Kazik continued by stating that he had no idea who it was Rawicz thought might come after him.

Despite Rawicz's oddities of behavior, Kajik felt him to be a friend and kept up contact with him. Kazik found Marjorie hard to fathom. She was a devoted wife and mother but could be intolerant at times, even to Kazik if he visited unannounced. (He had the same experience as Downing when the latter, on his monthly visits, occasionally found himself confronting a locked door and wondering if he would be let in, according to his nephews.) Kazik also found himself having to deal with Marjorie whenever Rawicz was in one of his depressed moods. Kazik wondered about those moods but was fain to tell her that Rawicz had allegedly developed a reputation as a lady's man when he was in the military. He didn't want to add another portion of worry to Marjorie's plate—by mentioning past gossip. Instead, Kazik let his wife deal with Marjorie and her plight, and it was Kazik's wife who heard details about the writing of the book and learned that Downing had been the motivator and principal scribe.

Once the book reached popularity and the royalties rolled in, the Rawicz family bought Cloud House, as mentioned earlier, and Kazik and his family did not see them as often as before. Kazik wondered about the book while in Rawicz's presence but no information from his friend was ever forthcoming except the odd comment that Kazik had been lucky in his life. Kazik explained that Rawicz envied him a little because Kazik's mother was reunited with him; also that Kazik came across one or two men from his village in Poland and they resumed their friendships in England. Thus, he was able to reunite with both his family (what was left of it) and two people from his hometown; Rawicz always commented on the loss he felt of his family and childhood friends.

At the risk of sounding like a broken record, I kept asking Kazik why he never questioned Rawicz about his past or about writing *The Long Walk*. He made many excuses—comments that his wife would have known much more about Rawicz than he; remembrances of asking an occasional question but never receiving a specific reply; and an acknowledgment of his general lack of curiosity, of his distaste for prying into someone else's life. I pointed out that Rawicz had bared his soul to the world in writing the book, so how could Kazik feel like he was prying?

Try as he might, Kazik could remember nothing that Rawicz ever said about his past, his family, or childhood friends. He did, however, corroborate what Levinson at the BBC learned from Rawicz's children, namely, that the Rusiecki part of Rawicz's surname had been dropped. Kazik remembered Rawicz stating that "Rusiecki" represented his past and he no longer wished to use it. Kazik couldn't recall when Rawicz dropped that part of his surname, nor could he explain why Marjorie and the children continued using it. I shifted tack and asked if he had met Rawicz's cousin while in Palestine. He replied that if Rawicz had a cousin in Palestine in 1943 or 1944, it was news to him. I then asked about Rawicz's first wife, named Vera in the book. Kazik was inclined to think Rawicz had mentioned his marriage before the War; but again, his friend never referred to the subject over the years, and Kazik never thought to bring it up.

What *was* brought up during our many conversations included the list of documents I received from "Memorial" concerning Rawicz. The BBC had already apprised Kazik of the contents of the amnesty, the travel permit, the questionnaire, and so on. Although Rawicz never confided in Kazik about his past over the sixty years of their friendship, none of this documentation came as a surprise or as a disappointment. Kazik had no opinion about the information one way or the other. When pressed, however, he did express his thoughts that after publication of the book, he and Rawicz drifted apart somewhat and were not as close as they had been previously. He accepted the situation as a fact of life, since both men were busy raising and providing for their respective families. Kazik did remark that, some years after the publication of the book, Rawicz gave him a signed copy but never really talked to him about the story. Finally, Kazik described Rawicz as a tragic figure when Marjorie died; and he wasn't surprised when Rawicz followed her to the grave just a few months later— leaving Kazik and thousands of others with a sense of loss and with many unanswered questions.

Chapter 23

Another Escape Story

Q uestions. What a bothersome word that became. There were so many questions, with more on the way, and so few answers. As 2006 drew to a close, I wondered what 2007 would bring in the way of those elusive answers.

In the event, answers didn't ring in the New Year; instead, intriguing information came pouring in. This time the information came from the Antipodes, specifically New Zealand, and it went like this: Once upon a time there was a handsome young man who found himself in the wrong place (Eastern Europe) at the wrong time (1939). Without needing to repeat this by now familiar chronology, suffice it to say that this particular young man, who died as an elderly man in December 2006, found himself embarked on a life-changing adventure. The man's name was Bronislaw Boguszewicz.

Boguszewicz died just a few weeks after the 2006 BBC Radio 4 broadcast. His family contacted the BBC and passed on Boguszewicz's life story. The link between his story and *The Long Walk* is a prison escape and subsequent walk across continents to freedom in India.

Boguszewicz was born in Lithuania during World War I; his personal story echoed Rawicz's and Glinski's. His grandparents were executed by the Soviets during the Russian revolution as their Polish-Russian background was aristocratic, leaving his father as the surviving member of the family. Boguszewicz grew up in Lithuania and studied engineering; then he joined the Polish army in 1939. He survived the blitzkrieg on the western front only to be captured by the Russians in Vilnius. He was subequently sent to a prisoner-of-war camp close to the place where the Katyn Forest massacres happened.

The following year, in 1940, Boguszewicz and another officer escaped from an unknown camp in southern Russia and fled across the steppes to the port of Baku on the Caspian Sea. They hid among a crowd of Russians on board the ship and made it to Krasnovodsk. From there they walked to Afghanistan, joining a band of nomads while crossing the Khyber Pass. They gave themselves up to British authorities when they reached Peshawar and were sent to the Polish Embassy in Bombay.

Boguszewicz volunteered to join the Polish Army once in India. He worked for a short time at General Motors in Bombay. Because of his refugee status, he was made known to the Banasinski family, which represented the Polish government-in-exile. He got along well with the Banasinskis but ran afoul of the vice consul, Dr. Tadeusz Lisiecki (referred to in some of the Banasinski papers at the Polish Institute in London as "Count" Lisiecki). During a conversation in which Boguszewicz mentioned his mother's family, Lisiecki suddenly realized his own family had been in dispute with that particular family over a property rights claim. Lisiecki was so worked up about this situation that he tried to get the British authorities to repatriate Boguszewicz to Poland or Russia. The British listened to Lisiecki and sent Boguszewicz to the internment camp for displaced persons and POWs at Dehra Dun where, according to his widow, the latter found himself to be the only Pole in the camp.

Boguszewicz was released but then sent back to Dehra Dun on more than one occasion until the end of the War. During the time he was in Bombay, he resumed working for General Motors and lived in an apartment building owned by the Firpo family. Towards the end of the War, he met his future wife at Kolhapur, one of the Polish refugee camps near Bombay. Boguszewicz stayed more than seven years in India. He and his wife left the country on the USS *General M. B. Stewart* in January 1948, pausing to unload and load Polish refugees who were in camps in Uganda and Tanganyika and reaching Europe a few months later.

❧

At the end of this intriguing saga, I asked myself how all of this was linked to *The Long Walk*. I soon found out that Boguszewicz recounted his story over the years to family and friends, including his remark that while in Bombay he came across a man with a very similar story to his: Zdenek Szara. Once settled in New Zealand, Boguszewicz and his wife learned of *The Long Walk*. He repeated to his wife and family that the man, Zaro, mentioned in the book was very probably the same man, Szara, whom he had met in Bombay. The man's name and story stuck in his mind all those years because Szara was the only other person he had ever met, besides himself and his fellow escapee, who had walked out of Russia. (Both Boguszewicz's wife and son remembered him talking about Szara in the plural, as in reference to "fellow escapees from Russia." Although no other names were ever mentioned when Boguszewicz retold his story, the impression he gave me was that Szara [a singular person] had escaped from Siberia with other men.)

I was agog at this revelation—but there was more to tell. I contacted Boguszewicz's son, who gave me an extensive outline of events, and afterward I got in touch with Boguszewicz's first wife. Boguszewicz and his first wife divorced and both remarried in the 1970s. Little by little, the details of his story unfolded.

Boguszewicz's first wife, Regina, spoke of her own harrowing history at the beginning of the War—of being sent to Siberia, being amnestied, making her way to Camp Pahlevi in Persia, and ultimately finding shelter in India. It was only at the end of the War that she met her husband and heard his story. After the War, her husband began working for the Polish Red Cross with the Banasinski family. He was put in charge of transportation in 1948 to escort Polish refugees to Mombasa, to pick up other refugees in Africa, and to look after all who wished to return to Europe. Some time later, Regina and her husband immigrated to New Zealand.

Fearful that I was not getting the whole story, I asked Regina to back up to the beginning. She repeated what I already knew, reviewing her husband's imprisonment and escape from Russia with a fellow prisoner. (Regina couldn't remember the man's name but thought he was Jewish—she also had no idea what happened to him once he and her husband reached India.) Suddenly, though, Regina recalled that during the escape, her husband and his comrade were helped by an old woman. Half starving, the two men came across a forlorn cottage on the way, and an old woman, who had a very good idea they were on the run, took them in and fed them for a few days. Boguszewicz was forever grateful for this act of kindness. The brief respite allowed the two men to regain their strength (and possibly their senses) and press on to Baku and Afghanistan.

(An interesting sidenote came up when I repeated Regina's narrative to her son. He remembered the story of the old woman and then added a few more facets to the tale—namely, that while in the labor camp Boguszewicz was asked to repair the commandant's radio and had become friendly with the man's wife! If true, it was an amazing coincidence, reminiscent of the help Madame Ushakov gave to Rawicz.)

While listening to this sequence of events, I kept wishing I'd known about this story while in London. I had no way to realistically dig around in the Banasinski papers at the Polish Institute, being so far away. Also, I wasn't sure I would locate any information on Szara at the Polish Institute. The one thing I kept turning over in my mind was that Szara or Zaro was not Polish—he was reputed to have been from somewhere in the Balkans. Yet, Boguszewicz stated that, at the time of meeting Szara, the latter was waiting to be shipped out to join the Polish Army. Could he have volunteered to join the Polish Army while in India? Perhaps Szara had a Polish connection or the Free Poles were willing to accept kindred spirits to fight the Nazis. This was another unanswered question of mine.

I also wondered about the mention of Firpo's. This was a famous restaurant during the days of the British Raj, but its location was in Calcutta, not in Bombay. This puzzled me, but Regina was adamant and mentioned having had the place pointed out to her by her husband before they left India. I subsequently discovered there was a Firpo's in Bombay—it was part of Firpo's holdings, more of a residence than a hotel, but such a place did exist. This was one answer I successfully obtained.

These were minor points, however. The major revelation was yet to come in Regina's narrative. Upon her remarriage, she and her second husband traveled to South Africa on business in 1977. They stayed at a large tourist hotel in Johannesburg. While there, one of the European managers of the hotel struck up a conversation with them. Idle chitchat revealed that Regina had spent the war years in India. She described her first husband's escape from Russia and his walk to India. The manager nodded throughout the story and then chimed in. He asked if Regina and her current husband were familiar with *The Long Walk*. The man named Zaro had been at the hotel in Johannesburg in the 1950s and had lived, or still lived, in South Africa.

Having lived in South Africa myself in 1975, my first thought was that Regina and her spouse stayed at the Carlton Hotel, or possibly the President Hotel. There were not many good hotels from which to choose for foreign visitors at that time. Regina thought the name of the place where they stayed sounded like Churchill Hotel. Her husband recollected there was a very large diplomatic function being held at the hotel during their stay, so it had to have been a large enough hotel to accommodate a crowd. With more digging, both online and in my memory, there appeared a reference to the "Churchill Room" at the Carlton Hotel. At any rate, I tracked down families in South Africa with similar surnames to Zaro or Szara; I contacted a Polish organization in Johannesburg, which kindly offered to help me by placing a query in their newsletter; in fact, I left no stone unturned, but I never found any information on a Zdenek Szara or anyone with a similar name. (I concluded that there was a very good possibility that Szara or Zaro had not settled in South Africa but had lived in Rhodesia [as it was then called] or Botswana. I kept in mind the fact that Boguszewicz had escorted refugees *to* Africa, as settlers, as well as picked them up for transport to Europe in 1948.)

Gathering all this data and sifting through it, tracking down the details and so on, involved weeks of effort. The story of Boguszewicz and his escape was fascinating; the possibility that he had actually met one of the men mentioned in *The Long Walk* was riveting. I contacted Glinski and repeated the story, but unfortunately it meant nothing to him. He restated that he never saw the other three men once they had arrived at the medical facility outside Calcutta; he was on his own, without his fellow escapees, in the convoy that left India for Persia. When pressed for any memories of what the other three had wanted to do once they arrived in India, he asserted they hadn't voiced any opinions, at least nothing specific that he could remember. Glinski was the only one who wanted to join the Free Poles and get back to Europe; he had no memory of the others stating any preference for their futures.

Many months after first having heard this story, I again jumped into the inner workings of Google and dug up information about the Banasinski family. As stated previously, both Mr. and Mrs. Banasinski were deceased; however, I discovered there was a daughter who was still alive. I contacted her and her husband, but they had no memory of the men of *The Long Walk* or of Boguszewicz. Frustratingly, another door was closed in finding out the truth of so many details.

Chapter 24

LEADS AND DEAD ENDS

A fter all the excitement revolving around my collaboration with the BBC, the spring of 2007 was comparatively quiet. Lots of names and speculations were in the air, but it seemed to me as if every avenue of information that opened up ended in a disappointing dead end. I could never quite get to the bottom of the leads that presented themselves to me over the months and years. Ultimately, I was back to my original question: How could I find proof to show the story of *The Long Walk* was true, and where could I find some concrete evidence that stated what happened and to whom?

It transpired that I became distracted and found myself walking down misleading paths for the next few months. Though misleading, the pathways I trod were nonetheless intriguing. I thought I might have been on the right track when I contacted an acquaintance in India who offered her services to help me look up names and documentation in the archives in New Delhi. This was information I wanted to pursue vis-à-vis the Banasinski papers in London. Shraddha Kumbhojkar helped and encouraged me to have a look at those archives, and she arranged for a graduate student to further the project. Nothing came of the effort, however.

While the archives in New Delhi had lots of documents pertaining to the Banasinskis and to Polish refugees and displaced persons, nothing surfaced regarding my specific focus. Interestingly enough, though, documents did come to light pointing to an extensive Polish "diaspora" in southeast Asia at the time of the War—Poles and other nationalities were spread out from India through Burma to Singapore, and they were all trying to get out of Asia. Documents detailing the arrival of Poles—Jews and non-Jews—who were evacuated from Rangoon and sent to Bombay made for interesting reading. (Coincidental to the receipt of these documents I became aware of a book with passages that included descriptions of the plight of some of these refugees from Burma: *The Road from Mandalay* by J. S. Vorley. I was soon in contact with Vorley's son, who was quite young at the time but remembered his father talking about the refugees who turned up in Rangoon during the War. His father reckoned they were the best workers he ever had, even though they could hardly speak a word of English and were absolutely penniless.)

There were also extensive documents pointing to an argument and eventual litigation between the Banasinski and Domeszewicz families. Mr. and Mrs. Domeszewicz were honorary consular officials based in Kabul, Afghanistan, who had been evacuated by the British to Bombay—for their own safety. They made financial claims on the Polish consulate in Bombay, and those claims resulted in a serious disagreement with the Banasinskis. Once again, an interesting sidelight into history surfaced that didn't help me to move any distance down my own road.

Another document that came to light in New Delhi mentioned a political officer who was chief secretary to the North West Frontier Police at the beginning of the War: Lt. Col. G. L. Mallam. Was this man in Peshawar at the time when Boguszewicz and his comrade came across the Khyber Pass and gave themselves up to the British? Would there be any records of such an encounter? I tracked down Mallam's son and listened to stories of his father's time in India. As always, the memories were poignant and evocative of times gone by. One more treasured nugget to add to my store.

Before refocusing my search, I had the inspiration to look again in the pages of *The Long Walk* and reflect on who the Polish translator for Mayne may have been when he interviewed the escapees near Calcutta. There was some speculation that the interpreter was Jewish. With that thought in mind I contacted the Jewish Genforum and typed out an inquiry to be put online. Replies came in with added suggestions, but no one remembered any relatives in the Calcutta area during the War, nor had they known or heard of any Jews working with the British military at that time. There was an interesting aside to my query, however. I was contacted by someone who suggested I take a look at *Jewish Exile in India 1933–1945*, by Anil Bhatti and Johannes H. Voigt. The book confirmed the names of people and incidents I had already uncovered but didn't disclose anything about Jews in the British military.

∽∽∽∽

Meanwhile, the Hollywood studio that held the film rights to *The Long Walk* contacted Levinson at the BBC with thoughts of making a movie. After the producers became aware of Levinson's Radio 4 broadcast and the positive response to it, their interest piqued. Levinson and several contributors to the broadcast, including myself, brought the producers up to date as best we could and suggested they look closely at the documentation the BBC and I had unearthed. We repeated, for their benefit, that although the story was very probably true, the book was questionable. This conclusion caused their interest to wane.

(As a separate side issue, thoughts of how to make a movie from the book have given pause to many people down through the years. The story is riveting, no doubt about it. But is it fit for a movie? Basically, the story is that of one man's unfortunate imprisonment, a switch to the imprisonment of a group of men, and then a long escape to freedom. There would certainly be enough tragedy and drama to go around but, Hollywood being Hollywood, there is no romance whatsoever in the story; there is no tension between the escapees [although deaths abound from natural causes]; and the idea of focusing on abominable snowmen toward the end of the film would deter the bravest of producers. The film would have the potential to become an instant comedy.)

The BBC pulled out as many stops as they could at the time. Because of the response to their radio documentary, they were hoping to have a follow-up broadcast. The word "hope" indicated the follow-up would only take place if more information came to light—more information meaning something definitive about the walk or the people on it. Families with the surname of Batko were contacted across England in the hope they might be related to the Jan Batko mentioned by Glinski; the Mayne family and the Downing family were again contacted on the off chance some bit of information may have been remembered; queries were placed in the Polish daily newspaper in London in hope that someone might come forward with memories of the walk; members of Koi-Hai offered to contact people whom they knew were in Assam during the War; the list of contacts and endeavors went on and on, as usual.

Regardless of all the effort put forth, no new material appeared from the above sources, but a tantalizing possibility came into view via the Missions Étrangères de Paris. I had previously invested some time and effort in contacting people at both the Missions and at the Order of St. Bernard in Switzerland. I didn't realize at the time, nor did these organizations ever state, that books about some of the fathers had been written. One such book came to my attention via a story on the Internet about Catholic missionaries in Yunnan province. The book, *Le Père Georges André*, was hard to come by but worth reading. It not only listed names of other fathers who were in the Yunnan–Tibetan area at the outbreak of the War but also included photos. Might one of the men in the photos have been the mysterious German-speaking missionary encountered by the escapees? Copies of those photos quickly found their way to Glinski. With his poor eyesight, however, he was unable to discern any resemblance to the man he met in 1942.

❦

As 2007 progressed, I sat back and let the e-mails, letters, and phone calls roll in. Not one of them led to solving the mystery of the story. This was one of those times when my interest waned and I set the project aside for awhile, answering queries but not instigating any new avenues of research.

During this lull, though, I did bestir myself to put out feelers concerning the U.K. publisher and editor of *The Long Walk*: Constable & Robinson.

My objective was to ask if the publishers had any original documentation regarding the book. In other words, was there any existing correspondence (rough drafts, notes, and so on) between the publisher and the co-authors, Rawicz and Downing, that could help answer the many questions I had? Neither the BBC nor I had much luck contacting anyone at Constable & Robinson, however. It seemed that any files pertaining to past publications were at a site outside London. When it was pointed out that "past" publication didn't apply in this instance as the book had never been out of print, there was some waffling but not enough to pique anyone's interest in locating the archived material.

Next, I contacted Aitken Alexander Associates, Ltd., hoping that I would find more information from that source. If contact with Constable & Robinson had proven chilly and uncooperative, the response from Gillon Aitken was the exact opposite. Aitken passed on the information that in 1956 the agency handling *The Long Walk* was Hughes Massie, Ltd. His agency bought Hughes Massie, Ltd. in 1984 from the children of the founder of the company, Edmund Cork. Aitken kindly put me in touch with one of those children, who worked with her father as an agent during the 1950s.

Cork's daughter always had the impression that her father thought the story was authentic. Her view of Rawicz was that of a very shy man whose wife, Marjorie, had done all the talking, writing, and business dealings. She remarked that Marjorie seemed to take charge and that Rawicz deferred to his wife in conversation, possibly because he still spoke with a heavy Polish accent and may not have felt comfortable talking business. Both father and daughter also had contact with Downing, who came across as very nice but terribly busy; they met his wife, Edna, and formed a favorable impression of her.

Aside from these remembrances, there was no other information. I then inquired about any archived records. I was told they were either passed on to Aitken or had been thrown out at some point. When I followed up with Aitken, he stated the file he inherited from Hughes Massie was slim with no relevant documents therein pertaining to *The Long Walk*. Between phone calls to these two people, however, another name was inserted into the mix—that of Ben Glazebrook, who bought Constable in 1962.

This time I had luck. Glazebrook was very patient in listening to my query and stated that his entry onto the scene was some years after the publication of *The Long Walk*. He knew of the book, of course, but had never been involved with either Rawicz or Downing. Glazebrook did think the editor who served as point person between Constable and Rawicz/Downing in 1956 was Richard Sadler; he wondered aloud if Sadler had already passed away. So I moved on once more, perusing accumulated data while searching for new possibilities to investigate.

Chapter 25

~〇

BARRACKPORE

A s I felt myself slipping behind in my research, e-mails continued to zip around the world. They were sent to J. P. Cross, who was currently living in Pokhara and who would possibly pass on suggestions about contacting people who were with the Gurkhas in the early years of the War; they were sent to an old friend of his, George Mackenzie in Australia, who was stationed in India during the 1960s and might remember stories of the past; and they were sent to Sterling Seagrave, son of Dr. Gordon Seagrave, the famous Burma surgeon. (From this latter contact came an interesting parallel to J. S. Vorley's story of having left Burma on one of the last ships out of Rangoon in 1942. Seagrave had memories of leaving Rangoon about the same time, just before the Japanese overran Burma.)

Not surprisingly, nothing came of all these efforts except for more stories of wartime grit and heroism. Some of those stories came to my attention via the Koi-Hai Web site. As previously discussed, this Web site was organized by and for the descendants of tea planters who were primarily in India and Ceylon before World War II.

At odd times during the ongoing research into *The Long Walk* I attempted to contact medical entities such as the RAMC (Royal Army Medical Corps), Queen Alexandra nurses, Lady Minto nurses, and other organizations. There was usually little or no response, excepting excuses about records having been lost, further suggestions as to where to look, and so on. I now decided to take a fresh look at the situation—from the Indian angle. Glinski described the nurses, doctors, and orderlies who cared for him while he recuperated as having been Indian or Anglo-Indian; mention is also made in Rawicz's book of native—i.e., brown-skinned— medical personnel.

So, with paper and pen at hand, I wrote to the *Nursing Journal of India* and the *Medical Journal Armed Forces India*, as well as to the Indian Red Cross Society. I felt this was an area of inquiry I had not fully turned my attention to until now. I hoped for a positive outcome as, to date, most of my letters to medical journals in India or medical associations in England never received a reply.

The impetus for this particular angle of inquiry came from Seagrave's recollections of his father's activities in Burma and later in India during the War, and it came from meeting missionaries on leave from India in 2007. While holding conversations regarding India and medical staff living in the country during World War II, I began to wonder if some of the medical personnel there in the 1940s were actually medical missionaries. These thoughts brought me back to the location in Calcutta where Glinski and the other escapees were brought to recuperate from their ordeal. I had raised that question before and remembered that the word "Barrackpore" was mentioned on numerous occasions.

❧❧

Barrackpore is a town within an hour's drive from Calcutta. More importantly, during World War II there was a large British military base located in the town. In 1942, the British were well ensconced and had a medical facility on the base. I discovered this when I found a reference on the Internet regarding the Barrackpore base, along with a name: Harry Tweedale. Another quick reference to the computer and Tweedale's story began to unfold, thanks to his niece, Jane Marshall, and another relative. After Tweedale's death, his relatives had laboriously transcribed his wartime journals and contributed them to the BBC WW2 People's War Web site.

During my perusal of Tweedale's journals, I was struck by the possibility of him being in the right place at the right time to have heard of the escapees from Siberia if, in fact, they were housed in the medical facility at Barrackpore while recuperating from their ordeal. I discovered that Tweedale was in Barrackpore during 1942; just as certainly he was on and off the base, visiting with local Methodist missionary families who lived across the Hooghly River on Riverside Road, and there was mention of medical missionaries to boot. Reading his journal entries proved fascinating, but there was no reference to emaciated survivors of a labor camp in Siberia. To be fair to Tweedale, though, I realized he was not at Barrackpore for the entire year; however, it is possible he heard about Siberian "guests" from some of the missionaries, medical or otherwise, who were in the Barrackpore area from before the War.

I contacted Tweedale's niece, and she very thoughtfully browsed through the journals looking for any additional tidbits, but nothing came to light. While she kept busy looking through journals, I investigated online for further information about where the Methodist missionaries had lived. It appeared there was a large compound owned by the Wesleyan Methodist Church with several houses (read "villas" complete with armies of servants—this was the India of the Raj, after all) in which missionaries and medical personnel lived. During the War, some of those houses were commandeered by the British military. After the War, missionaries continued to inhabit the compound but, as the years progressed and their numbers dwindled, the compound was leased to the BKP Rastraguru Surendra Nath College. Since the early 1950s, the college has gradually taken over the compound and incorporated it into its campus grounds.

The word "Methodist" kept cropping up in this research, and, with the help of many Methodists along the way, I located someone in the London headquarters of the Methodist Church who pointed me to the *Methodist Recorder*. I was encouraged to submit a request asking for help in my search. With just one reply, I was off and running once more, chasing one set of names after another.

My query in the *Methodist Recorder* pinpointed one particular name mentioned by Tweedale in his memoirs: Rev. R. Brown. I also included the name of a doctor living in a nearby villa, Dr. John Lowe. Soon after the query appeared, I received a reply from Jean Parton, a member of the Church of North India. She passed on several names, both of active church members in India and of retired missionaries in England. At the same time, someone at the Methodist office in the U.K. looked up the names of missionaries stationed in Barrackpore during the war years. Each name seemed to give rise to another.

Into this swirling mix came one more reply, this time from the widow of Rev. John P. Hastings, who had been employed by the Methodist Missionary Society, albeit after the War, in the 1960s. Mrs. Hastings was knowledgeable about Methodist history and gave me as much information as she could. She and her family had lived at 6 Riverside Road, Barrackpore, during the time in which her husband was busy with a variety of pastoral duties in the Barrackpore area.

Mrs. Hastings had done some digging of her own in an effort to pass on as much information as possible to me. To that end, she had come across references to Dr. Lowe in a book about leprosy missions in the eastern part of India. It appeared that Lowe had been an expert on leprosy (and this was later confirmed by articles on Lowe available on the Internet, his obituary in *The Times*, and by one of his sons whom I was able to contact). Although Mrs. Hastings never met nor heard of Lowe prior to this finding, she knew the occupant of 6 Riverside Road during the War was Rev. Reg Brown and his family—and, as it turned out, Reverend Brown's two sons were alive and well, living in England.

My phone calls to the two brothers caught them by surprise but elicited wonderful memories of their childhood days. They recalled their years living on the compound and attending St. Paul's School in Darjeeling; they spoke of their father's friends (especially Bernard Glover, who was involved in jute manufacturing and whose hobby coincided with Brown's—driving toy trains around the compound), fellow missionaries (Rev. Quentin Snook and his doctor wife, Maire, and their daughters), and playmates. They also gave me references to journals their father wrote during his lifetime; about the early death of their mother, Dora; their father's remarriage; and the loss of whatever papers their father kept during his life.

Then the conversation took a sharp turn and went off in an unexpected direction. Though one of the brothers did not recognize the name of Dr. Lowe, the other brother did. Both brothers remembered accompanying their father onto the Barrackpore military base during the War when Reverend Brown served as chaplain on the base. Although the brothers were too young to remember whether their father had ever mentioned escapees from Siberia, they remembered the base as a fantastic place—it was like being in another world. One brother remembered watching his first film there, *Ali Baba*; the other brother talked about chewing gum and Life Savers that were given to him by the American GIs, who were sharing the base with the British military.

The memories tumbled one after another, though neither brother clearly remembered Dr. Lowe and his wife living at 26 Riverside Road—not until Tweedale's niece scanned some old photos of her uncle's and e-mailed them to me. Those photos contained snapshots of the Brown family, Tweedale, Dr. Lowe, his wife, and their spotted dog. The Brown brothers saw the photos and one of them vividly remembered the spotted dog but little else about the Lowe family. (I subsequently discovered that Lowe and his wife moved to Africa after the War. In the mid-1950s, while back in the U.K., Lowe died suddenly of a heart attack.)

❧❧

Phone calls such as the above were in many ways emotionally draining, for me as well as for the people reliving memories half a century old. At the same time, they were truly fascinating and rewarding, even if no solid information came forward that would help me in my research. I say no solid information but there was the inevitable litany of names. The outcome of tracking down those names was that I got in touch with the daughters of Reverend Snook (who remembered playing with the Brown brothers), and with Reverend John Clapham (now retired) who made a list of most, if not all, of the missionaries in Bengal over the years. I kept trying one name after the other but without any luck in attaining new information. No one had any memory of the Siberian escapees.

Exhausting the possibility of finding answers in India, I briefly turned northward, to Siberia. In letter after letter to Karta Indeks and to "Memorial," I asked for information about the labor camps, the gulags, and of World War II Siberia, but a reply was never forthcoming. Therefore, I decided to reassess my efforts and contacted a group exploring what happened to POWs from Finland (another group had pinpointed POWs from the Baltic states and still other groups were interested in Lake Baikal, studying ecology and climate change); and I tried to find out who to contact in Siberia with information about airfields. In *The Long Walk*, there was mention of the commandant using a small plane to get in and out of the camp area during the winter; therefore, I figured, small plane meant a landing strip. Whatever the focus, my e-mail queries elicited several responses but no hard information.

Part VIII

A WALK ENDED

Chapter 26

≈⌒

THE PINSK CONNECTION

In the summer of 2007, the explosive information I was hoping for finally appeared. The BBC had received documents from the Pinsk archives in Belarus the summer before, in response to their inquiries about the Rawicz family. At the time of the interview with three of Rawicz's children, Levinson was shown a photograph of their paternal grandmother and grandfather, Yulia and Feodor, with their names printed on the back.

Levinson kindly passed on the basics of that documentation to me but it took months to find a contact. Eventually I became acquainted with a very generous woman in Pinsk: Elena Romanovich.

Elena turned out to be a person of generosity, kindness, patience, initiative, and curiosity. She was a person after my own heart. It was difficult at first for her to understand *why* I was researching Rawicz, due to our language barrier. With my Russian skills at zero, we had to rely on her English, which was well above zero but unused to bizarre requests from overseas strangers. I shall always be thankful she took me at face value and was ever eager to help me with my research.

Initially, I inquired about Yulia and Feodor Rusiecki-Rawicz. I knew Yulia's maiden name but the Latin (i.e., Western) spelling was all over the place, as were dates of birth, marriage, and other important events. So, what started out as Yulia Vasilievna Krichevskaya (spelled as such) encompassed the possible spellings of that surname as Krzyzewski, Kryczewski, and other permutations. Along with the muddle in spellings came the need to make a decision. Elena sent me names and phone numbers attached to all of the above spellings and I needed to decide where to start.

I pinned my hopes on contacting someone in Rawicz's mother's family who could relate details about the family's history. This would be a wonderful window to discovering facts about Rawicz's early years. With the help of Russian exchange students and a Russian-speaking friend, I began to make phone calls to Pinsk. Despite the incredulity expressed by some of the people I phoned, I ultimately connected with a member of the Krichevskaya family who remembered Rawicz's mother, Yulia.

Over a period of two or three weeks, several phone calls were made to this particular Krichevski family in Pinsk. I was informed that Krichevski's father was Boris Petrovich and his grandfather was Peter. Krichevski recalled that Peter had a brother named Vasili whom he thought was Yulia's father. As it turned out, he had never met any of these people, having been born after the War, but heard stories of them. Krichevski stated his father and grandfather were priests in the Russian Orthodox Church; he knew his grandfather's brother, Yulia's father, was also a Russian Orthodox priest; and there was some kind of falling-out in the family after the War.

Krichevski was not very informative, but his wife was blessed with curiosity. It was she who insisted we call back and she would let us know what she had discovered. She was true to her word. Mrs. K must have canvassed large swaths of the population of Pinsk as she related her research efforts to us over the phone. She made inquiries of relatives, friends, neighbors, and anyone who would talk to her—and her inquisitiveness paid off. One thing led to another, and information began to stream in my direction.

Every time my translator and I phoned Mrs. K she had a new piece of information for us. My problem was cataloging all the new findings within some sort of framework that made sense. First she mentioned someone named "Inna"; then she talked of someone living in Brest; then there were names of people (relatives, friends, acquaintances) living in Pinsk, followed by a list of streets that had all, seemingly, changed their names since World

War II. At the end of those phone calls, my translator and I were worn out coping with the deluge of information.

Little by little the jumble of data began to make sense. Firstly, Mrs. K's husband, Mikhail, was the great nephew of Yulia Rusiecki-Rawicz's father, Vasili. The entire male population of the Krichevski family appeared to have been Russian Orthodox priests—at least until World War II erupted. Mrs. K was told by several people that Yulia's husband, Feodor, had been an Orthodox priest, as had his two brothers. She discovered that Yulia and Feodor had three children, all daughters she thought; and one of the daughters was known by her nickname "Inna." Then came the important news: Yulia and Feodor were both buried in the Old Russian Orthodox Cemetery on Spakoynaya Street in Pinsk. Mrs. K had gone to the cemetery and noted down the names and dates of both people. Yulia Krichevskaia Rusiecki was born in 1890 and died in 1972; Feodor Antonovich Rusiecki (the name Rawicz did not appear on the tombstone) was born in 1881 and died in 1962.

After each phone call there was a lot of information to untangle and digest. Mrs. K had the energy of ten people coupled with the instincts of Sherlock Holmes. At the time of our final conversation, Mrs. K referred to someone in Brest who was closely related to Yulia and Feodor—possibly a cousin or grandson.

Reflecting on the relative in Brest, I reassessed what I had learned so far about Rawicz's parents and siblings. It seemed that Yulia and Feodor had survived the War, contrary to what Rawicz wrote and affirmed over the years; there were siblings; and now it appeared there might even be a grandson. I wondered how the family had survived the War, whether they knew Rawicz had escaped Siberia and ended up in England, and if they had information about Rawicz's first wife.

While communicating every week or so with Mrs. K, my Pinsk contact, Elena, had sent me a long list of people with the surname Rusiecki. As I had done so well with the K's, I could now start on the R's. The R list was rather daunting, though, with many more names on it. As I started contacting people, they were all curious and helpful in trying to point me in the right direction for additional information.

Meanwhile, Elena was busy tracking down addresses. In the pile of papers the BBC received in 2006 were copies of census reports and other documents listing the pre-war address for Yulia and Feodor as Dominiskaya Street. Once Elena began looking into that address, she discovered the street name was changed to Gorky Street. Somehow, she came across a phone number for an establishment on that street that turned out to be a convent. We phoned the convent, Matrushka Yekaterina, and were told that in its present manifestation the building and site had been a convent only since 1993. Prior to that date, it was a psychiatric hospital. Unfortunately, the voice on the other end of the phone had no idea what the building had been used for before the War. My search there was complete.

As Elena passed on her findings to me, I passed on Mrs. K's information to her. Before I knew it, I received an e-mail with an attachment. The attachment consisted of photos of both Yulia and Feodor's graves, side by side, with deeply etched and very legible tombstones. Elena also had a good look at the information in the Pinsk archives—the same information sent to the BBC—and began to interest herself in the three children born to Yulia and Feodor, one son and two daughters: Slavomir, Predislava, and Susanna. Slav was the eldest, born in 1915; Predislava, his sister, was born in 1917; and Susanna was the baby, born in 1920.

Elena was able to track down a bit more information about the Rusiecki family as well. She discovered that Yulia had had a sister named Eugenia, whose daughter, Leonila, was still alive at age ninety-seven. Sadly, Leonila's memory was not what it had once been; but her daughter and grand-daughter did confirm that they had heard of Yulia and Feodor many years ago but never met them. We phoned the granddaughter on two occasions, and the second time she stated that when she tried to ask her grandmother about Yulia, Feodor, and their children, Leonila immediately started calling for "Slavka" and continued speaking that name for several days thereafter. She also mentioned that she was in touch with a cousin who currently lived in Brest and who might have more information about the Rusiecki family.

The Brest connection, Mr. Dunets, was most emphatic that his grandparents were Yulia and Feodor, his mother Predislava, his aunt Susanna, and his uncle Slavomir Rawicz. Not only was he the grandson of Yulia and Feodor Rusiecki-Rawicz but so was Yuri, his cousin whom he had not yet met.

To clarify the situation before speaking with Dunets, Elena contacted me with his name and phone number, and the information that he was, indeed, a grandson of Yulia and Feodor: his mother had been the eldest daughter, Predislava. (It was never made clear if Predislava was the daughter with the nickname "Inna" or if it had belonged to her sister, Susanna.) At any rate, before making more phone calls, I sat down to get my facts in order and organize questions. My translator and I then dialed his number.

When Dunets answered and my translator and I posed our questions, he explained that the war years had been a hard time for everyone. Yulia and Feodor, along with their two daughters and their respective families, moved to Poland during the War, either in 1943 or 1944. Once the War was over, they had stayed in Poland as life was a little easier for them in that country. Then, in 1949, the entire family moved back to Belarus—to Brest instead of Pinsk—and Yulia and Feodor continued to live with Predislava and her family until their deaths. The younger sister, Susanna, had married a Pole and was reunited with her husband in 1953, when she returned to live in Poland.

When we asked about Rawicz, Dunets stated he had never met him; and the family had always been circumspect when mentioning his name, as he was the only one arrested in the Rusiecki family in 1939. My translator pointed out to Dunets how difficult it had been to track down any family information concerning Rawicz as it appeared no one in his family continued to use the double-barreled surname of Rusiecki-Rawicz or of Rawicz on its own. Dunets explained that the latter part of the name gradually ceased to be used after the Russian Revolution.

Then Dunets stunned me by claiming that he and the rest of the family knew all along that Rawicz had made it to England and settled there after the War. While Dunets and his family resided in Poland during and after the War, Rawicz sent them food parcels via the International

Red Cross. Postcards and letters were also exchanged, with difficulty. I informed Dunets that Rawicz's children had some of those postcards but had trouble understanding what they meant, as Rawicz never spoke about his family. (These were the postcards shown to Levinson when the BBC interviewed the Rawicz family.)

Dunets accepted this comment and remarked that his aunt, Susanna, was the one person in the family to continue her contact with Rawicz. It was easier for her, in Poland, to keep in touch with Rawicz and pass on news between the far-flung members of the family. Because both sisters, Predislava and Susanna, died in the 1980s, Dunets decided to write to his uncle outlining their lives and deaths, and simply making an attempt at contact. He received a reply from Rawicz, a note on a card, thanking him for getting in touch but stating that he did not wish to recall the past—it was too painful.

Furthermore, Dunets explained that Susanna's husband—Dr. Pavel Kaminsky (or Kaminski)—had been in touch with Rawicz and Marjorie since the 1980s or early 1990s. Dunets wasn't sure about this information; however, he knew that either Kaminsky or a close friend or relative of Kaminsky's had gone to England to visit Rawicz. (While the translator was reciting the story to me in English, I couldn't keep my mouth from gaping as my jaw dropped lower and lower.) I subsequently confirmed with Levinson that the Rawicz children had come across an address for a Pavel Kaminsky among their parents' possessions, and they had heard their mother speak of him, but they didn't seem to know who he was. Kaminsky, who died in 2005, had, after all, been their uncle.

(Eventually I relayed this information to Rawicz's old friend, Kazik. He is still close to the Rawicz family and would be able to translate should the Rawicz children wish to speak to their relatives. I brought up the name Kaminsky, and Kazik immediately recognized it. Evidently, Marjorie had mentioned a visitor from Poland to Kazik and his wife some years ago. Kazik remembered Marjorie saying she kept in touch with Kaminsky . . . without ever explaining that he was her brother-in-law.)

Towards the end of my lengthy conversation with Rawicz's nephew, Dunets stated his plans for an upcoming trip to Poland to meet his cousin, Yuri, for the very first time. When we asked why he had not met him before, he replied that when his aunt died his uncle remarried and moved to another part of Poland. However, the families kept in touch over the years and, finally, Dunets was going to meet his cousin.

Several weeks later, I spoke to Dunets again and he confirmed everything he previously stated. He had met Yuri, who produced no new information pertaining to Rawicz, but he confirmed what Dunets had already told me, namely, that Susanna had kept in touch with Rawicz until her death. Both Yuri and Dunets agreed they had heard of their uncle's fame as the author of a book many years ago and they also knew that Rawicz had died in 2004. So, although having lived behind the Iron Curtain for decades, they were aware of their uncle in England—which was more than could be said of Rawicz's children, who remained in ignorance about any possible family members until contacted by the BBC in 2006.

Chapter 27

SEARCHING FOR SMITH

After learning that Rawicz had, in fact, been in touch with his Polish family, I contacted Levinson with the results of my phone conversations and he was absolutely amazed. He was still sitting on a pile of documents sent to him by the Pinsk archives, and he had already learned of Rawicz's extended family.

The outcome of the contact with the Rusiecki families in Belarus and Poland was to lay to rest Rawicz's allegation that his family had all perished in the War. Simultaneously, it gave his children the opportunity to pursue their own research if they chose to do so. The "why" of the actions Rawicz took to portray himself as a sole survivor, in more situations than one, may never be answered, and at this point, I knew I still faced the problem of finding out what had happened to the *other* survivors of the walk.

I became increasingly frustrated in my search. I had already canvassed wide expanses of the globe in search of answers, from Polish translators in Calcutta to air strips in Siberia to forgotten relatives in Belarus, with side journeys to New Zealand, South Africa, and many points in between. I wondered where to turn next.

My first thought was to renew my search for Mr. Smith. Of all the escapees, Mr. Smith was the most thought provoking; and he was the one who sparked the most interest in readers of *The Long Walk*. I looked again at the possibility that Mr. Smith had worked in Moscow in the 1930s. Referring to a number of books and periodicals pertaining to American and foreign workers in the Soviet Union before World War II, I came across references to a Charles Smith. Such a common name caused confusion when I later came across the name in *The New York Times* with a middle initial B. and, in another instance, with a middle initial H. It transpired that Charles B. Smith of St. Louis, staff member of the American Railway Commission, was arrested in Siberia in 1917 and immediately released—with no explanation given. Charles H. Smith appeared to have been a clone of Charles B. Smith, so I wondered whether the initial was simply misplaced.

In time, I learned, there *was* a Charles H. Smith. He and a William Smith were both involved with the U.S.–Russian Chamber of Commerce in the 1930s; an Alfred Smith, industrialist, resided in Moscow then as well; and there was a Homer Smith, author of a book focusing on his experiences as a black American in the Soviet Union. There was also an Andrew Smith, a Hungarian engineer and author of *I Was a Soviet Worker*, who immigrated to the United States, changed his name, and then followed the siren call to the U.S.S.R. before becoming disillusioned and returning to the United States once again. And, last but not least, there was a Fitzgerald Curtis Smith, journalist, who was in Moscow during and after the War. (This last person was intriguing because of the reference by Rawicz to the name Herbert or Fitzherbert aligned with Smith, but nothing came of it as I learned the journalist had not been in Russia in the 1930s.)

No record of a Mr. Smith had been found among the sparse remains of the Amtorg files. The Hollywood folks also had no luck in finding out about him after hiring a researcher at NARA to look into whether Mr. Smith's name came up in correspondence between Washington and the U.S. consulates in India in 1942. That is not to say there was *no* reference in the files to engineers with the surname of Smith. The Hoover Institution had an extensive list of documents recording the experiences of Americans in the Soviet Union in the early part of the twentieth century. With the help of a researcher in California, documents in the Russian subject section were perused and two names jumped out from the pages: Lloyd E. Smith of Staten Island, who had been in Russia as an engineer, and Dr. Warren F. Smith of Massapequa, Long Island. Both men were in the U.S.S.R. in 1935 but returned thereafter to the United States. In the Pelliken collection, there was correspondence regarding the problems Pelliken had encountered trying to "legalize" his Russian wife to enable her to leave the Soviet Union with him. There was additional information that about one hundred American engineers had married or were living with Russian women and could not leave the U.S.S.R. with them. Although Mr. Smith might have been one of these men (with reference to that passage in the book stating he had been living with a Russian woman at the time of his arrest) his name was not mentioned in the correspondence.

Further questions to answer arose: Had Mr. Smith actually worked on the Moscow Metro? Was he in fact a qualified engineer? What happened to the girlfriend mentioned in the book? Was his name really Mr. Smith; and if not, was it Herbert, as Rawicz suggested? Glinski remembered the man as speaking Russian without an accent; in other words, he spoke Russian as a native-born speaker would. Notations to that effect appeared in the book as well. Rawicz later told interviewers that Mr. Smith spoke of Mexico on occasion and of distant family; Glinski had no memory of Mr. Smith ever speaking about his life before becoming a victim of Stalin's tyranny. The man was simply a mystery—that much was certain.

Then, by a fluke, I stumbled across an online article from 1997, which dealt with those unfortunate Americans who "disappeared" while working and/or living in the Soviet Union under Stalin. The article listed several names of American citizens who were executed in the 1930s as well as one or two names of people who were sent to prison and lived to tell the tale. The article suggested other avenues of exploration in my quest to discover the identities of the Americans working in Moscow in the 1930s—those Americans who offered their skills and services in the interests of building Socialism and who ended up being shot in the head for their efforts.

The article listed quite a few names, many of them showing Russian roots. Almost all of those names belonged to men and women who were executed during Stalin's purges of the mid-1930s. One of the names, Thomas Sgovio, had fortuitously survived his imprisonment and wrote a book about his experiences. It was no longer possible to ask him about those experiences, however, as he had died in the late 1990s. Another survivor was Frank Hrinkevich. As the name was unusual, it took little time to make contact with the Hrinkevich family. Again, though, I was too late to speak to the man himself. Hrinkevich died many years ago and his children knew little about his experiences as a young man in the Soviet Union. They stated that he was based in Minsk, working in a factory, and had gone back to the land of his birth (Belarus) in the 1930s for several reasons, one of which was to look for a wife. As horrible as his story was—in that he was imprisoned when he asked to return to the United States and take his new wife with him—at least he survived the ordeal.

⁂

This somber list was compiled by Alan Cullison, an Associated Press reporter, while working in Moscow. With the usual amount of muddling around, I managed to make contact with Cullison. His replies to my e-mails complemented what I already noted in his article, namely, that he was sympathetic to the plight of those Americans who had suffered so greatly, both at the hands of a tyrannical regime and from the indifference and callousness of their own U.S. Embassy officials. The remarks attributed to some of those American officials showed a degree of prejudice that is hard to fathom today, as their inaction to assist American citizens caused the imprisonment and death of many Russian Americans arrested at that time. Diplomatic relations with the Soviet Union had just gotten off the ground after a decades-long freeze, and the U.S. government was still trying to find its diplomatic footing. Because of this past history of no contact and a "careful as she goes" mentality, the embassy had no wish to help or aid people it deemed not quite American and very obviously didn't want to be bothered with such vexatious questions as dual citizenship.

It appeared, from reading Cullison's article and other articles on "lost" Americans, that the vast majority of men (and women) who went to the Soviet Union were inspired by idealism. It was also true that much of that idealism came from feeling "left out," from wanting a better life, from wanting a job at a time when the world was going through one of its darkest hours: the Great Depression. The only bright economic light, regardless of one's politics, seemed to be the Soviet Union. That shining beacon attracted all kinds of people from all walks of life and with all kinds of political affiliations. Initially, that beacon fulfilled the expectations of many of the people who made their way toward it. It lifted up everyday workers from around the world and, because of their expertise and know-how, made them into supervisors, teachers, and instructors—people in leadership positions who had come to show their Soviet cousins how to get on in the world. Later, however, as jealousy of the perks given to "foreigners" seeped through the Soviet bureaucracy and corruption became rampant, that same bureaucracy felt it necessary to harden its grip on its own society and disillusionment set in among the foreign guest workers. Even the ones who held to their values of socialism or communism for years after having been to the Soviet Union had sense enough to get out while they could. No one will ever know how many just kept going to work, trying to stay out of politics, and ultimately disappeared.

Was that what had happened to Mr. Smith? Had he been one of the hundreds of "disappeared" Americans mentioned in Cullison's article who had simply soldiered on, had tried to keep out of politics, and had tried to keep his thoughts to himself? And how was I to begin to understand his history if I didn't even know his true identity?

Cullison was very patient with me and my questions. He pointed out that it would be nearly impossible now, in 2008, to do what he and others had done in the early 1990s—namely, to do extensive research in the former Soviet Union. After the breakup of the Soviet Union, he explained, it was possible (as Adam Hochschild and Professor Wolf had described) to do research into many aspects of Soviet history. It had been possible to look at NKVD or KGB files on Americans who went to Moscow and were caught up in the Soviet purges. Over time, however, the KGB changed its name to FSB and stipulated that only bona fide family members could look at the files of purge victims, making it almost impossible for a non-relative to do any research into this area of Soviet history.

Cullison said that perhaps he could help with the information he had already researched. I outlined the little I had collected about Mr. Smith and passed it on to him. The basics were that he was a Russian speaker; he had worked in Moscow; he might have worked on the Moscow Metro; he had lived the life of a foreign guest worker complete with Russian girlfriend; and he had been oblivious of the looming danger to himself right up to the time of his arrest in the mid-1930s when he was sentenced to prison, sent to Siberia, and escaped. I anxiously awaited Cullison's reply.

One of Cullison's first responses was that he had a copy of *The Long Walk* and was familiar with the story, although he had never read the book. His next comment was to inquire about abominable snowmen! Once beyond that fascinating hurdle, Cullison got down to facts. As in his article, he suggested that many of the U.S. Embassy staff had considered Russian-born Americans or left-leaning Americans of whatever parentage to be less than full citizens. The question of dual citizenship was one the U.S. Embassy kept at arm's length, in step with the Soviets. Cullison further stated that although the U.S. Embassy tried to keep track of Americans who were in the Soviet Union as the purges began, embassy officials were sending assurances back to Washington (in 1938) that no Americans were under arrest.

This diplomatic assertion by the U.S. Embassy was a blatant lie. It flew in the face of the arrests of thousands of foreigners, with or without dual nationality, during the purges of the 1930s. However, if the U.S. diplomatic corps pretended that a problem didn't exist, that no "Americans" were being arrested, then there was no extra work or aggravation to deal with in the form of aid to distressed nationals. Bluntly speaking, the U.S. authorities considered there *were* no distressed U.S. citizens in the Soviet Union at that time, and left those mentioned earlier to their respective fates.

Cullison and I tried to narrow our conversation to focus specifically on Mr. Smith. He recommended delving into the U.S. consular files at NARA, although I reminded him that Hollywood already paid a researcher to do just that, with no results. He went on to suggest that Mr. Smith was a phony name but, like me and many others, he couldn't figure out why a Russian speaker would use that name. Then I remembered Andrew Smith, the Hungarian engineer mentioned earlier, who did exactly the same thing—namely, he adopted a very American name when he immigrated to the United States. He never gave an explanation for doing so, leaving the field wide open to future speculation.

The outcome of these e-mail messages was that Cullison stated he had U.S. Embassy registration lists dating back to the mid-30s when the embassy opened in Moscow. He cautioned, however, that the lists were only as good as the people who came to the embassy to register their names. It was a point well made. After some false starts, we made contact by phone, Cullison informing me that he had the citizenship registries for the U.S. Embassy for the latter half of the 1930s and they contained the names of all U.S. passport holders in Russia at the time. He stated the lists showed something like 1,800 names beginning in 1935 but that by 1939, after the purges had come and gone, less than half that number of U.S. citizens were registered.

So according to Cullison's list, in 1936 three men living in Moscow with the last name of Smith appeared on those registry lists: Anthony, a Russian native who was listed as a machinist in Moscow; Charles Hadley, an engineer whose hometown was Rushville, Indiana; and Homer, a journalist and native of Mississippi. The latter name was already familiar to me as Homer Smith wrote about his experiences as a black American in the Soviet Union. Charles Hadley Smith was an unknown, but the name came up on the Social Security Death Index, so it was definite he returned to the United States at some point in time. Therefore, I was left with Anthony Smith.

Chapter 28

THE RUSSIAN MR. SMITH

With my list of choices being narrowed to one name—Anthony Smith—I asked Cullison what information he had on the man. He responded with Smith's number on the list of American citizens registered with the U.S. consular authorities: number 719. Smith's passport number was 653519, issued in Washington, D.C., on November 28, 1928; Mineola, New York, was listed as his U.S. residence. Then there was a pause on the other end of the phone. I inwardly groaned, thinking that was the end of the flow of information. However, Cullison continued talking, stating that more than 1,800 Americans were registered with the U.S. Embassy in 1935, and that the numbers dwindled dramatically as the years rolled by: 1,047 for 1936, 872 for 1937, 596 for 1938, and only 400 for 1939. The significance of those dwindling numbers was not lost on me. Interesting as the list sounded, though, I had to make sure I kept myself and Cullison focused on the fate of Anthony Smith.

Looking through his lists, Cullison remarked that in 1937 there was a notation next to Smith's name. The man was under "rule P," meaning a person listed as being under a presumption of non-citizenship. As I mulled over the statement I wasn't sure the explanation made the meaning any clearer. Was Smith a non-U.S. citizen, then? Did that make sense? It was confusing, as Cullison had just passed on the man's U.S. passport number to me with the date and place of issue. Ignoring my mutterings, Cullison kept going down his lists and stated that in 1938 another notation was placed next to Smith's name: a U.S. passport was authorized but not issued; and Smith was considered a dual national with a Soviet wife and two children, one of whom had just recently been born (in either late 1937 or early 1938).

Cullison and I discussed the concept of dual nationality, namely that this was frowned upon by both the Soviet and the U.S. governments. With diplomatic relations between the two countries only recently out of the deep freeze, neither one wanted to deal with this particular situation. Both countries harbored suspicions toward people of dual citizenship and perhaps divided loyalties, concerned that such individuals could be coerced into espionage activities.

Cullison continued to look at his list for 1939 and remarked that there was an additional notation next to Smith's name for that year. While in 1937 he was listed under "rule P," by 1939 the notation by Smith's name was reduced to the initials "d.n.," dual national. There was a comment with the initials "s/w" meaning Soviet wife, and a further notation that he was the father of two daughters, both of whom were registered with the U.S. Embassy as Rosa and Harriet (the youngest one born a year or two earlier). His occupation was listed as that of a machinist and his address in Moscow was on Novaya Bashilovka Street, Bldg. 9, Apt. 30.

As usual, I waited for more information to come through from Cullison but the silence that followed the address wasn't broken. That was practically all Cullison had on the man known as Mr. Smith, beside the fact that Smith may have originally come from Seredue and Leuzen. Cullison said he had looked up the town names in a Soviet atlas and couldn't find them, speculating they were probably mis-translations of Smith's home village somewhere in the Soviet Union.

My initial impression was that Anthony Smith couldn't have been the Mr. Smith I was researching because his name came up as late as 1939 on the U.S. registration lists. Cullison had a different opinion, familiar to me from what I had read in accounts of life during the era of the purges. He was inclined to think that because a U.S. passport had been authorized but was never issued in 1938, it was possible Anthony Smith could still be *the* Smith in whom I was interested, keeping in mind that something had obviously happened to Smith to prevent him from picking up that precious passport. By 1938, Smith might already have been arrested and imprisoned, he reasoned; and although his Soviet wife was not mentioned in the lists by name, it was entirely possible she was the one who had registered their daughters and kept up contact with the U.S. authorities for as long as she could. In other words, there was no indication that Smith needed to go to the U.S. Embassy to keep in touch with that entity; his Soviet wife or a friend with connections could have done that.

(There are many notations in past and present publications indicating that family members, close friends, and people with connections could intercede on behalf of those unfortunates arrested at that time. It seemed to Eugene Lyons, Russian-born American journalist and author of *Assignment in Utopia*, that there were armies of Russian Americans who were virtual prisoners in the Soviet Union; other authors used words such as "captured," "stranded," or "derelict" Americans on Soviet shores. By whatever designation, their plights were living nightmares, especially for the children of those dual nationals. The Soviet Union did not recognize U.S. sovereignty over people of Russian birth; and there was no treaty to deal with this issue. People caught in this nightmare of statelessness, as it were, begged for help from whatever source possible. Accounts of intercessions on behalf of these unfortunates were mentioned by Lyons [who personally interceded more than once himself], Zara Witkin, and other well-known American figures in Moscow at the time.)

At the end of my conversation with Cullison, I was left with my thoughts and they were in a muddle. In the midst of that muddle was the phrase "authorized but not issued." Why was the passport not issued? What had happened? Above all, though skeptical, I had to consider Cullison was right—that Anthony Smith just might be the man I was seeking.

To verify the information I'd received, the usual assortment of phone calls to government offices were made, with one call leading to another, until I finally had an address for an office within the U.S. Department of

State, Research & Liaison Branch, that dealt with passport inquiries. I wrote the letter the first week of March 2008 and received a reply in August.

In the meantime, I trawled the Internet looking for information on naturalization procedures for the 1920s in New York State. Having found the correct office that would have handled naturalization proceedings for people living in Mineola, New York, I asked if there were any men named Anthony Smith in their records. Unfortunately for me, there were several. I would have to wait until I received additional information from the State Department to help me pinpoint the correct man.

While waiting for that reply, I reviewed several years' worth of the *Economic Review of the Soviet Union* for the 1930s. The name of Charles Hadden Smith came up as being that of the vice president of the American-Russian Chamber of Commerce. With a correction in spelling of the middle name, this was the man cited on the lists Cullison reviewed with me. There was little information about the man himself in the *Review*, as that publication kept to the straight and narrow of economic news. Originally in the mid-1920s, the Review had single-mindedly sung the praises of the Soviet economic miracle. There were lots of photographs each month of life before and after the Russian revolution. There were stories of dreadful hardship with positive punch lines: the U.S.S.R. was going through difficult times in order to shake off the past and rise like a phoenix from the ashes to a glorious future. The call was for everyone to put his or her shoulder to the grindstone and help lift the new country out of the mire and into the radiant sunshine of world attention. After all, while the Great Depression was throwing millions of workers out of work in the West, the Soviet Union was the one country looking for and hiring workers.

The *Review* expanded in size and quality in the early 1930s, with issues coming out twice a month, until about 1934. There were many references to foreign workers and their lives and contributions to the ongoing Five-Year Plan. One American farmer, George McDowell of Kansas, was actually awarded the Order of Lenin for his contribution to the Soviet economy. There were also indirect references to the grumblings of many foreign workers about living conditions, with the assurance that life was getting better under communism for everyone, guest workers and Soviet citizens alike—they just needed patience and hard work. These grumblings echoed those included in the book *60 Letters*, published in 1936 in Moscow. Although the guest workers uniformly praised the chance to work or pursue their careers, they had generally negative views of their living conditions.

While reading about people of all nationalities flocking to the Soviet Union to escape poverty at that time, I kept wondering what had happened to them. Specifically, I wondered what had happened to Smith. What had he done to be arrested? What had happened to his family? I couldn't answer any of these questions until I knew something more about the man. As things transpired, I had to wait five months to receive a reply from the U.S. Department of State regarding Smith. When the reply did arrive, the mystery of Smith's identity only deepened—something I had thought impossible.

Chapter 29

THE AMERICAN MR. SMITH

A month or so before receiving anything from Washington, I answered a phone call from the State Department asking *me* if I knew anything about Anthony Smith. Rather than offer any information that might be false or on the wrong track, I equivocated and promptly received an explanation to overcome my surprise. In a nutshell, there was a folder of documents on Smith found by the State Department. The documents, however, didn't contain much information about who the man actually was. (This had obviously intrigued the State Department which was why it had taken them so long to reply to my query.) Without seeing the documents, however, I really couldn't offer any comment on Smith's identity beyond mere speculation.

A few weeks later, a large manila envelope appeared in the mailbox consisting of some twenty-odd pages of photocopied documents. My hopes were high as I pulled out the papers and the accompanying letter. Going through them, one by one, did not bring enlightenment, however; rather, my perplexity grew the more I read.

The passport application for Anthony Smith, dated August 28, 1928, gave basic information about the man, including his birthdate, his place of birth, when he had emigrated from Russia to the United States, where he currently lived, when he was naturalized, what he had been doing for the past couple of years, and so forth. I turned the page to continue reading on the backside . . . and came face-to-face with Smith. A good-sized black-and-white photo, very clear, was at the bottom of the page. Could I be looking at Mr. Smith? The photo captivated my attention. It showed a youngish man, in his mid-thirties, looking solemnly into the camera. He was wearing a suit and tie for the passport photo and appeared well groomed. The photo showed a clean-shaven rectangular face with thick swept-back hair, a high wide forehead, deep-set eyes, a noticeable nose, broad cheekbones, and a full mouth. In many ways the photograph was typical of the era: an unsmiling, no-nonsense direct look at the camera.

With the face of the man I had been trying to find for many years firmly imprinted on my mind, I turned back to page one of the passport application and began reading more carefully. At the top of the page was a big stamp stating that Smith's passport had been issued on November 28, 1928. There was a notation that a fee was paid on August 30, 1928, right after the application for the passport had been made. I noted that Smith's previous passport, issued on July 22, 1926, had expired, and the reason he was applying for a new passport was to allow him to return to Russia. He wrote that he planned to return to Russia via Europe on September 25, 1928, on the Cunard Line, but he obviously had to postpone that booking as his passport was not issued until November. The reason for the delay in issuance soon became clear.

Before wading through pages of documents attached to the passport application, I checked Smith's personal information in hopes that I might spot something relevant, something familiar to me from the course of my research. Initially, this didn't appear to be the case. Smith claimed that he came from Saratov State in Russia; that he was born on December 22, 1890; and that he had emigrated from Russia to the United States on or about December 22, 1913. He went on to affirm that he had lived on Long Island during his time in the United States, was naturalized in 1926, and had returned to Saratov in 1926 to visit relatives. He had apparently been away almost two years when he came back to the United States in July 1928 and asked for a new passport, with the intention of turning around and immediately returning to the Soviet Union.

His father's name was a bit smudged, but the spelling looked like Muscy Smith. Owing to some misunderstanding, perhaps, next to his father's name Smith had again written his own birth date, December 22, 1890. The following line was even more doubtful. It wasn't clear if his father lived in the United States as on the line below this family information Smith had listed his father's address as being Elkhorn Street, Howard Beach, Long Island, New York—which was Smith's address. Was that his father's address as well?

Continuing to read on the backside of the passport application, I noted Smith's self-description: height 5 feet, 2 inches; age 38 years; hair brown; eyes blue; no distinguishing marks; occupation carpenter. All this was followed by a very legible signature: Anthony Smith. There was nothing on the application, save for a couple of smudges and blotches caused by excess ink from a fountain pen, that caused it to look any different from thousands of others filled in at that time. It was not the look of the application that was intriguing, however, but its content.

Had I finally discovered the identity of Mr. Smith? When I was able to refocus my thoughts, I began turning page after page of the enclosed documents.

The first letter was dated January 22, 1929, on Department of State letterhead, Office of Special Agent in Charge, Mr. R. C. Bannerman to Mrs. R. B. Shipley, Chief, Passport Division. There was an accompanying large purple date stamp on the letter belonging to the Division of East European Affairs, dated January 25, 1929. The letter simply stated that, with reference to a previous report dated November 12, 1928, there was no more information on "IN-CO." In-Co stood for Industrial Co-operative; but that discovery was hardly illuminating. What was In-Co?

Working backward from the last half of January 1929, there were pages of questions and answers within the State Department: "Reference is made to your memorandum of . . ." "In response to your letter of . . ." What several of those pages boiled down to was an attempt by the U.S. authorities to discover who Smith was. In other words, they could not find a convenient category in which to pigeonhole him. Who he was and what he was doing in the United States were the themes of the correspondence.

Another thread that ran through the file was that of urgency. Remarks such as " . . . very much interested in obtaining any possible information concerning . . .," "Has it been possible to obtain any further information . . . ?," and "Anything further which you may be able to obtain regarding Mr. Smith and his company will be of interest to the East European Division" proved this. The need for answers rang through, loud and clear.

References to In-Co or the Company were perplexing. Somehow I had never developed an image of *The Long Walk*'s Mr. Smith in any other, earlier persona, such as a businessman. Rather, I saw him simply as a victim of injustice, one of the escapees who walked to freedom in India. I realized I even found it hard to imagine him as an engineer. To me, and perhaps to thousands of readers around the world, he was a survivor—no thought was given to examining those aspects of his personality dealing with his profession.

Continuing to browse through the documents, I noticed that approval was given for his passport application by late November. On this particular page there was a comment alleging that "Mr. Smith's activities show that they are promoting American trade interests."

Buried halfway down a densely typed page was the sentence that caught my eye: "You may also desire to consider the fact that the applicant, before naturalization, changed his name without Court order; and the fact that his application gives his father's residence as the same as his own, while his affidavit states that it (is) his intention to visit his father, 'who is ill in Russia.'" The next sentence stood out as well: "It may also be noted that the liquidation of the Society for Technical Aid to Soviet Russia (mentioned herein) has recently be (sic) announced in the DAILY WORKER." (The *Daily Worker* was the mouthpiece of communism for many decades, until 1991.)

I suddenly had flashbacks to my college days in the 1960s when most self-respecting students around the world liked to read the *Daily Worker*. There was always some scurrilous article on the evils of the capitalist system. Here I was at this point in time looking at references to that long-ago "rag" in the middle of my search for Mr. Smith. It then dawned on me that the U.S. authorities were looking at this man as a possible communist.

This was ironic in view of the Soviet's arresting and imprisoning him as a political prisoner, a fate usually befitting a capitalist spy. Again, I had never thought of Mr. Smith in any kind of political light whatsoever despite the fact that I had read many books by people with similar stories to his own, who had very obvious and forthright political views.

The next page in the file referred to Smith as a naturalized U.S. citizen and noted that on his original U.S. passport " . . . issued on July 22, 1926, (he) gave his real name and intimated that he had changed his name at the time of naturalization. I note also in the present application, he gives his father's name as Murcy Smith, whereas his father never had any such name." What *was* Smith's real name?

I found it in the next set of documents dated November 12, 1928, referring to more special agents who were investigating Smith, namely Special Agent A. R. Burr and Special Agent LeRoy Mullen. The latter, Mullen, had obviously put in a lot of time and effort trying to discover some solid facts about Smith and about In-Co, the Industrial Co-operative. His efforts served to point out that Smith either lied on his initial passport application in 1926 or had not understood how to properly fill out the form. A special delivery letter was dispatched to the address given by Smith at that time only to be returned to the State Department marked undelivered, as the mail carrier had never heard of either Smith or In-Co. The next paragraph piqued the interest of the authorities: "Since the address in question harbors a nest of Bolshevik propaganda organizations, such as Rose Baron and her International Labor Defense, famous for their activities at the time of the Sacco-Vanzetti frenzy as well as their activities in supporting striking miners and mill-workers, it was deemed advisable to approach the investigation . . ." Sacco-Vanzetti? I wondered. It transpired that the investigators in 1928 believed Smith was involved in espionage activities.

Agent Mullen learned that Smith's real name, transliterated from the Russian Cyrillic script, was Abdul Chumjlakef. He had changed his name to Anthony Smith after he arrived in the United States in 1913. Abdul was a Muslim name, wasn't it? And Chumjlakef was a tongue twister. I had a difficult time understanding all of this.

I continued reading Agent Mullen's report, hoping for additional clarification. Mullen questioned Smith about his professional abilities and was told the latter was both a carpenter and a machinist, self-employed, who lived in the Mineola, Long Island, area between 1913 and 1926. Smith confirmed the time he spent in Russia and stated he was currently living with his longtime friend, John Alexander, on Elkhorn Street, Howard Beach, Long Island. In fact, a letter from the State Department addressed to him, care of Alexander, had brought Smith to the interview with Mullen in mid-November, 1928.

During that interview, Mullen caught Smith off-guard when he asked him why he had never mentioned In-Co to the State Department. He inquired if there was another man named Anthony Smith who was associated with In-Co, because a letter from the State Department sent to Smith using In-Co's address at 799 Broadway, New York City, "was returned as undeliverable, as In-Co and Anthony Smith were unknown at that address." Mullen prodded Smith, asking why he was so reluctant to mention In-Co; Smith then admitted he was returning to Russia as a representative of that company.

Pressed for details, Smith offered that In-Co was a cooperative Russian affair with a branch in Moscow. He planned to accompany machine tools that were being shipped to Moscow for installation in In-Co's factory, and he claimed that he would work in the factory or machine shop once there. He further stated the shipment of tools (lathes, jigs, shapers, milling machines, planers, pressers, etc.) had a value of approximately $25,000 and were purchased from the Dewitt Tool Company on Lafayette Street, New York City. Then, suddenly, he seemed to clarify his statements. He claimed he was *not* going to accompany the tools; rather, they had already been shipped. Smith stated he would catch up with the shipment in Moscow where he would be working for In-Co with a salary of 160 rubles per month. He pointed out that any delay in receiving a new passport was very costly, as he had kept his rooms in Moscow while paying rent to his friend, Alexander, here in the United States.

Agent Mullen was as bemused as I, stating he "was unable to get an intelligent answer as to how long he [Smith] worked for them [In-Co] in

Moscow, and just what he did there. He denied being a member of the Communist Party, denied going to any classes or school in Moscow, and denied that he had attended similar meetings in this country." Smith must have squirmed under that barrage of questions and accusations! Eventually, though, Mullen realized he wasn't going to get the confession he was looking for.

Smith was asked more questions attempting to tie him to communist organizations in the States. He was asked if he worked for Amtorg, but Smith stated that Amtorg was a Soviet government proposition and that In-Co was a private company. He denied having anything to do with Amtorg. He stated the tools were bought from Samuel DeWitt of S. A. Dewitt Tool Co. as well as from Morey & Co., in New York City. DeWitt, a former Socialist assemblyman in the New York legislature, vouched for Smith when contacted by the State Department. He confirmed that Smith was a bona-fide mechanic and was thoroughly honest. When questioned about Smith's political leanings, DeWitt replied that Smith was not a propagandist but was "a native Russian of the peasant class who has invested money in a co-operative scheme along with others of his class in the expectation that he ultimately will make a good profit." The scheme required Smith to return to Russia and take a hand in its operation.

The back-and-forth between Mullen and DeWitt in establishing Smith's character continued for many paragraphs. Ultimately, Smith came across as a man who bumbled along, never gave thought to politics, lived in one country while keeping ties to another, and who seemed to be innocuous. But was he? Reading between all those lines I got the distinct impression that Smith may have been playing some kind of game of his own. Did he, like so many ex-pat Russians, want to go back to Mother Russia to show solidarity with a young, vibrant nation that had recently shaken off monarchy and feudalism? Or was he just an honest businessman, albeit a peasant, as alleged by DeWitt? The former thought suggested a possible interest in politics; the latter described a shrewd workman only interested in making money. I asked myself where, for instance, Smith had laid his hands on the $25,000 reported in these documents to invest in the purchase and shipment of tools to Russia. The many references to communism and to money didn't quite gel. There was mention of other people having gone into this venture with him, but it was unclear just how much money was invested individually—keeping in mind that $25,000 then would be nearer to quarter of a million dollars in 2010. How had a simple Russian immigrant of the peasant class accumulated that sort of money between 1913 and 1926?

Further reports and affidavits were attached to the documents about Smith, all affirming what a "good fellow" he was. On the final page, I came across a comment by the Passport Division pointing out to Smith that his new passport would "be valid for a period of two months only, and should you continue to remain in Russia after the expiration of the passport which may be issued to you, you should apply for registration or for the extension of your passport through the nearest American consul. It may be added, however, that as this Government has not recognized the Soviet regime, no American diplomatic or consular officers are stationed in territory over which that regime claims to exercise control." Then came a warning: "Upon applying to the consul for registration or for the extension of your passport, it will be necessary for you to submit satisfactory documentary evidence to show that the reasons for your residence in Russia come within the rules prescribed by the Department to overcome *the presumption of having ceased to be an American citizen.*" (The italics are mine.) The warning was portentous if, indeed, Smith was *the* Mr. Smith.

Chapter 30

THE SMITH CONUNDRUM

While mulling over the clairvoyant nature of the warning to Smith from the Passport Division, a piece of paper slid from the pile and landed on the floor. It looked like a copy of the passport application; but when I glanced over it, I realized it was an Affidavit to Explain Protracted Foreign Residence and to Overcome Presumption of Non-citizenship. Smith was asked to fill out the affidavit and explain his long absence from the United States between 1926 and 1928. The several paragraphs on the form indicated that Smith could write fairly well in English, with only a few spelling errors. His sentences showed a degree of articulateness and thought that pointed to a good education of some kind. Yet the man was a simple carpenter or machinist by his own account, and a peasant according to Samuel DeWitt. Something did not add up.

Once again, scanning all those papers included in the packet from Washington, I settled on my next step: I'd write to the Supreme Court of Mineola, New York, and ask for a copy of Smith's naturalization papers. I phoned the court first to check the address and inquire about the fee, then sent my request. Luckily I didn't have to wait five months for a reply—it arrived the following week.

The rapidity of the response did not, however, include insights into Smith's identity. If anything, the naturalization document (Declaration of

Intention, U.S. Department of Labor, Naturalization Service) considerably muddied the waters, and made me wonder if some of the run-around hadn't been deliberate. It was evident at a glance that the document was written by the Clerk of the Supreme Court and not by Smith himself. The signature was clearly Smith's, though, albeit a rather shaky and uncertain signature dated August 1919. His writing ability and self-confidence had obviously improved by 1928. But what of the information itself? In 1919, he declared he was twenty-nine years old, but I noticed his birthdate was different on the naturalization document than on the passport application: December 28, 1889, instead of December 22, 1890. Instead of carpenter, he had put machinist as his occupation. His personal information seemed to be the same: not married; color white; complexion fair; height 5 feet 2 inches; weight 137 pounds; color of hair brown; color of eyes blue. He stated he was born in Saratov, Russia and resided in Hempstead, New York, in 1919. Smith went on to affirm, "It is my bona fide intention to renounce forever all allegiance and fidelity to any foreign prince, potentate, state, or sovereignty, and particularly to Russia or any independent state within the bounds of the former Russian Empire of whom I am now a subject."

Last but not least, the information on the document gave his date of original arrival in the United States as February 22, 1913. The ship he was on arrived in New York from Hamburg, Germany, on that date. Frustratingly, the name of the ship (a two-word name) was indecipherable; but I felt I had enough information to consult the Ellis Island records, which were now accessible online.

One of the easiest and most encompassing ways to look at the Ellis Island immigration records is to use a Web site set up by Steve Morse. On that Web site one can choose to search by passenger name, vessel name, date, nationality, and so on. As I had no idea what Smith's original name was, having already discovered that no such surname as Chumjlakef seemed to exist, and I was unable to read the ship's name on the naturalization document, I had to settle for using the date: February 22, 1913. However, as I soon learned, no ship had arrived in New York on that date.

Before I could despair (one more time), I noticed there *had* been a ship arriving from Hamburg the day before, on February 21, 1913. I searched the passenger list using the criteria of Smith's age, his nationality, his bachelor status, and anything else I could think of. Nothing remotely similar to Chumjlakef surfaced. I consulted Russian friends who suggested other spellings: instead of the "ch" as in church, we thought of "tch" as in Tchaikovsky; then there was "dzh" as in Dzherzinsky. I tried every permutation I could think of including zh, sh, sch, dj, and dz. Nothing even close to the many spellings we thought of appeared on the computer screen.

The passenger list contained hundreds of Russian names; the vessel carried a few thousand immigrants. I felt so near yet couldn't pinpoint Smith. (Needless to say there were no "Smiths" from Russia on board.) What to do next? All I could do was go back and look at the documents from Washington and hope something striking would emerge.

❧❧

Buried in the documents was the name of Smith's friend, whose address he had used on his passport application. John Alexander lived on Elkhorn St., Howard Beach, Long Island, in 1928. (I noted the two variant spellings for Elkhorn St. on Smith's paperwork.) I wondered if he had continued to live there for many years and whether any neighbors might still be alive who remembered him. Without further delay, I immediately opened a genealogical Web site, wrote out the information I had on Alexander, asked for help with the 1920 or 1930 census for Howard Beach, and sat back to wait for a reply.

Not one but two replies initially came, followed by others with additional information. Based on my experiences over the past few years, though, I should have guessed that John Alexander wasn't the man's real name. On the census record for 1930 the man's name appeared as John Alexandrow. The record showed that he was married with four children, that he was born in Krolevets, Russia, in 1887, and that he had arrived in America in 1913. My immediate thought on reading that last date was that Alexander was more than an "American" friend to Smith—he was someone Smith knew in the old country and who possibly accompanied him on the trip to the United States.

Back at the Ellis Island Web site, I typed in the name of John Alexandrow, Russia, 1913, and hit "search." A minute later, up popped dozens of choices. I couldn't believe just how many variations of John Alexandrow appeared on the screen for 1913. On second glance, however, I noticed that only one man born in 1887 fit the bill: Iwan Alexandrinkow (possibly John Alexandrow) from Kŗoliwecki, Russia (possibly Krolevets, Russia).

As I absorbed this information, I noticed another name directly below that of Alexandrinkow: Abeduto Szumgalakoff from Lusan, Russia. I just about jumped for joy. Even with the misspellings of both names, I knew in an instant I had located my Mr. Smith. In all of 1913, there was no other name even remotely similar to Abdul Chumjlakef. With a little thought, and considering the vagaries of transliteration between Russian and English, it was clear this was "Anthony Smith" immigrating to America with his friend "John Alexander."

The word "Lusan" also rang a bell and I looked again at the information Alan Cullison gave me concerning Smith. On the U.S. consular registration lists, Smith's birthplace was listed as Leuzen, Seredue. Could his birthplace have been Lusan, Saratov? Was there such a place? Plugging those words into the computer brought up an instant result: Lusan spelled as Luzern, aka Remmler, one of the German settlements on the Volga River in Saratov province. This was confusing, as Szumgalakoff was not a German or Russian name. I suspected that it was probably Kazak or Tartar. After looking at a map of the entire area, I realized how close Luzern was to Kazakhstan.

Pleased that I had tracked down information on Anthony Smith, I still needed to verify that he was *the* Mr. Smith from *The Long Walk*. The first thing that came to mind was the knowledge Cullison passed on to me from his registration lists. They had accurately described the man about whom I received so many documents from the State Department and who arrived in the United States in 1913 on the *SS President Grant*. Anthony Smith and Abeduto or Abedulo (as the name appeared on the scanned manifest rather than on the typed text) Szumgalakoff were one and the same man. I looked again at the photo of Smith, noting his broad open face, his square shoulders, and his direct look into the camera. Did he look Russian or Kazakh? I reread the warning from the Passport Division in 1928 concerning the need to renew or extend his passport *within two months* of his arrival back in Russia or he may very likely lose his American citizenship. According to Cullison's registration lists, he had waited not two months but nearly ten years to apply for a new passport, which was then never issued.

I went back to the ship's manifest to check what little information there was on Smith and his friend Alexander. In one instance, it appeared that Smith had been married as there was an "M" in the marital status box, while Alexander seemed to be single. It also appeared that Smith and Alexander were the same age, twenty-six, even though their birth dates were two years apart. Smith's father's name was written as "Musy," a close spelling to the Muscy on the passport application I received.

I then began to focus on the other notations on the manifest. At one point it seemed as if half the men on board the ship had dark blond hair and gray eyes, such was the sequence of ditto marks, name after name. (While sympathizing with the immigration authorities and the babble of languages they dealt with every day, interpreting their remarks nearly one hundred years later was daunting. The immigration officials made extensive use of ditto marks throughout the ship's manifest. In other words, if a name at the top of the list had a description written next to it denoting "blond hair" and "gray eyes," ditto marks under those categories were often used to describe the next dozen or more immigrants. Obviously this left me wondering about the number of passengers, one right after the other, with the same hair and eye color!)

One note that did *not* fit into the normal scheme of things was made next to Smith's name on the manifest. Under "Marks of Identification" it was written that Smith/Szumgalakoff had "scars on neck." Needless to say, there were no extra comments to explain why the man had scars on his neck or where precisely they were; and it appeared that the next dozen arrivals also had scars on their necks, courtesy of the ubiquitous ditto marks. (On seeing the comment, my first thought took me back to *The Long Walk* and the statement therein about Mr. Smith having a scar from his head to the nape of his neck. The scar may well have existed even though Glinski did not remember any such distinguishing mark when he recalled how long their hair grew during the walk.)

Continuing to scrutinize the ship's scanned manifest showing the original handwritten pages, I looked for comments and names. Nothing else pertaining to Alexander or Smith came to light. No surprises showed up. Then I went back to the home page in the Ellis Island records and typed in surnames starting with Smith, Jones, and Alexander, coupling those names with the word "Russia" and the date of 1913 to see what might come up. I had already searched for Smith on the SS *President Grant* with no luck. Using the broader spectrum of choices, up popped more than one Smith or Jones—born in Russia—who arrived in America in 1913. I was amazed. There were too many such names to have been a coincidence in my opinion. Where had these names come from? Were they, as in Smith's case, a matter of using his initials, A. S., and choosing a common English/American name with the same initials? Was there any other reasoning behind this commonality?

I would never have questioned the change of name as anything but an oddity had there not been so much made of it in the Department of State papers trying to establish a link between Smith and communist radicals in New York. Could an American name have been chosen for or suggested to Smith before he left Russia? Had the man been active in politics in Europe before coming to America, as suggested by the State Department? (I thought back to Andrew Smith, writer of *I Was A Soviet Worker*. There was no explanation as to why, coming from Hungary, he chose such an innocuous Anglo-Saxon name. Like Anthony Smith, Andrew Smith immigrated to the United States in his mid-twenties as a manual worker/machinist. Like or unlike Anthony Smith, Andrew Smith was dedicated to communism and became a member of the American Communist Party before going to the Soviet Union. Was there any parallel with Anthony Smith?)

Then I leapt to my next question: Why did Anthony Smith leave Europe from Hamburg and not from a port in Russia? Had he been visiting or living in Hamburg? What was his connection, if any, with Germany? In looking through available records, it appeared that immigrant ships left the port of Hamburg on a regular basis, catering to Russians and

Germans almost exclusively before World War I. So, presumably there was no mystery there. (I later learned that Alexander had been working in Germany before coming to the United States and that he and Smith may have worked together or planned to meet and emigrate from Germany.)

Resorting once again to the people who had responded to my appeals for information on Alexander through the census reports, I asked for suggestions on how to track down any family members or neighbors of his. Responses came back quickly concerning the 1930 census. Names of family members were listed; then a separate e-mail arrived stating that one of Alexander's children, who continued to live in the family home on Elkhorn St., had died in the 1990s. One step led to another and details of the will came to light, including the names of those family members still alive.

Before long, I was on the phone speaking to Alexander's daughter-in-law. She spoke to me at length about Alexander and then suggested I speak to his son, her brother-in-law, who was alive and in reasonable health. As on so many past occasions, once questions were asked about the past, the outflowing of stories and memories wouldn't stop. Before the phone calls ended, I had learned quite a lot about the Alexander family, though very little about Smith. The identity of Smith remained unknown. All was not lost, however, as Alexander's son had a memory of an older man, a family friend, living with his family in the late 1920s when he was a small boy. When I suggested he might have known Smith as "Tony" or "Uncle Tony," he immediately repeated the name and it brought back a memory of an older man teasing him as a small boy.

Once that door opened, I probed some more but he couldn't remember anything else about Smith. Many of his father's friends had come and gone over the years, some staying with the Alexander family, as Smith had done, while others simply visited. Alexander had been a sign painter with the United Cigar Company in New York as well as with J. I. Hass in Jersey City. From Smith's State Department documentation, it appeared that Alexander was never interviewed on Smith's behalf—the information Smith gave about Alexander appeared to have been taken at face value, possibly because no one realized Alexander was actually Iwan Alexandrinkow.

I stayed in touch with the Alexander family for some time in the hope that dormant memories would come to light, and I sent them copies of Alexander's immigration records from Ellis Island. In turn, I received photographs of Alexander as a young man in the uniform of the Russian Imperial Army. He was seated in a group photo with other young men, all in uniform. None of the others, however, had the features of Smith. The town where Alexander was born, Kroliwecki, was in Ukraine, far from Luzern in Saratov, which was Smith's hometown. Considering the distance, how had the two men met? The only rational answer pointed to them having met in the army. This assumption also coincided with Glinski's description of Smith as appearing to have been in the military: he had the bearing and intelligence of someone who had received military training.

Going over these facts and suppositions with the Alexander family took us once again to the scanned, handwritten ship's manifest of 1913. Alexander was listed as having been 5' 7" with dark blond hair and gray eyes; Smith/Szumgalakoff was listed as having been 5' 6" with the same dark blond hair and gray eyes plus the notation about "scars on neck." Alexander's son most emphatically disagreed with the above description. He stated his father was a tall man, on the order of 5' 10", and had dark hair and eyes, as shown in the photos. (At the same time, I read from the census record of 1930 that Alexander was forty-two years old, 5' 9" tall, 173 pounds, with gray eyes and gray hair.) I had to reassure Alexander's son that there were many discrepancies on the list, including basic information about size, shape, and hair color. I also advised him that Smith's passport and naturalization affidavits showed him to have been short, 5' 2", medium weight, 137 pounds, and with brown hair and blue eyes.

Considering all the misinformation on the ship's manifest, I wondered about marital status for the two men. Alexander's son stated that his father was betrothed when he arrived in America and had married into a German family shortly thereafter. It would be pure guesswork to state with any certainty whether Smith was married or not. One thing that was clear, however, was that both men used the name and address of the same referee in America. Though the handwriting was a little indistinct, it appeared that the man who welcomed Smith and Alexander to America was named

Makewski or Minkeski, living on 15th Street in New York City. More than anything else, the fact that both men used the same name and address as their contact information confirmed that Smith and Alexander knew each other before arriving in America. Now came the tough question—did Alexander's son know anything about his father's early political leanings? Had there been communist sympathies in the family?

The answer was immediate: No. Alexander had no time for or patience with communism, according to his son and, in fact, his father's entire family was wiped out at some point between the Russian Revolution and World War II. Also, his parents had been devout churchgoers. He never remembered any sort of political discussions concerning communism, socialism, or any other "ism." At home, his parents spoke English to each other and to their children, following the maxim that "when in America, speak English." Of course, it might have been possible that Alexander, as a young man—a young man in the military—may have dabbled in radical thinking. Once grown older and in a new country, it appears he put aside any such youthful tendencies. What about Smith, though? Had he been a communist sympathizer? One could only hypothesize.

Chapter 31

Who Was Mr. Smith?

Nearing the end of my research trail, I was still asking: Who was Mr. Smith? Had I really discovered his true identity? That was the burning question at the end of the day, with conjecture running rife. The man was truly a chameleon. Either he was as naïve and innocent as he appeared on the surface or he was a master of subterfuge. Either he was a simple man who worked with his hands—a jack of all trades—or he was an educated man with a hidden agenda. He professed to have worked with the Dewitt Tool Company to further American business interests in the Soviet Union while declaring his affiliation with In-Co, an entity known for its communist sympathies. On different applications and affidavits, Smith stated that his father lived with him at an address in New York, while pointing out his intention to visit his seriously ill father in Russia during a different interview. The circumvention of rules governing his change of name to Anthony Smith without the benefit of bureaucratic niceties was never adequately explained. The State Department investigation into all these discrepancies held up the authorization and issuance of Smith's passport for three months in 1928. As late as January 1929, there were still inter-office memos showing up in his file with questions as to who Smith actually was. The suspicion, of course, centered on Smith being a communist sympathizer, cutting the cloth for his coat to fit the occasion. His cavalier attitude toward the truth obviously caused consternation within the State Department.

What about the man himself? Mr. Smith was described by both Glinski and Rawicz as having been quiet, contained, and disciplined; a man with an apparent military background; a man who seldom spoke, but when he did, everyone listened to him and heeded what he had to say. The only remarks in the book about Mr. Smith's appearance were in reference to his obvious age, namely, that he definitely appeared to have been an older man, somewhere in his late forties or early fifties, and had looked his age. In looking once again at those remarks in *The Long Walk*, I glanced back to the interview between Rawicz and the scriptwriter in 2002. When Rawicz had been asked about Mr. Smith's personal information, his one comment was that the man was fifty-one years old. Upon further questioning, Rawicz couldn't say why he chose that particular age; he just knew Mr. Smith had been that old at the time. As I reviewed those comments and looked at the documentation I had on Smith, it struck me that if the date on his passport application were correct, and if Smith and Mr. Smith were one and the same man, then Smith would have been fifty-one in 1941/42, keeping in mind that his actual birthday was in December.

The only other reference to Mr. Smith's appearance in the book had been the statement regarding the scar on his head and neck, supposedly caused during his work on the Moscow Metro. Could it have been there earlier, before he worked in Moscow? With such an odd notation as "scars on neck" written on Smith's immigration papers as a distinguishing mark, could the two references indicate the same man? More to the point, if they did, then how had Rawicz known about the scars as well as Smith's exact age? Had he met Smith somewhere in the Middle East after Rawicz left Russia and joined Gen. Anders's army in Tehran? Or had he run into Smith somewhere in Palestine, at one of the camps where he trained recruits to perform parade ground maneuvers? If Rawicz knew so much about Smith and the story of the escape from Siberia, where, and how, had the transfer of stories and information taken place? Where should my next avenue of research take me?

With all the restrictions imposed by the present Russian government on requesting and releasing information, it would be difficult to discover any more concerning the people named above and who did what, when, where, and how. In fact, it might soon be impossible to do further research at all in Russia. That wonderful organization "Memorial" found itself on the wrong side of someone in the current Russian bureaucracy and its offices in St. Petersburg were raided in 2008, with its entire archive of records "removed." Obviously, the Soviet Union is still alive and well, but it may be some time before the Russian people wake up and realize they're back where they started from not so long ago.

Again, I returned to Mr. Smith. He started from Russia as a young man. He came to the United States to do what? Was he looking for a better life, a new start? During his time here from 1913 to 1926, he was unmarried, living in the New York area, performing a variety of odd jobs, and becoming involved with radical influences and people. In 1926, he returned to the Soviet Union accompanying a shipment of equipment. He stayed there for nearly two years, returning to the United States in the summer of 1928. His time in America was limited to less than six months, during which period he organized another shipment of equipment, applied for and was granted a new U.S. passport, stayed with his friend Alexander, and then left for the U.S.S.R. While back in his home country, he remained in Moscow, working as a machinist, living on Novaya Bashilovka street with a wife and two small daughters, and he eventually applied for a new U.S. passport ten years later—a passport that was authorized but never issued. Had the application prompted his arrest? Was that the sum total of all I knew about Mr. Smith? Very nearly.

I put out a few feelers over the Internet to addresses in Moscow, asking for suggestions as to how I might augment the information I had on Smith. Suggestions were made but nothing ever came of them. Then I was contacted by someone who had seen my queries on a genealogical Web site. Although he had no knowledge of the Smith family, the man who contacted me did know that the address on Novaya Bashilovka Street (i.e., building 9) no longer existed—part of that particular section of the street was torn down in the 1950s to make way for a sports stadium.

When I explained why I was seeking information about the address, he speculated that if Smith was arrested and sent to a labor camp, then his children may have been sent to an orphanage outside Moscow. (He didn't refer to the possible fate of Smith's wife; he didn't have to.) Further, he pointed out that children sent to such places in the 1930s were given new names and it would be next to impossible to locate them now. When I countered that the children were U.S. citizens registered with the embassy at that time, he reminded me that Soviet officialdom would not have recognized them as such. So, once more I was confronted by another wall of impenetrable obfuscation thrown up by the Russian bureaucracy. (I couldn't help but wonder how different this research might have been had I come across *The Long Walk* ten years earlier, right after the break-up of the Soviet Union, when access to long-secret archives was possible. I've had to restrain myself many times from playing the "what if" game over the past ten years.)

Not wanting to give up until I turned over every stone, I contacted the State Department one more time in hopes that something about Smith's passport application in the mid-1930s might have come to light. The reply was that nothing more was discovered about Smith/Chumjlakef/Szumgala-koff. The officials had used Smith's various birthdates and looked through their files but came up with nothing. Whatever passport application had been submitted to the U.S. consular service in Moscow in the 1930s was either lost or buried by 2008. "Authorized but not issued" indicated an application was made, a fee paid, and paperwork submitted; but then what? If Smith had been arrested and imprisoned, would he have asked his wife to find an advocate for him? Would that person have been someone like Eugene Lyons, or someone like Samuel DeWitt back in New York?

I managed to track down the DeWitt family and, after overcoming his initial amazement, one of DeWitt's grandsons was keen to help and find out what he could. He knew about his grandfather's activities as a Socialist legislator in the New York State Assembly of the 1920s, but had little idea, and no record, of his other activities aside from having heard that DeWitt was connected somehow with the Spanish Civil War in the 1930s. The information from the State Department that DeWitt was shipping equipment to the Soviet Union in the 1920s came as a real surprise. The upshot of my contact with the DeWitt family was that they had no idea who Smith was or whether their grandfather had helped the man in the 1930s—if, in fact, such a request for help had ever occurred.

One more question needed to be asked: What had happened to Smith? If Mr. Smith and Anthony Smith were one and the same person, could he have adopted a new identity in India as he had done when he immigrated to America years before? Being a master of adaptability, and therefore of survival, did Smith take a leaf from his previous book of experiences and simply reinvent himself? In the turmoil of British India in 1942, with no papers or documents to prove who he was, it might have been a fairly easy thing to pull off. (That observation goes for the other survivors of the walk as well as for thousands of displaced persons and refugees who found themselves in India without benefit of documentation. Their word about who they were would have to suffice unless the authorities discovered otherwise.) And if Smith had chosen a new identity, where had it taken him? Certainly not back to the Soviet Union, and probably not back to America either.

Putting aside the question of Mr. Smith's identity for a moment and looking back over the past several years of research, I reflected on the story of *The Long Walk*. I felt the escape from Siberia and the long trek to India had most definitely taken place. I also felt Glinski had been on that unique journey. As for Rawicz, document after document showed him to have been elsewhere during the dates the walk to freedom occured. It was difficult to draw any other conclusion but the obvious—Rawicz had not been on the walk to India. What about the other escapees? Batko and Zaro seemed to have been real people. The former was remembered and discussed by Glinski and there was a court document noting his arrest in England for theft; the latter was remembered and discussed within the Boguscewicz family. Had there been a Kolemenos, Paluchowicz, Makowski, Marchink-ovas, or a Kristina Polanska? Very probably, although their names might not have been exactly as stated in the book. Surely there was a comman-dant at the camp in Siberia. His name may have been Ushakov or some variant of that spelling; and the commandant had a wife named Maria, who, according to Glinski, was sympathetic to the plight of the prisoners and their intention to escape.

Reviewing names brought me to the point of trying to rationalize the two versions of *The Long Walk*. So much of what Rawicz wrote and what Glinski said dovetailed, despite a couple of major descrepancies, yet the two men had supposedly never met. How could two men tell more or less the same story, each claiming to have been part of a daring escape, but never have known one another? Going by the documentation from "Memorial," the Hoover Institution, the Belarus archives, and Pinsk records, it appeared that Rawicz started out in life as he related in the book: a young Polish man from a good family who found himself drawn into the nightmare of World War II as a prisoner destined for a Siberian labor camp. Almost the same words could be used to describe Glinski's background. Once in Siberia, both men told the same story of the commandant's wife befriending them and ultimately helping them to flee the camp.

In a similar manner, they also described the group of men who escaped with them, as well as the people they met and the incidents that happened along the way. Finally, with the walk completed and their safety assured in India, they parted from their comrades and led their own lives, with neither Rawicz nor Glinski knowing anything about the other until I began researching their stories within the last ten years. How were the two versions of the story to be resolved?

It could be argued that Glinski made up his story after having read *The Long Walk* more than thirty years ago. If so, what did he gain? He never spoke about his wartime experiences except to his family and a few close friends. Glinski never dreamed of writing a book or talking publicly about his past. That left me with the question of who to believe—Rawicz or Glinski?

The only way to tackle my confusion was to look at the remarks made by both men that were *not* included in the book. Were there any such points of similarity? Unbeknown to the general public, Rawicz admitted one of the survival techniques used during the escape was to eat earthworms. Glinski noted eating earthworms as a necessity, a vital source of protein, and commented that they were "gritty." He had no way of knowing that Rawicz stated a similar fact privately; nor could he have known about Rawicz's remarks concerning that passage in the book dealing with the escapees walking thirteen days across the desert without water. When I first spoke to Glinski about crossing the desert without water, he immediately said it was rubbish—without knowing that Rawicz had privately disavowed this part of the story as well, suggesting it was the result of an editorial misunderstanding.

Once in India, Rawicz described being cared for in Calcutta at a medical facility. Privately, he emphasized that he was not in any kind of large hospital but in a ramshackle type of place. Glinski mentioned to me that he also was not in a hospital but rather in a makeshift camp with a medical facility, outside Calcutta. Again, these private descriptions tally in respect to the non-institutional appearance of wherever the survivors were treated.

At the end of the arduous walk to freedom, Rawicz blessed the sight of a "native" patrol led by a British officer. In private, he thought the patrol was comprised of Gurkhas. Glinski had not batted an eyelash when retelling his story, stating the rescue patrol was made up of Gurkhas, whose uniforms included their famous knives.

Discussion of the German-speaking missionary described by Rawicz coincided with how Glinski remembered the man—with one difference. The difference between the two accounts concerning the missionary was that Glinski thought he was definitely a Roman Catholic priest because of the way he was dressed; Rawicz referred to him as a non-conformist. Glinski also thought the meeting with the priest took place toward the end of the long trek across China and Tibet. In the book, Rawicz outlined his encounter with the missionary and soon thereafter stated the escapees came across a vast inland lake. As detailed in an earlier chapter, there was only one lake that would fit such a description: Qinghai Lake. If that were the case, then Rawicz's meeting with the missionary was right after crossing the desert and way to the north and east of Lhasa. One would like to give the benefit of the doubt to both men with regards to geographical details on a trek for which they had no maps and tried to recall decades later.

In summary, and not to take further guesswork away from the reader, how could each man's recounting of little details coincide so well when those details were not discussed in public? Glinski spoke of them as he recited his personal history to me, with no prompting on my part and no reference to the book—those details were not included in print anyway. Rawicz spoke of the same details to family and friends and never made those corrections to the book. Where was the point of contact, then, between the two men? Or should I ask "who" the point of contact was? That may be an unresolved question for future researchers to tackle, unless or until more information is unearthed.

◦◦◦◦◦

Was there anything else I could learn about *The Long Walk* before calling it a day? I felt I had looked into every nook and cranny I came across, found many answers, but there were still lots of questions remaining. I had to make a decision. After all these years of research, it was time to type up my notes and present the outcome to the reading public—with a request for their help. If the mysteries and enigmas of what took place during the walk and the people who "walked the walk" were ever to be resolved, I needed help from a worldwide audience, from readers in Poland, Belarus, England, Siberia, India, and perhaps as far away as Canada, Australia, and New Zealand.

With that appeal in mind, I'll end this researcher's tale. What a wild ride it's been! My hope is that some reader will come forward with additional information about the people mentioned herein so that their individual stories will not be forgotten and their role in one of the most remarkable endeavors ever undertaken will be remembered for future generations. Somewhere, someone has the key that will help unravel the mystery of *The Long Walk*.

Afterword

My interest in *The Long Walk* began more than ten years ago. At that time curiosity combined with another interest, family research, prompting me to look for the story behind the book and perhaps, in time, to write my own book detailing the research adventures I encountered along the way. One of my aims in gathering all the material I could about *The Long Walk* was to use my efforts at seeking the true story of the walk as a backdrop to outlining the progress of a budding researcher—such as myself.

The fumbling and bumbling I experienced, the dead ends as well as the exhilarating finds, pointed me in a direction that went beyond just getting at the backstory of the men who walked to India; rather, my effort at research became something of a tale unto itself. That is not to say I wanted to write a "how-to" book. What I wanted from this experience was to tell a tale of research, to solve mysteries along the way, to recount the steps it took to move from goal to goal, to learn from my lessons, to pass on any thoughts or gems of wisdom to the reader, and to enjoy both the research and the writing phases. Whether all my intentions were fulfilled or not, I believe that each step of the way was certainly an adventure. I also wanted to present my research in a way that would encourage others to take heart, follow through with any projects they might have, and enjoy the experience, no matter how daunting it first appears or how difficult that first step seems.

～❦～❦～

I certainly learned many lessons on my own walk. This first full-scale experience of researching a specific topic was an eye-opener. Whether I used new, modern methods—computers and the Internet—or older methods—the card catalog, pen and paper, or the telephone—I had to make contact with other human beings. In order to win the trust of people who might be of help to me, I learned to emphasize the word "research" and expand its definition to include geographical areas, the war years, and the interviewees' own personal histories in the hope of establishing a confiding relationship between myself as a researcher and the respondent.

While seeking information from the people I contacted, I quickly learned to be conscious of my manner toward them and aware of how I accepted or questioned what they told me. For instance, the lesson of treading lightly and not trampling on emotions and feelings when interviewing a respondent wasn't lost on me; fortunately, most people didn't mind talking about the past, but there were a few who objected, whose histories stirred up unwanted memories. This is an area which each and every researcher has to delicately negotiate on an individual basis, as defined by the research subject's personality and experiences. Also, the information imparted by the person on the other end of an e-mail or the phone must be digested with a certain amount of open-mindedness. Solid facts are, of course, welcomed and form a basis for further investigation; but the facts are often difficult to elicit and verify. Too often, it seemed there were no facts, no information of any sort; replies to my questions were all in the negative. In the back of my mind, however, lurked the suspicion that the information I sought was there, somewhere, just not remembered or cross-referenced, or remembered under a different name or category. It was difficult to accept that, occasionally, some data from the past would never be forthcoming, despite speaking courteously or using modern research aids.

Continuing this train of thought, the concept of digging into the past using modern technology sounded wonderful when I began researching *The Long Walk*. I was quick to learn that a good proportion—in fact the majority of research I did—dealt with contacting the elderly. Thus, any technology beyond the telephone was usually not an option. Beautifully written or typed letters were received at my end; in turn, I brushed up on my penmanship in order to reply. The formal dance revolving around pen, ink, and good-quality stationery was repeated many times over; it was a tried-and-true supplement to the phone call.

Yet the telephone call was a good way to break the ice and then lead on to a leisurely exchange of thoughts and ideas via letter or e-mail. Nine times out of ten it was an effective mode of communication. There were only a few rare instances in which the recipient of my call did not understand or could not hear properly and hung up. On one or two occasions the response I received was frosty because of the nature of my call, as when asking people who knew Rupert Mayne what they remembered about his intelligence work during the War. The informant followed Mayne's example and hid behind the Official Secrets Act, making the speaker sound important while pointing to his ignorance of Mayne's career.

Interestingly enough, occasionally I would connect with the wrong number and end up speaking to someone's children or grandchildren rather than the intended contact. These family members generally had no idea what I was asking when I launched into my introduction; and they voiced concerns that their elderly relative would not speak to me, as the latter had never spoken of his/her past experiences. What a surprise then when I finally made contact with the elderly relative in question, listened for more than an hour to reminiscences, and later was asked by the family, "What happened? Dad hasn't stopped talking about the past since he spoke to you last week." This declaration points out the need to ignore objections from family members, such as, "My dad won't talk about the War." I can almost guarantee that the elderly person in question will not mind talking about his or her past, if asked the correct questions. More than once an aged informant said to me, "I didn't want to burden my family with the past. And now I have no one to talk to. Friends and family from my generation have all died." (The unstated reality is that the interviewee may not be around much longer as well.)

Somehow the interviewer has to convey reassurance that the elderly respondent's conversation is still worth listening to and is actually sought after. Oddly enough, the interviewer, as a stranger, has an advantage—the interviewee often does not feel any constraint talking about the past to someone outside the family. For whatever reason, during the interviews I conducted, the majority of elderly people opened their hearts to me and told me tales they had not spoken of for more than fifty years. In some cases they had forgotten about them entirely. More than once someone would say, "I forgot about that. I'm glad you asked because . . ." or, "I wanted to get back to you because you got me thinking and now I remember . . ." So it went.

❧❧

As I wrap up this research tale, I can only look back in amazement at all the work I put into it and how much I accomplished. What had I, a fledgling researcher, known about investigation at the start? Over time, I learned to use the computer. It became an ideal tool and workmate in the twenty-first century. While stating that fact, I never lost sight of the human touch when investigating the recent past. The best information I obtained usually came from letters, phone calls, word of mouth, photo albums from attics, shoe boxes full of small handwritten index cards, and, above all, face-to-face conversations.

The human touch can mean picking through the memories of literally hundreds of people. My processing skills had to be honed to a fine edge, filtering abilities needed to be learned, and repetition of the same question from different angles to check and cross-reference responses were talents I gradually acquired. Just the simple art of listening blossomed into an experience involving subtleties of accent, mood, depth, nuance, hesitation, volume, and so on.

With no standard method for interviewing people, anyone delving into research for the first time has to sort out which approach, angle, or technique fits the occasion and how best to use one's skills as well as one's personality. What works well with one person may not be the best approach with the next. What every researcher should keep in mind can be summed up in one word: patience. The art of interviewing rarely allows for one to practice a "cut to the chase" approach. Thus, the researcher should work at demonstrating patience and the ability to listen while asking questions.

For instance, during interviews I had to remind myself to speak slowly, to pose questions that weren't leading (or misleading), to listen for changes in tone and mood, to figure out when to push for specifics and when to keep quiet, and to let the conversation proceed as naturally as possible. Juxtaposed to practicing patience is the matter of keeping the interviewee on task and nipping any tendencies to fly off on irrelevant tangents in the bud. (The researcher probably does not want to add one more story about a tiger shoot in India to his or her repertoire.)

Another challenge when pursuing interviews is perfecting the simple ability to ask questions. Often the interviewer will realize he or she is receiving answers from the interviewee that do not ring true. A sense of miscommunication frequently boils down to what the interviewer wants to hear and what the subject wants to tell, leaving a gap in the middle. Alternately, there arises the situation in which the subject tells the interviewer what he or she *thinks* the questioner wants to hear. In that case, second-guessing is extremely frustrating.

Occasionally the researcher is lucky enough to "click" right away with the research subject, and questions and answers follow each other in an orderly, intelligent fashion. More than once while researching *The Long Walk,* I had the privilege of speaking to and meeting with people who had never spoken of their memories and experiences to anyone. Once the interview minuet began, though, it would often continue for hours. When asked why their memories had been locked away for so long, I frequently received the reply, "Nobody asked me before," or, "I didn't think anyone would be interested." My rejoinder would be to point out that, even though I was a stranger, the interviewee seemed willing and eager to talk about his or her history. The reply I often heard was, "Oh, that's O.K. I feel like I've known you all my life. I could say anything to you." I took this as the highest compliment any researcher could ask for—and a spur to continue doing research.

~~

ACKNOWLEDGMENTS

I offer my sincerest thanks and gratitude to the hundreds of people who helped me along the way while I researched this book. I only wish there was unlimited space to include everyone's name who took the time and had the patience to encourage me over the years. My special thanks go out to Paul Rossiter, Joan Gabbeday Kirby, Noel Clark, and Jeffrey Blyth, friends and colleagues of Ronald Downing; Shirleyanne Cumberledge, Faith Spencer Chapman, Ian Gardiner, Terence O'Brien, Ian Gemmell, and Lady Jardine Patterson, friends and acquaintances of Rupert Mayne; Elizabeth Kaegi, Len Thornton, Sandy Cleland, Mrs. Alison Ross, Col. J. P. Cross, George Mackenzie, Shraddha Kumbhojkar, Anuradha Bhattacharjee, Francis and Elaine Obradovich, Bob Younger, the Sadleir and Cross families, the Kaulback and Hanbury-Tracy families, and the Betts family provided insight and help with my research regarding India; Bill Brough and Martin Davies (Friends' Ambulance drivers); Ruby Johnson and Labang Loo (Burmese nurses); Jan Cesarczyk, Dr. Andrzej Suchcitz, Eva Garcelon, Tatiana Smorodinskaya, and members of the Kresy-Siberia Web site helped with all things Polish and Russian; Shirley and Milek Masojada and Barbara Kukulska helped with searches in South Africa; Margaret Michelmore, Christine Westren, Rosemary Tootle, Jean Parton, Jane Marshall, and the families of Rev. Reginald Brown and Dr. John Lowe aided me in researching Methodist missionaries and medical staff in the Barrackpore area; Nancy Wilson, Sterling Seagrave, Dr. John Grindlay's family, Dr. Myles Johnson's family, readers of the Ex-CBI Roundup and of *Dekho*, and members of the Koi-Hai Web site were instrumental in helping me research the Assam/Burma area during the war years; George Tippett, Alison Campbell, and Joanne Laing, who became very familiar with my search for Batko; Father Jean Charbonnier for his help with missionary records for western China; the Boguszewicz family for sharing their father's story; Walter Alexander for sharing his father's history; the Krichevski and Rusiecki families in Pinsk and Brest; to genealogists the world over; and to those staff members who came to my rescue at all the institutions, associations, libraries, and archives named herein.

My own seemingly endless walk along the research trail couldn't have been accomplished without the help and support of Michael Anstead, Rob Lawrence, Joe Walker, Bob Turner, Stan Whittlesey, Jeff Maguire, Lance Visser, Maj. Alan Edwards, Alan Cullison, Alan Lathrop, Pete Lutken, Hugh Levinson, Kazik Zuzmak, Witold and Joyce Glinski and their family, John Downing and his brothers, James Mayne and his sister, Susan Boyd, and, as ever, Lt. Colonel Patric Emerson, OBE.

INDEX